T0360936

ROUTLEDGE LIBRARY EDITIONS:
BUSINESS AND ECONOMICS IN ASIA

Volume 13

THE FINANCIAL MARKETS OF HONG KONG

THE FINANCIAL MARKETS OF HONG KONG

ANDREW F. FRERIS

Routledge
Taylor & Francis Group

LONDON AND NEW YORK

First published in 1991 by Routledge

This edition first published in 2019
by Routledge
2 Park Square, Milton Park, Abingdon, Oxon OX14 4RN

and by Routledge
52 Vanderbilt Avenue, New York, NY 10017

Routledge is an imprint of the Taylor & Francis Group, an informa business

British Library Cataloguing in Publication Data
A catalogue record for this book is available from the British Library

ISBN: 978-1-138-48274-6 (Set)
ISBN: 978-0-429-42825-8 (Set) (ebk)
ISBN: 978-1-138-61759-9 (Volume 13) (hbk)
ISBN: 978-0-429-46157-6 (Volume 13) (ebk)

Publisher's Note
The publisher has gone to great lengths to ensure the quality of this reprint but
points out that some imperfections in the original copies may be apparent.

Disclaimer
The publisher has made every effort to trace copyright holders and would welcome
correspondence from those they have been unable to trace.

The Financial Markets of Hong Kong

Andrew F. Freris

London and New York

First published 1991
by Routledge
11 New Fetter Lane, London EC4P 4EE

Simultaneously published in the USA and Canada
by Routledge
a division of Routledge, Chapman and Hall, Inc.
29 West 35th Street, New York, NY 10001

© 1991 Andrew F. Freris
Typeset by Columns Design and Production Services Limited
Printed and bound in Great Britain by
Biddles Ltd, Guildford and King's Lynn

British Library Cataloguing in Publication Data

Freris, Andrew
    The financial markets of Hong Kong.
    1. Hong Kong. Financial institutions
    I. Title
    332.1095125

    ISBN 0-415-02079-4

Library of Congress Cataloging-in-Publication Data

Freris, Andrew F., 1945–
    The financial markets of Hong Kong/Andrew F. Freris.
        p. cm.
    Includes bibliographical references.
    ISBN 0-415-02079-4
    1. Financial institutions—Hong Kong. I. Title.
HG187.H85F74   1991
332.1'095125—dc20   90–35380
                                                         CIP

To my wife, Anabella

Contents

List of figures ix

List of tables xi

Preface and acknowledgements xv

1 Introduction **1**
1.1 *Basic outlines* 1
1.2 *Hong Kong's economic growth: an outline* 4

2 Banks **15**
2.1 *Introduction* 15
2.2 *Market morphology and competition* 17
2.3 *Portfolio structure and dynamics* 42
2.4 *The demand for bank loans: an exercise in estimation* 58
2.5 *The developing environment* 68

3 Deposit-taking companies and the capital market **75**
3.1 *Introduction* 75
3.2 *Morphology of the deposit-taking companies market* 78
3.3 *Portfolio structure and dynamics* 83
3.4 *The development of the debt market* 87
3.5 *The developing situation* 94

4 The stock exchange **97**
4.1 *Introduction* 97
4.2 *Quantifying the characteristics of the market* 99

Contents

4.3	*Measuring market activities: stock indexes*	105
4.4	*Risk and returns in the Hong Kong stock market*	113
4.5	*Flow of funds and the role of the stock market*	119
4.6	*Analysis of the efficiency of the Hong Kong stock market*	126

5 Futures, gold, investment management and regulation **141**

5.1	*Introduction*	141
5.2	*Futures markets*	142
5.3	*The gold market*	157
5.4	*Unit trusts and investment management*	160
5.5	*The regulatory framework*	172

6 The foreign exchange rate, monetary and fiscal policy **179**

6.1	*Introduction*	179
6.2	*The foreign exchange market*	180
6.3	*Foreign exchange rate policy*	184
6.4	*The pegged system in operation*	190
6.5	*An appraisal of the arbitraging process*	196
6.6	*Determination of the stock of money and external flows*	215
6.7	*The pegged exchange rate and the monetary–fiscal policy mix*	221
6.8	*Measuring the budget surplus or deficit*	226
6.9	*Measuring the fiscal impact: a simple approximation*	229
6.10	*Conclusions*	231

Summary and conclusions	237
Notes	242
Index	262

List of figures

Figure 2.1   The banking firm   17
Figure 2.2   Effects of costs and demand changes on the
             banking firm   31
Figure 2.3   Market for loans and deposits   34
Figure 2.4   Interest rate controls   34
Figure 2.5   Lifting of interest rate controls   35
Figure 2.6   Demand for loans and deposits   62
Figure 2.7   Identifying demand for loans   62
Figure 2.8   Identifying demand for loans   64
Figure 5.1   Efficiency frontier of combinations asset   167
Figure 5.2   Retirement fund performance in Hong
             Kong 1983–8   168
Figure 6.1   Summary of the cash arbitrage mechanism   195
Figure 6.2   The Exchange Fund and the stock of
             money in Hong Kong   216
Figure 6.3   Fiscal–monetary policy mix   224

List of tables

1.1	GDP growth rate, 1975–88	5
1.2	Inflation rates, CPI (A), old series 1980 = 100, 1979–88	5
1.3	Contribution of economic sectors to GDP, 1980–7	6
1.4	Structure of domestic exports by type of goods, 1980–8	7
1.5	Current balance of trade, 1978–88	8
1.6	Structure and direction of re-exports, 1980–8	9
1.7	Distribution of trade by countries, 1981–8	10
1.8	Foreign investment in Hong Kong's manufacturing sector, 1980–8	11
2.1	Banks in Hong Kong, 1988	19
2.2	Market shares of the top five local banks in Hong Kong, 1983–7	20
2.3	Estimates of relative shares of the Hongkong Bank group of the total banking and DTC market in Hong Kong	21
2.4	The relationship between size and profitability of local banks in Hong Kong	25
2.5	The influence of market share on the profitability of Hong Kong local banks	26
2.6	Ranking of banks according to size, profitability and liquidity, 1986	29
2.7	Trends in costs and income sources of all banks in Hong Kong, 1981–6	30
2.8	Interest rate spread, 1984–8	32
2.9	Problem banks in Hong Kong, 1983–7	40
2.10	The portfolio of all banks in 1988	44
2.11	Loans and advances to non-banking customers as a	

	percentage of all assets, 1980–9	46
2.12	Loans and advances to non-banking customers in HK dollars as a percentage of HK dollar assets, 1980–9	47
2.13	Proportion of all assets of banks denominated in forex, 1980–9	47
2.14	Sectoral allocation of HK dollar bank loans for use in Hong Kong, 1980–9	48
2.15	Price indexes of different types of property, 1980–8	48
2.16	Net loans by banks to DTCs, 1980–9	51
2.17	Inter-bank and DTC deposits and loans by banks in HK dollars and forex, 1980–9	52
2.18	Inter-bank and DTC deposits and loans by DTCs in HK dollars and forex, 1980–9	53
2.19	Net inter-institutional position of all banks and net forex position of all banks and DTCs as a percentage of assets, 1980–9	54
2.20	Deposits in forex and HK dollars as a percentage of total deposits, 1980–9	55
2.21	Spread of interest rate on bank deposits, 1981–8	56
2.22	Estimation results	65
2.23	Behaviour of the BLR and inter-bank overnight rate, 1978–88	66
2.24	Results of regression analysis of sectoral demand for bank loans	67
2.25	Major offshore market size, 1984–8	72
3.1	Numbers of LDTCs and RDTCs in Hong Kong, 1980–8	78
3.2	Morphology of DTCs, 1986–8	79
3.3	Ownership and size in terms of deposits of RDTCs, 1987	80
3.4	Ranking of LDTCs and RDTCs in terms of assets and net profit, 1981–6	81
3.5	Share of LDTCs and RDTCs in total deposits and assets of banks plus all DTCs, 1980–8	82
3.6	Assets and liabilities of DTCs, 1988	84
3.7	Comparative holdings of debt instruments, 1988	86
3.8	HK dollar capital markets: distribution and totals issued, 1982–8	89
3.9	HK dollar capital markets: types of instruments	

	and institutions, 1984–8	90
3.10	Average size and allocation of FRCDs in Hong Kong, 1985–8	92
3.11	Holdings of NCDs, 1980–6	94
3.12	The ranking of Hong Kong's DTCs amongst the top five merchant banks in Southeast Asia, 1982–5	96
4.1	Value of turnover in the stock market(s), 1980–8	98
4.2	Sectoral distribution of market capitalization and turnover, 1986–8	100
4.3	Market capitalization, top twenty firms, 1988	101
4.4	Distribution of turnover in terms of number of securities and value of transactions, 1987	101
4.5	Share activity of the top twenty shares in terms of market capitalization, 1987	102
4.6	Turnover in terms of volume of shares traded, 1979–86	103
4.7	Average comparative costs of trading securities, 1988	105
4.8	HSI components, 1987	108
4.9	Constituents of the HKI, 1988	110
4.10	Comparison of percentage changes of the three stock indexes	113
4.11	Dividend yields and average price-to-earnings ratios of HKI constituents, 1982–8	114
4.12	Beta values of HSI stocks	115
4.13	Sectoral returns and risk, Stock Exchange of Hong Kong, 1986–7	117
4.14	Sources of finance for selected HSI constituents, 1983–7	121
4.15	Estimates of capital raised by new issues in the stock market(s) of Hong Kong, 1975–88	123
4.16	Gross private domestic capital formation and stock exchange financing, 1976–87	124
4.17	Merchant banking activities in Hong Kong, 1980–5	126
4.18	The evidence for market efficiency in Hong Kong	139
4.19	Seasonality effects of the Hong Kong stock market, 1975–87	139
5.1	Turnover in the HKFE, 1986–8	144
5.2	HSI futures contract: trading volume in contracts, 1986–7	145

5.3	White noise and stability tests of inter-day and intra-day index changes	155
5.4	First and second moments of inter-day and intra-day HSI changes	156
5.5	Hong Kong's comparative position in fund management, 1987	162
5.6	Data on selected locally incorporated life insurance companies, 1984–5	164
5.7	Correlation, risk and return: Hong Kong and other major stock markets, 1971–85/6	169
6.1	HK dollar effective exchange rate index, 1975–88	185
6.2	The cash arbitrage system and the pegged exchange rate	189
6.3	Spread (minimum and maximum) of inter-bank interest rates in Hong Kong, 1983–8	199
6.4	Correlations between the exchange rate and the cash-to-asset ratio of banks	204
6.5	The money stock and its components, 1982–9	217
6.6	The public's cash-to-HK dollar deposits ratio, 1982–8	220
6.7	Banks' cash-to-HK dollar savings deposits ratio, 1982–8	220
6.8	The monetary base and its impact on money stock, 1961–78	221
6.9	Surplus or deficit in the Government's budget, 1977–87	228
6.10	Surplus or deficit in the current account balance as a percentage of GDP, 1977–87	229
6.11	The average and marginal propensity to surplus in the consolidated budget, 1970–87	230

Preface and acknowledgements

A great deal of the research undertaken in the writing of this book was supported by grants from the City Polytechnic of Hong Kong during 1986–9. In particular Chapters 2, 4 and 5 draw freely from the data collected and results obtained from these funded projects. A vote of thanks is therefore due to the research assistants involved, Henry K.N. Lee (now Lecturer in the Department), Louis Chan, Connie G. Ng and Chris W.K. Chow.

The Director of the Polytechnic until 1989, Dr D.J. Johns, provided constant support whilst the book was being written.

Colleagues in the Department were liberal with their time and advice. It would be convenient to claim that whatevern errors or misinterpretations remain in this book are their fault. This would be worse than unfair, it would be untrue. My thanks to Kenneth K.K. Chow, Daniel K.P. Chan and K.Y. Cheung for all their help. Last but not least thanks are due to Vincent H.C. Cheng of Hongkong Bank and to T.C. Thompson of Wardley Investment Services. They provided invaluable material and moral help at various stages. So did P. Sowden of Routledge who was willing to listen, and perhaps believe, my excuses over delays. The permission of HSI Services Ltd to reproduce the data in Chapter 4, Table 4.12, is gratefully acknowledged.

To my speedy, patient and always cheerful secretary and PA Indy K.Y. Chan Ching another vote of thanks for producing tangible evidence from my tangled manuscript.

Finally, and as always, none of this would have been possible without the support and help of my wife Anabella.

Andrew F. Freris
Head, Department of Economics and Finance
City Polytechnic of Hong Kong

P.S. Since the completion of the writing of this book I have taken up the post of senior economist with GT Management (Asia) Ltd. The views expressed herein are strictly my own.

Chapter one

Introduction

1.1 Basic outlines

Hong Kong's economic performance has elicited a whole list of superlatives. Coupled with its spectacular rise from a sleepy colonial port to a world commercial centre is the fact that this bastion of capitalist free enterprise will be handed back to the People's Republic of China (PRC) in 1997. What perhaps characterizes Hong Kong most is the pace of change, the shortness of any planning horizon and the speed by which the events are frequently overtaken by Hong Kong rather than the other way around.

To write a book about Hong Kong's financial markets and to try to keep it up to date would be a futile enterprise. Therefore, what this book aspires to do is not to produce an up-to-date essay in the sense of incorporating all the more recent statistics or events just before going to press, but to present a picture which draws together the current understanding and analysis of the markets' behaviour. This does mean that commentary or description of institutions, events and controversies are often given second place to the quantification, empirical investigation and analytical treatment of what appear to be long-term trends or paths of development. In a similar vein, trying to predict the course of future events or the shape and behaviour of these markets by 1997 and beyond is also given second place to a comprehensive survey of all serious and quantitative investigations of these markets over the last 10 years or so. The perceived benefit of this approach is that it allows trends to be delineated which are not submerged under the welter of current developments, some of which may turn out to be only of temporary importance. In a broad sense this book is about applied financial economics with examples drawn from Hong Kong's experience.

Despite its reputation for rapid change and volatility, judicious application of economic analysis helps to map out a relatively coherent picture of the way in which Hong Kong's financial markets developed. This is also assisted by the emergence of a small group of scholars and observers of Hong Kong's economy who have taken the longer view and have also taken the time and trouble to apply the tools of financial analysis and econometrics in order to explain and understand rather than just describe Hong Kong's financial dynamics.[1] Predictably, many of their findings were not dissimilar to those encountered in other developed or developing countries. In this sense Hong Kong is not unique and this bodes well for its future. A truly unique experience in financial development may well have contained the seeds of its own destruction in dealing with the vagaries of the international market place and the stresses imposed by the 1997 handover. But even so, given Hong Kong's dependence on international trade, it would have been unlikely that its financial markets would have developed along lines very different from those of its customers and competitors.

The book examines each of the major financial markets by outlining their development, quantifying their key characteristics and using empirical and statistical evidence to analyse their dynamics and evolving patterns. The commercial and merchant banking sectors come under scrutiny first in Chapters 2 and 3 as they represent the more mature and developed of the financial sectors. The emphasis here is to discern evolving patterns of competition and quantify the characteristics of a market which is wide open to international competition but which is also, on a local basis, dominated by a few large institutions. Separate sections in Chapter 3 trace out the recent rise of the non-equity capital market in Hong Kong, an area on which a great deal of hope has been pinned to ensure Hong Kong's continuing ascendancy as a regional financial centre. The stock market, recently unified and recovered from the shock of the October 1987 crash is examined next in Chapter 4. The Hong Kong Stock Exchange has received a disproportionate amount of poor publicity and attention – disproportionate not only in terms of its relative importance as a market where firms may raise capital, but also in terms of the accuracy of the descriptions of its operations and dynamics. The evidence presented should go some way towards restoring realism in the discussion about Hong Kong's most glamorous market. It is shown that the equity market shares a great deal of common characteristics with other much larger and developed markets and that its dynamics and efficiency may possibly have been underestimated. The picture that emerges may not be altogether flattering, but it is based on facts and quantitative research rather than opinion.

The following Chapter 5 deals with the futures markets, gold, investment management and the issue of regulation. Here, again, and in particular in the section concerning the stock index futures market, financial research restores realism and allows a fascinating insight in the birth, maturity (and near death!) of the Hang Seng Index futures contract. This discussion is followed by sections on the reform of Hong Kong's regulatory framework as well as the emergence of Hong Kong as a regional investment management centre.

The penultimate chapter deals with two particular aspects of policy which have been crucial in Hong Kong's economic and financial development. One is the decision since 1983 to peg the exchange rate to the US dollar and the other is the deliberate policy of surpluses in the government's budgets. The reasons for the importance of these two policy decisions to the financial markets are obvious. A pegged exchange rate has direct implications for the determination of the stock of money and of interest rates. Coupled with the fact that Hong Kong has no formal central bank type of institution, the implementation of the pegged exchange regime required some very special arrangements. Hong Kong is still perhaps unique in that the note issue is controlled by two private banks, the Hongkong Bank and the Standard Chartered, the latter not even incorporated in Hong Kong.

The pegged exchange rate system was also bolstered by a cartel arrangement amongst all banks which limited interest rate competition for retail deposits. Although this arrangement predated the decision to peg the HK dollar in 1983 it has come to play an important role, according to the authorities at any rate, in maintaining both the orderliness of competition in the banking market and in supporting the exchange rate at appropriate occasions via the manipulation of the market interest rates.

The conservative, if not deflationary, fiscal stance of the Hong Kong Government has resulted in successive years of budget surpluses. The absence of a central bank generated some interesting problems regarding the monetary impact, or absence of monetary impact, of these surpluses. It also meant the almost complete absence of government debt in the money and capital markets which had serious repercussions on their development.

The concluding chapter draws all the evidence together and summarizes the direction and paths of these particular markets in the context of the macroeconomic policies pursued.

Since 1984 when the Sino-British agreement was signed, the role of China and the impending handover of Hong Kong to the PRC in 1997 has cast a giant shadow over most of the developments outlined. But perhaps the major shock to confidence was the May–June 1989 events in the PRC culminating with the Beijing massacre. As stated before, any prediction about Hong Kong is risky and almost certain to be instantly overtaken or proved false by events. This must also apply to the consequences of the unrest in China on Hong Kong's future as a financial centre. As pious platitudes and statements concerning the 're-establishment of confidence' in Hong Kong are just that, pious and platitudes, in the next section we shall try to quantify some of the consequences and draw conclusions based on what Hong Kong knows and trusts best – dollars and cents. Political power grows indisputably out of the barrel of a gun, but the finger which pulls the trigger may well be the same which pushes the buttons on the till. If this statement sounds obscure, the following section, which outlines Hong Kong's economic development in the context of the financial markets and the links with the PRC, may help to clarify it.

1.2 Hong Kong's economic growth: an outline

Table 1.1 shows the salient feature of Hong Kong's economy over 14 years – sustained growth, frequently at double digits with only one year of relative stagnation. At the average rate of growth achieved in the 1980s, Hong Kong's gross domestic product (GDP) would double nearly every 10 years, no mean achievement for an economy with no natural resources except an excellent harbour.

Table 1.1 GDP growth rate (per cent (1980 constant prices)), 1975–88

1975	0.2	1981	9.4	1987	13.6	
1976	17.1	1982	2.9	1988	7.0	
1977	12.5	1983	6.5	1989	2.5	
1978	9.5	1984	9.5	Average for 1970s	10.2	
1979	11.7	1985	−0.1			
1980	11.0	1986	11.2	Average for 1980s	7.3	

Sources: Hong Kong Annual Digest of Statistics; budget statements

Equally, this rate of growth was achieved with very low rates of inflation. Hong Kong official statistics contain three different cost of living indexes to choose from, leaving aside the GDP deflator. Table 1.2 shows the rate of inflation over 1979–88 using the most popular of the three.[2]

Table 1.2 Inflation rates, CPI (A), old series 1980 = 100 (year on year per cent) 1979–88

1979	6.0	1984	8.1
1980	6.9	1985	3.1
1981	10.2	1986	2.8
1982	10.5	1987[a]	5.4
1983	9.9	1988[a]	7.4

Sources: Hong Kong Monthly Digest of Statistics; Hong Kong Annual Digest of Statistics
Note: [a] The rates for 1987 and 1988 are on a recalculated base with 1985 = 100 and hence are not comparable with the previous years.

The high rates of growth were achieved by a combination of productivity growth and capital accumulation. However, the factors contributing to growth changed over time.[3] Aggregate production functions of the Cobb-Douglas type estimated over 1955–70 indicated that capital accumulation contributed 46 per cent to the overall growth rate, labour about 20 per cent and total factor productivity 33 per cent. For 1971–84 capital accumulation increased its significance considerably to 46 per cent, with labour and total factor productivity contributing about 26 per cent and 27 per cent respectively. To that extent Hong Kong's experience is not significantly different from that of other Western developed nations which also experienced a productivity slowdown in the

1970s. Labour immigration has been of undoubted importance to Hong Kong, as it contributed to the overall growth of the labour force. The high rate of capital accumulation, particularly from the 1970s onwards, can also be explained by the development of Hong Kong's financial sector which contributed by its inter-mediation role and eased access to savings. Government policy also contributed in two different but related ways. First, it kept income and business taxes low, thus increasing the net expected returns from investment. Second, the policy of 'neutral fiscal stance', as expressed in budget surpluses rather than deficits, meant that private investment would have direct access to private savings. It also kept the Government out of the loans market thus keeping interest rates lower than they would have otherwise been.[4]

The process of growth and accumulation was also reflected in the structure and pattern of economic activity. The share of the manufacturing sector in the GDP stood at 31 per cent in 1970 and dropped to 25 per cent in 1975. Table 1.3 shows the experience for 1980–7 with the services sector showing an increasing tendency from the mid-1980s onwards.[5] This is not surprising and it reflects the experience of other developed countries where a rising standard of living shifts the emphasis to quality rather than quantity with a consequent move towards services rather than goods.

The shift in the pattern of the activities and production in Hong Kong requires closer examination. The structure of exports indicates a relatively stable distribution amongst classes of goods, with clothing still being the most importance commodity (Table 1.4).

Table 1.3 Contribution of economic sectors to GDP (current prices), 1980–7

	1980	1981	1982	1983	1984	1985	1986	1987[a]
Manufacturing (%)	23.8	22.8	20.7	22.8	24.1	21.9	22.3	22.1
Services (%)	63.2	64.1	65	62	61.8	63.5	63.3	65.2

Source: *Estimates of GDP 1966–88*, Census and Statistics Department, Hong Kong, 1989, p. 30

Notes: Services include wholesale, retail, import and export trades, restaurants, hotels, financial and related services and social, community and personal services; ownership of premises would add, on average, an extra 10 per cent on these estimates.

[a] Estimates.

Table 1.4 Structure of domestic exports by type of goods (per cent of total domestic exports, at current prices), 1980–8

	1980	1981	1982	1983	1984	1985	1986	1987	1988
Clothing	34.1	35.1	34.7	32.9	33.8	34.5	33.8	33.4	30.9
Watches	9.2	8.8	8.6	7.9	6.4	7.1	7.3	6.8	7.6
Textiles	5.0	5.1	4.6	5.2	4.8	4.7	5.8	6.9	6.0
Toys etc.	7.2	8.3	9.9	7.6	7.8	7.1	6.8	5.5	3.8
Electronic parts	2.1	2.6	2.0	3.6	4.4	3.4	2.8	2.5	3.2

Source: *Hong Kong Monthly Digest of Statistics*

However, this simplistic approach, which concentrates on sectors or classification of goods may easily miss out some broader and more important developments. It has been repeatedly stated that Hong Kong lives or dies by its foreign trade activities. On the purely merchandise balance base, Hong Kong has experienced a cumulative deficit of more than HK$82 billion over 1978–88. It was the exports of services which reduced and finally reversed this deficit into an increasing overall surplus in current balance of trade by the late 1980s (Table 1.5).

The Hong Kong Government does not collect statistics on the movements of capital, and so it is not possible to have an overall figure of either Hong Kong's accumulation overseas or its indebtedness. Some of the available estimates are discussed in Chapter 2, Section 2.5. Even more important perhaps than the growing current balance of trade surplus has been the rapid rise of re-exports in Hong Kong's trade. Re-exports are classified as goods which are imported into Hong Kong but are then subjected to no further processing and are exported again. As Table 1.6 shows, re-exports have come to account for more than half of the total of Hong Kong's trade, with China taking the lion's share as both the source and the destination of re-exports. This is a development very closely related to the role of Hong Kong as the main entrepôt for China which still lacks the world-class port facilities of Hong Kong, including its superb container docks.

Re-export trade does generate income for Hong Kong in the form of port fees, insurance, transport services, etc., but is of far more direct importance to China. Having said that, however, China has progressively become the second most important direct trading partner for Hong Kong (Table 1.7). Hong Kong's exports to China as a percentage of domestic exports rose fourfold within

Table 1.5 Current balance (HK$ billion, current prices), 1978–88

	1978	1979	1980	1981	1982	1983	1984	1985	1986	1987	1988
Domestic exports	40.7	55.9	68.1	80.4	83.0	104.4	137.9	129.8	153.9	195.2	217.6
Re-exports	13.1	20.0	30.0	41.7	44.3	56.2	83.5	105.2	122.5	182.7	275.4
Imports	63.0	85.8	111.6	138.3	142.8	175.4	223.3	231.4	275.9	377.9	498.7
Merchandise balance	−9.1	−9.9	−13.4	−16.2	−15.5	−14.7	−1.9	+3.7	+0.5	+0.08	−5.7
Exports of services	14.7	19.2	22.1	27.1	30.6	36.9	43.8	45.8	53.6	67.3	NA
Imports of services	8.2	11.9	14.9	19.3	20.9	25.2	30.0	33.5	38.9	45.7	NA
Invisibles balance	+6.4	+7.4	+7.2	+7.8	+9.6	+11.6	+13.8	+12.3	+14.6	+21.5	NA
Current balance	−2.7	−2.7	−6.2	−8.4	−5.9	−3.1	+11.9	+16.0	+15.1	+21.5	NA

Sources: Hong Kong Annual Digest of Statistics; Hong Kong Monthly Digest of Statistics
Notes: The figures do not add up because of rounding.
NA, not available.

Table 1.6 Structure and direction of re-exports, 1980–8

	1980	1981	1982	1983	1984	1985	1986	1987	1988
Re-exports as % of total exports[a]	30.6	34.1	34.8	35.0	37.7	44.7	44.3	48.3	55.8
Re-exports from China as % of rex	27.9	30.7	33.1	34.9	33.6	32.8	42.1	46.1	47.7
Re-exports to China as % of rex	15.4	19.2	18.0	21.1	33.6	43.7	33.3	32.9	34.4

Sources: *Hong Kong Annual Digest of Statistics; Hong Kong Monthly Digest*
Note: [a] Total exports = domestic exports plus re-exports.

8 years (1980–8). Equally, imports from China into Hong Kong rose by more than 60 per cent during the same period. On the other side of the coin, Hong Kong is now China's single most important export market accounting for more than 35 per cent of its own exports. These are the direct results of China's modernization and 'open door' policy which led to rapid links developing with the West. However, the USA remains the largest buyer of Hong Kong's goods, with the European Economic Community (EEC) overall also showing an increasing share.

Hong Kong's trading economy is also developing close links with the other fast growing economies in the region, namely the ASEAN countries (Association of South East Asian Nations, Indonesia, Singapore, Malaysia, Thailand and the Philippines) and the so-called newly industrialized countries (NICs) (Taiwan, Korea, Hong Kong and Singapore). The original linking point between these groups was Japan. In 1988 Japan took on average 12.2 per cent and 21 per cent respectively of the exports of NIC and ASEAN 4 (i.e. excluding Singapore) and supplied 25 per cent and 24 per cent respectively of their imports. As the figures in Table 1.7 indicate, Japan is the largest exporter to Hong Kong after China. However, it is important to stress that all these trading links are now fostering inter- and intra-regional trade flows which point to a Pacific rim economy which is becoming relatively more independent of both Japan and the USA. For example, total trade between the ASEAN 4 and the NICs grew by more than 60 per cent between 1978 and 1988 as compared with the 45 per cent growth of trade between Japan and ASEAN

Table 1.7 Distribution of trade by countries: percentages of domestic exports to (DX) and imports from (M) other countries (at current prices), 1981–8

	1981		1982		1983		1984		1985		1986		1987		1988	
	DX	M	DX	M	DX	M	DX	M	DX	M	DX	M	DX	M	DX	M
USA	36.3	10.4	37.6	10.8	41.9	10.9	44.4	10.9	44.5	9.4	41.7	8.4	37.2	8.5	33.4	8.2
PRC	3.6	21.3	7.4	23.0	5.9	24.4	8.1	24.9	11.7	25.4	11.7	29.5	14.2	31.0	17.4	31.2
FRG	8.7	2.4	8.4	2.4	7.7	2.5	6.9	2.4	6.1	2.8	7.1	2.9	7.6	2.6	7.4	2.6
UK	9.5	4.5	8.6	4.8	8.1	4.2	7.6	3.8	6.6	3.6	6.4	3.3	6.6	3.0	7.1	2.5
Japan	3.6	23.2	3.8	22.0	3.7	22.9	3.7	23.5	3.4	23.0	4.0	20.4	4.8	19.0	5.2	18.6

Sources: Hong Kong Annual Digest of Statistics; Hong Kong Monthly Digest of Statistics

4 over the same period, although this is still well below the 105 per cent increase in Japan–NIC trade over this period.[6] These regional trade flows are augmented and complemented by direct foreign investment. Japan has a cumulative US$13 billion invested in the ASEAN 4 and NIC over 1951–87. The amount of Japan's direct foreign investment in these countries has been declining as a proportion of Japan's total outflow of investment and it has progressively been shifting towards the services rather than the manufacturing sectors. In the case of Hong Kong, as Table 1.8 shows, the USA continues to be the largest foreign investor in the manufacturing sector. Japan has been a steady second with an accumulated total of US$4.07 billion of investment in Hong Kong over 1982–7, representing about 3.3 per cent of total overseas Japanese investment.

Table 1.8 Foreign investment in Hong Kong's manufacturing sector (per cent of total), 1980–8

	1980	1984	1985	1986	1987	1988
USA	43.6	53.7	36.4	41.0	36.4	34.0
Japan	31.5	21.0	21.0	20.5	26.5	26.6
PRC	NA	NA	18.3	15.2	8.2	11.2
UK	6.9	6.9	6.7	5.5	7.0	9.0

Source: 'Report on the survey of overseas investment in Hong Kong's manufacturing industries', Industry Department, Hong Kong, 1989

Note: The investment figures on which these percentages are based are cumulative totals based on original costs. Figures for China were not collected before 1985.

China's role in Hong Kong's economy requires further elaboration for a number of reasons, not least because of 1997 and more recently because of the blow to confidence that the May–June 1989 events in China dealt to Hong Kong and the potential retrenchment of China's 'open door' policy to the West.

The figures and facts outlined so far are indicative of the tight links which have developed between Hong Kong and China. It is equally easy, however, to over emphasize these links in assessing the short- and long-term repercussions on Hong Kong's economy of adverse political or economic events in China.

First, as already indicated, the re-export trade may not have a major macroeconomic impact on Hong Kong. At present there are no systematic calculations for the value added generated by re-exports. Therefore any slowdown in China's economic growth or retrenchment away from the open door policy may impact primarily on the domestic exports from Hong Kong. This will have an adverse impact on the GDP but its long-term effects may well be cushioned by the diversified nature of Hong Kong's trade. The USA is still the main trading partner in terms of domestic exports, and it is unlikely that these exports will be abruptly or arbitrarily curtailed as could be the case with a centrally planned economy. In other words Hong Kong's broad export base is not dependent solely on economic or political developments in China.

Second, Hong Kong has been the main source of direct investment into China. This has taken the form of joint ventures and setting up production and processing facilities in China (particularly in the Pearl River delta adjacent to Hong Kong) as well as provision of credit, loans etc. In 1987 out of the 7,800 foreign enterprises set up in China, 6,600 were from Hong Kong and accounted for 65 per cent of all foreign investment there.[7] It has been variously estimated that nearly two million workers in China are directly employed by Hong Kong enterprises. This is also reflected in the fact that nearly 55 per cent of Hong Kong's exports to China are for outward processing. This means that more than half of all Hong Kong's exports to China are used there as inputs for further production which is usually re-exported to Hong Kong. China is therefore becoming not so much a market as a convenient production and processing stage for Hong Kong's own output. This implies that the export trade link with China must be appraised against a processing rather than a purely consumption background. If the links with China were considerably weakened, one of the consequences would be that Hong Kong would export its unemployment to China. Equally, however, China has invested extensively in Hong Kong. A simple example illustrates the magnitude of this commitment. The Bank of China group (BOC) is now the second largest local banking conglomerate in Hong Kong. Its activities and related developments are examined in detail in Chapter 2. As the figures in Table 1.8 indicate, China is now the third most important foreign investor in Hong Kong's manufacturing sector.

Finally, the financial links with China, as opposed to the processing and trading links, are less easy to quantify. Given the present state of complete underdevelopment in China's banking and financial system, the links are almost certainly one-sided, with Hong Kong providing both the instruments and the outlet for China's foreign financial dealings primarily through the activities of BOC in Hong Kong.

The foregoing discussion is not meant to underplay the importance of China's economy to Hong Kong but it is designed to show that this has become a two-way link. Hong Kong has as large a stake in China as China has in Hong Kong. Much has been made of the assumption that the communist leadership in China will not 'kill the hen which lays the golden egg'. This perhaps misses the point, not just because the communist cadre appears to be oblivious to any consideration other than maintaining their power but also because any severe repercussions on Hong Kong will generate an immediate impact on China other than just loss of revenue. The hen, in a sense, is not now an independent entity to the economy of the PRC which can be lifted or lowered on demand so that the eggs can be removed. It is for this reason that hasty or alarmist statements about the future of Hong Kong's economy following the Beijing massacre should not be made. The picture is considerably more complex and the links run in both directions. What is undisputed is that the 'confidence factor' is of great significance for the stability of the *local* financial markets and for the morale of the labour force. The word 'local' must be emphasized because Hong Kong has now developed its financial system along directions which are not all related to or linked with China. These will be explored in the following chapters.

The major confidence impact, however, has been on the labour force. The political uncertainty has forced hundreds of thousands of Hong Kong residents to emigrate. The so-called 'brain drain' involves primarily the professional and better-off classes who are, in general, more mobile and more welcome in the countries of their destination. The impact of the brain drain will have a long-term effect on Hong Kong's economy. The drain will exacerbate the already tight labour market situation in Hong Kong.[8] It is also likely to be accompanied by export of capital. The effect of the latter will be very difficult to estimate because there are no data on capital movements in Hong Kong and because the Government has repeatedly stated that the pegged exchange rate to the US dollar will not be severed or altered under any circumstances. Whether the brain drain is reversible is a disputed issue, with most of the opinions on the side that emigrants are permanently lost to Hong Kong. A productivity miracle aside, some of the effects of both the labour market shortage and the brain drain can be ameliorated by training and education in order to increase professional mobility and by selective import of migrant workers, although the latter solution has been rejected by the Government. Restoring confidence in the long-term prospects of Hong Kong has to be a long-term exercise.[9] The very pessimistic analyses and predictions which followed the events of May–June 1989 in China do not stand very well under the light of facts and quantification. But perhaps therein lies the most imponderable question of all – the quantification of loss of confidence.

This introductory chapter opened with the statement that predictions about Hong Kong's future are always hazardous. Hong Kong's greatest asset has been the ability and willingness of its entrepreneurs and labour force to meet challenges by changing fast and adapting even faster. This ability will be put to its ultimate test in the run-up to 1997.

Chapter two

Banks

2.1 Introduction

Financial markets exhibit all the traits and behaviour of any other market for goods and services. Competition is dependent on ease of entry and absence of barriers to it, on the degree of concentration in the market, on the stability of oligopolistic or cartel arrangements and on product innovation. The pattern of demand for financial assets and services changes over time as the tastes of the consumers (asset holders) change, incomes increase and perceived risk-adjusted yield differentials widen or narrow. Financial innovation differentiates products but also provides different instruments for risk spreading and flexibility in re-arranging the structure of portfolios.

Banks as financial intermediaries have been perceived as fulfilling a number of functions in an economy. They can be considered as 'asset transformers' primarily in terms of filtering risk for their depositors. They can also be looked on as suppliers of deposits, a standard medium of exchange. These two approaches examine the assets side and the liabilities side respectively of banking operations. Logically, an approach that synthesizes both will look simultaneously at the lending and borrowing activities.[1] In one of the more simplified approaches to the behaviour of banks they are seen as firms attempting to maximize their profits or their market share in the process of bidding for funds and charging interest for lending them. This type of model yields fairly straightforward solutions to the size of assets and loans (output) and interest rates charged (price) for the operations of banks. Although elements of risk and issues of intertemporal choices need to be addressed, these models serve well in both explaining and predicting the simple dynamics of bank behaviour and their interest rate implications.

Banks operate in two markets, one where they borrow, i.e. attract deposits, and one where they lend, i.e. attract borrowers. From the point of view of the banks, the counterparts of these two markets are the suppliers of deposits, the asset holders, to the banks' demand for funds and the borrowers to the banks' supply of credit. In addition to capital, liquidity and reserve requirements banks are also constrained in their operations by the willingness of people to borrow from or lend to them. The profitability of their operations, given interest rates, is determined by their cost structures. Figure 2.1 sets out the simple analytics of this model where the supply of loans is S_L and the demand for credit is D_L. The analysis here abstracts from the demand for and supply of deposits as these will be examined separately. The operating costs of a bank can be allocated to areas specific either to the administration of loans (salaries, wages) or to the supply of funds which are primarily the interest rates paid on them. However, given the multiproduct nature of banking operations this allocation may not be possible. Subtracting these costs from the demand for funds and adding them to the supply of funds yields the average revenue and cost curves (AR and AC) respectively and their respective marginal revenue and cost relations (MR and MC). The profit-maximizing level of funds lent and interest rate charged is OF and OA. The cost to the banks is OB + BC (interest rate paid plus operating costs) and OA − AD where AD are the costs associated with lending. The difference DC = OD − OC is the surplus net of costs. Equivalently the gross interest margin return per Hong Kong (HK) dollar lent is AB with the net margin DC. Banks attempting to increase their market share will end up charging lower rates for borrowers (HF′) and lending more funds (OF′).

This model can be made more realistic by allowing for several different markets for loans and deposits. Therefore, for example, in systems where government debt is an important asset, the opportunity cost of loans to the private sector can be equated to the yield of government bonds of an equivalent maturity. Similarly, supply of deposits can be separated into time and current account deposits, with the latter being potentially more interest elastic than the former. The analysis can then incorporate

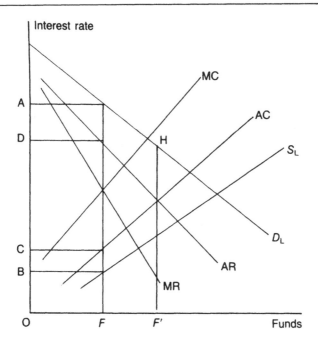

Figure 2.1 The banking firm

aspects of price discrimination by charging different borrowers different interest rates and similarly offering depositors different rates.[2]

The model presented here needs to be adjusted in two major ways with respect to Hong Kong. First, the local retail side of the banking market is highly concentrated in the hands of five banks, and in particular those of the Hongkong Bank. This raises the question of the degree of competition in the market and the possibility of an oligopolistic market leader imposing conditions or defining the limits of competition. Second, interest rate competition in the retail banking side is limited and controlled by a cartel arrangement which also has legal binding force. The influence of these particular factors on the behaviour of the banks will be examined separately.

2.2 Market morphology and competition

An interesting aspect of the structure of the bank market in Hong Kong is its division between the locally incorporated banks and overseas banks. Another is the division between banks and deposit-taking companies (DTCs). The difference between the latter institutions are sufficiently great for DTCs to merit their own chapter in this book (Chapter 3). Briefly, however, DTCs are banking type institutions primarily owned by banks and restricted by law as to the type of deposits they can accept. This means that their operations are almost exclusively limited to the wholesale side of the borrowing and lending markets with the largest of the DTCs operating as merchant banks and being active in the equity and capital markets. There are two types of DTCs, licensed which are few and large, and registered which are many and relatively small. This division, however, is now being phased out with the licensed DTCs becoming restricted licence banks. The DTCs do not come under the ambit of the interest rate agreement which applies primarily to retail deposits.

All banks in Hong Kong have to be licensed and there are regulations which apply to all of them irrespective of origin or of place of incorporation. To be specific, all banks have to maintain a 25 per cent liquidity ratio and observe certain restrictions on the type of loans they can make. A capital-to-assets ratio of 8 per cent is imposed on local banks. Hong Kong has now adopted the Basle Agreement rules with a transitional period arrangements to full implementation by 1992. The rules specify which assets are classified as part of the capital base and the risk weights attached to them. These weights vary from zero to 100 per cent depending on the degree of risk attached.[3] The Hong Kong Association of Banks (HKAB) has a statutory power to enforce an interest rate cartel on all banks, the Interest Rate Agreement (IRA), which covers most retail HK dollar deposits. One of the differences between the local and overseas banks is the obligation of local banks to report publicly and in some detail their assets, liabilities and structure of their portfolios. In addition, foreign banks are restricted as to the number of branches they may open and operate. Furthermore, for most locally incorporated banks the focus of their activities is on the retail side, whereas the overseas banks concentrate more on the wholesale side. As overseas banks are not obliged to report publicly any details of their activities in Hong Kong it is very difficult to obtain an accurate picture of the scale of their individual operations and of the relative significance of their activities. Indeed, the Banking Ordinance exempts these banks from publishing their balance sheets in Hong Kong. The office of the Commissioner of Banking publishes information on banks regarding their national origins but no more than that. Table 2.1 shows the basic breakdown of the licensed banks in Hong Kong in 1988.

Table 2.1   Banks in Hong Kong, 1988

160 licensed banks

125 incorporated outside Hong Kong of which	32 incorporated in Hong Kong plus 3 local unincorporated banks. Of these
Japan: 28 Europe: 45 USA: 20 PRC: 15 Others: 17	(i) 3 are affiliated to the Hongkong Bank (ii) 6 are members of the Bank of China Group (iii) 3 owned by the Hong Kong Government as a part of a rescue operation (iv) 10 more than 50% owned by non-PRC non-Hong Kong interests (v) 5 have minority equity participation by foreign banks (vi) 4 are completely independent and local

Sources: Commissioner of Banking, Hong Kong, *Annual Reports*; The Chinese Banks' Association, *Hong Kong's Banking System: Problems, Prospects and Policies*, Hong Kong, 1988

Entrance to the Hong Kong bank market is relatively unrestricted. Following moratoria between 1967 and 1972 and between 1975 and 1978 during which no further licences were issued, foreign banks were allowed to open in Hong Kong subject always to the provisions of the Banking Ordinance. The number of licensed banks in Hong Kong increased from 123 in 1981 to 160 in 1988, a rise of 30 per cent with an average of about five banks entering the market every year. In 1988, nineteen out of the top twenty banks in the world had offices in Hong Kong, or similarly seventy-five out of the top hundred were present. In terms of branches, about one third of all branches in Hong Kong (442) belonged to banks not incorporated in Hong Kong as opposed to the 955 which belonged to those which were.

The banking market in Hong Kong is highly concentrated, especially in terms of the locally incorporated banks and the retail side of the business. Taking only the locally incorporated banks for which consistent and published data exist, a five-bank concentration ratio in terms of deposits averages about 95 per cent over a 4-year period. Table 2.2 shows the relevant details.

Table 2.2 Market shares of the top five local banks in Hong Kong (per cent of the relevant totals of all local banks), 1983–7

Bank	1983			1984			1985			1986			1987		
	D	A	NW	D	A	NW	D	A	NW	D	A	NW	D	A	NW
Hongkong Bank	74.0	70.3	61.7	79.8	78.5	68.4	80.1	79.7	75.8	81.8	81.3	72.1	81.1	80.5	70.6
Hang Seng	8.2	8.6	6.8	9.9	9.7	8.2	10.5	10.3	10.0	10.8	10.5	9.7	10.9	10.7	11.5
East Asia	1.6	1.7	1.8	2.0	2.0	2.1	2.3	2.2	2.4	2.3	2.2	2.1	2.3	2.3	3.1
Nanyang	1.4	2.1	1.2	2.5	2.4	1.9	2.8	2.7	2.1	2.3	2.2	2.3	2.5	2.5	2.3
Shanghai Commercial	1.7	1.8	1.7	2.1	2.1	2.3	2.0	2.0	2.8	1.8	1.8	2.5	1.7	1.7	2.6

Source: Hongkong Bank, *Performance of Financial Sector*, several issues
Note: D, deposits; A, assets; NW, average net worth.

The Hongkong Bank and its subsidiary the Hang Seng Bank (61.5 per cent owned by the Hongkong Bank) dominate the market sector irrespective of the definition or measurement of size used. The role of the Hongkong Bank is extremely important in both the banking market and the execution of the monetary policy in Hong Kong. As this chapter concentrates on the microanalysis of the banking sector, the role of the Hongkong Bank as one of the note issuing banks and as the *de facto* central bank of Hong Kong is examined in detail in Chapter 6.

Data for the total banking sector, which includes the foreign banks, are scattered and unsystematic since, as indicated, foreign banks do not need to publish their local balance sheet. However, there are some data which give an indication of the relative size of the Hongkong Bank group in the banking and DTC markets (i.e. Hongkong Bank, Hang Seng Bank, Wayfoong and Wardley). These are summarized in Table 2.3.

Table 2.3 Estimates of relative shares of the Hongkong Bank group of the total banking and DTC market in Hong Kong (per cent)

	1985	1986	1987
Deposits	24.4–26.7	28.9–29.4	29.0
Loans	20.5	21.7	Not available

Sources: BT Brokerage Research, *Hong Kong's Banking Sector*, Hong Kong, September 1988; Commissioner of Banking, Hong Kong, *Annual Reports*; Chinese Banks' Assocation, *Hong Kong's Banking System*, pp. 103–6

The group's overall market share is not declining, although it is hard to draw conclusions from 2 or 3 years' observations. However, it would not be inaccurate to claim that the local banking sector in Hong Kong is dominated by a very small number of banks with little evidence of major changes or shifts in the distribution. The Bank of China group has made consistent and determined efforts to increase its market share and penetrate specific sectors or activities such as mortgage loans. The group's share of deposits in the total banking sector increased from 15 to 18.1 per cent between 1985 and 1986.[4] The events of May–June 1989 in China were a setback to the efforts of the Bank of China group to expand and maintain a substantial market share as there were significant deposit withdrawals.

Japanese banks as a group maintain a very important presence with twenty-eight out of the 160 licensed banks in 1988, six out of the thirty-five licensed DTCs and thirty out of the 216 registered DTCs. The group as a whole has maintained a relatively steady proportion of deposits (both HK dollars and foreign exchange) to total customer deposits (banks and DTCs) at about 9.5 per cent, and assets at about 52 per cent over 1986–8 (in both cases classified in terms of country of beneficial ownership). Not surprisingly Japanese banks dominated the inter-bank market (both forex and HK dollars) by lending on average 56 per cent and borrowing 68 per cent of all funds (1986–8).

One of the more controversial and extensively researched aspects of bank economics and market morphology has been the relationship between size and profitability. The standard predictions of industrial economics concerning the positive link between concentration and performance did not, apparently, apply to banks.[5] Attempts to establish a link between various measures of performance, usually defined in terms of profitability, and concentration in banking markets in the USA proved difficult. Concentration can be measured in a number of ways, usually by estimating the market share of the top three or five banks. The theory tested was based on the assumption that high seller concentration lowers the cost of information and fosters tacit or explicit collusion amongst firms. This may result to firms earning monopoly rents.[6] This approach was later criticized along the lines that greater concentration in markets results from greater efficiency rather than elimination of competition. Firms which are efficient end up obtaining a higher market share and as a result the concentration in the market increases. These firms will also be able to extract a monopoly rent from their operations.[7] It would now also follow that the observed relationship between concentration and profits is, in a sense, spurious since what matters is market share. Market share can be defined in terms of the individual bank's share of either total deposits or loans or assets. Efficient firms all have a higher market share and will also be more profitable. This relationship between market shares and profitability has been termed the 'efficient structure hypothesis' and has been applied to banks:

> The efficient structure hypothesis provides a potential
> explanation of the failure to find evidence of a consistently

positive concentration – profitability relationship in banking. . . . According to the efficient structure hypothesis, some firms will earn supernormal profits because of superior efficiency. This efficiency is reflected in high market shares. Since markets containing such firms will tend to exhibit high concentration, it is possible a spurious relationship between concentration and profitability will be observed when market share is not properly considered. When observed, however, one might expect this relationship to be quantitatively weak, which is exactly what is reported in banking literature.[8]

Using data spanning 4 years (1984–7) and covering the performance of thirty-two locally incorporated banks in Hong Kong a number of tests were run to investigate the links between size, market share and performance. This test covered thirty-two licensed banks incorporated in Hong Kong excluding three small local but unincorporated banks. All the accounting information was on a consolidated basis. Two measurements of profitability were used: percentage return on average assets and percentage return on average net worth. Net worth was defined as the sum total of share capital, share premium and capital reserve, general reserve and profit and loss plus minority interest but excluding loan capital. The returns are defined in terms of the ratio of average assets or average net worth to net profits.

The period covered by the data (1984–7) included two years 1985 and 1986 during which a number of banks exhibited negative returns, in some cases as high as −1,884.2 per cent! These figures were likely to distort the calculations by introducing extreme outliers. The existence of negative returns was allowed for in the regression models by running tests for equations which used all the data and then rerunning these tests excluding all negative returns.

Two models and their variations were run incorporating tests of efficient structure hypothesis.

Model I:

$$\%\mathrm{RAA}_i = \alpha + \sum_{j=1}^{6} \beta_j Z_{ji}$$

$$\%\mathrm{RANW}_i = \alpha + \sum_{j=1}^{6} \beta_j Z_{ji}$$

and the logarithmic forms on the versions which excluded negative returns

Model II:

$$
\left.
\begin{array}{l}
\%\mathrm{RAA}_i + \alpha + \sum_{j=1}^{6} \beta_j Z_{ji} + \gamma S_i \\[2em]
\%\mathrm{RANW}_i = \alpha + \sum_{j=1}^{6} \beta_j Z_{ji} + \gamma S_i
\end{array}
\right\}
\begin{array}{l}
\text{and the logarithmic forms} \\
\text{of the versions which} \\
\text{excluded negative returns}
\end{array}
$$

where $\%\mathrm{RAA}_i$ is the percentage return on the average assets of the ith bank, $\%\mathrm{RANW}_i$ is the percentage return on average net worth of the ith bank, Z_j, $j = 1 \ldots 6$ are different variables which may influence profitability, such as (i) percentage growth of assets (% GA), (ii) percentage growth of net worth (% GNW), (iii) percentage growth of loans (% GL), (iv) liquidity ratio (LIQ), (v) total assets and (vi) total deposits, S_i is the share of the deposits of the ith bank in the sum total deposits of the thirty-two banks. The inclusion of S_i according to the efficient structure hypothesis is expected to yield more accurate results and to draw out any underlying relations between profitability and size. The minimum number of Z_j variables was selected consistent with high R^2 and maximum number of significant coefficients with the right sign.

The results of the tests are shown in Table 2.4 and 2.5. A number of equations are included, some yielding reasonably good results and, for comparison, some which do not. Total deposits and assets were consistently non-significant in explaining either measurement of profitability and hence are not shown. Table 2.4 excludes S_i; Table 2.5 includes its effects. The logarithmic form of the equations did not improve the results. A number of tests for multicollinearity using stepwise regressions did not produce any strong evidence for it. A further attempt to eliminate the potentially distorting effect of the presence of data for the Hongkong Bank and the Hang Seng Bank by removing these from the sample yielded, in general, almost identical results for the models and equations that included them. The most obvious conclusion from these tests is that the non-relationship between size and profitability, so prevalent in similar US studies, also holds true for Hong Kong. The size of deposits or assets is not correlated with profitability. Large banks are not systematically more profitable than their smaller counterparts.[9]

The inclusion of the share variable S_i did not change the

Table 2.4 The relationship between size and profitability of local banks in Hong Kong

Year	Equation	%GNW	%GA	%GL	LIQ	C	R²	N	SSR	SEE
1984	%RRA	0.023 (1.04)	-0.025 (-0.88)			0.21 (0.27)	0.13 (0.04)	32	114.3	2.02
	%RANW	0.066 (0.47)		0.22 (1.65)	6.38 (2.19)	0.14	0.14 (0.08)	32	6342.0	14.78
	%RAAᵃ	-0.0049 (-0.40)	-0.0032 (-0.18)		0.019 (4.19)	0.44 (1.18)	0.49 (0.43)	26	11.48	0.72
1985	%RAA	0.13 (7.35)	0.067 (1.73)			-1.30 (-1.74)	0.85 (0.84)	32	363.0	3.53
	%RAA	0.14 (9.93)		0.056 (2.13)		-1.18 (-1.71)	0.85 (0.84)	32	346.31	3.45
	%RAAᵃ	-0.02 (-1.55)	-0.016 (-1.87)		0.02 (3.97)	0.72 (2.41)	0.54 (0.45)	20	4.34	0.52
1986	%RAAᵃ	-0.0015 (-0.30)	0.0010 (0.27)		0.17 (6.06)	0.15 (0.77)	0.66 (0.60)	23	2.74	0.38
	%RAAᵇ	0.0015 (0.21)	0.10 (2.36)		0.06 (1.53)	-5.5 (-2.32)	0.28 (0.19)	28	815.37	5.82
1987	%RAAᵃ	0.012 (8.81)	-0.0069 (-1.71)			1.10 (6.20)	0.79 (0.77)	24	6.71	0.56
	%RAA	0.012 (7.32)		-0.011 (-3.15)		1.11 (6.98)	0.65 (0.62)	32	15.85	0.73
	%RAAᵃ	0.010 (6.47)				0.97 (6.62)	0.59 (0.58)	30	16.0	0.75

Notes: Figures in parentheses are t ratios; the figure in parentheses under R^2 is the adjusted R^2.

Table 2.5 The influence of market share on the profitability of Hong Kong local banks

Year	Equation	Share	%GNW	%GL	%GA	LIQ	C	R^2	N	SSR	SEE
1984	%RRA	0.004 (-0.01)	-0.02 (-1.02)		0.02 (-0.86)	0.01 (1.36)	0.21 (0.26)	0.13 (0.01)	32	114.33	2.05
1985	%RAA	0.005 (0.10)	0.13 (7.07)	0.045 (1.22)	0.024 (0.45)	-0.00006 (-0.002)	-1.33 (-0.91)	0.85 (0.83)	32	343.2	3.63
	%RAA	0.005 (0.11)	0.15 (12.10)				-0.67 (-0.95)	0.83 (0.82)	32	400.7	3.71
	%RANW	-0.31 (-0.11)	5.40 (7.12)				-13.82 (-0.34)	0.63 (0.61)	32	0.13×10^7	213.93
1986	%RAA[a]	0.0071 (0.094)	0.0015 (0.21)		0.10 (2.28)	0.061 (1.50)	-5.54 (-2.26)	0.28 (0.15)	28	815.05	5.95
	%RANW[a]	0.053 (0.10)	0.023 (0.47)		0.80 (2.56)		-14.88 (-1.46)	0.22 (0.12)	28	41217.0	41.44
1987	%RAA	-0.0079 (-0.66)	0.010 (5.76)				0.89 (5.43)	0.53 (0.50)	32	20.9	0.85
	%RANW	0.0026 (0.019)	0.11 (3.55)		-0.15 (-2.06)		13.56 (5.05)	0.32 (0.24)	32	2534.0	9.51
	%RAA[b]	-0.01 (-0.98)	0.012 (4.48)		-0.0045 (-0.64)		1.12 (4.87)	0.61 (0.57)	30	15.36	0.76

overall picture because, as Table 2.5 shows, the coefficients were not significant in all the tests. This, in a sense, may not be surprising since in the case of Hong Kong S_i must be very highly correlated with deposits or assets in view of the extremely skewed distribution of both these variables. We could envisage a bank market with a more evenly distributed shares of deposits and assets where relatively small differences in market shares were reflected in relatively larger differences in profitability. In Hong Kong, with five banks holding in excess of 95 per cent of all deposits and assets, the remaining share amongst the thirty or so banks is so small that even if it varied amongst them the changes are unlikely to appear statistically related to changes in profitability.

From all the results two variables stand out as best explanators of profitability: growth of net worth and the liquidity ratio. Banks that are highly liquid and whose overall capital base has risen over the previous years are likely to exhibit consistently higher returns on their assets or their capital base. This holds true irrespective of whether banks with negative returns are included or excluded from the sample. The explanation for this is relatively simple. Higher liquidity can be associated with flexibility in the allocation of earning assets but also with avoidance of potential non-performing longer-term debts. Growth of net worth in itself may not offer an explanation of the more than proportionate growth of net profits. However, it may stand in as a proxy for dynamic efficiency in the sense that banks with a rapidly growing capital base may also be capable of earning profits at a higher rate as well.

These findings cast an interesting light and raise a number of additional questions as far as the morphology and efficiency of the banking market in Hong Kong is concerned. To be specific, small may, after all, be beautiful since larger is not better. This statement must be carefully qualified because the evidence presented here can be equally interpreted the other way. Since there is no systematic variation of size with profitability, the smaller bank could be equally unprofitable. Some evidence, however, may well reinforce the argument that for Hong Kong there is no proof for either argument. The comparison between the five largest, the five most profitable and the five most liquid banks in 1986 is quite revealing in so far as no consistent pattern emerges (Table 2.6). Similar results hold for other years as well. Absence of systematic and bank specific data for Hong Kong on banking cost structures does not allow a more detailed analysis of the causes and trends in the relationship between costs and income. This is an area of particular importance to Hong Kong given both the large number of branches in relationship to the total population and market, and the very high concentration of market power in the local banking market.

There is a wealth of evidence on the relationship between size and costs for the unitary and fragmented banking system in the USA. A comprehensive survey of the state of the knowledge of this area produced a somewhat confused picture concerning the relationship between size, cost behaviour and minimum size for minimum cost – the efficiency issue:

> Studies in 1960, and 1970, . . . reported evidence of diseconomies for branch banks at higher output levels, which were normally attributed to problems in coordinating a decentralised organisational form. The consensus of this literature was that small banks were at cost disadvantage compared to large banks but that the difference was not so large as to prevent them from competing effectively in their particular market niches . . . . Recent studies reported U-shaped cost curves for banks, with scale benefits exhausted at only US$10 million to US$23 million deposits. There was some evidence of flat cost curves in branch states also. To a certain degree, these results are contrary to earlier studies; that is very small banks were found to be cost efficient for the most part, and in the case of branch bank states, instead of diseconomies at higher output levels, a flat cost curve was encountered . . . . The findings of our research on bank costs (produced) cost curves in unit banking (which) were consistently flat, with no economies or diseconomies evident. In branch banking states, the cost curves were normally either U-shaped or upward sloping.[10]

However, this survey did find evidence of economies of scale where technology could influence operations or products. Therefore, for example, larger banks had cost advantages over smaller banks in the production of demand deposits and credit card services. But perhaps the most aposite conclusion was arrived at in a study which utilized data covering all the commercial banks

Table 2.6 Ranking of banks according to size, profitability and liquidity, 1986

Banks ranked by size	D (%)	%RAA	LIQ
1 Hongkong	81.8	12.9	45.4
2 Hang Seng	10.8	25.4	20.2
3 East Asia	2.3	18.9	63.0
4 Nanyang	2.3	7.8	65.9
5 Shanghai Commercial	1.8	14.9	64.3
Banks ranked by profitability	%RAA	D (%)	LIQ
1 Wayfoong	37.9	0.9	25.6
2 Hang Seng	25.4	10.8	20.2
3 Wing Lung	20.0	1.0	63.8
4 East Asia	18.9	2.3	63.0
5 Chekiang First	17.6	0.6	61.2
Banks ranked by liquidity	LIQ	D (%)	%RAA
1 Tai Sang	140.3	0.05	3.6
2 Tai Yau	126.6	0.05	7.6
3 Union	78.0	0.1	−14.7[a]
4 HK Chinese	67.8	0.1	2.5
5 Nanyang	65.9	2.3	7.8

Source: Hongkong Bank, *Performance of the Finance Sector*, 1986
Notes: For the meaning of symbols see Table 2.4
[a] Inclusion of extraordinary items would turn the loss to a profit return of 18.5 per cent and rank the bank as sixth most profitable.

in the USA. The study demonstrated that differences in the costs between banks of similar size are greater than those between the costs of banks of different sizes. In a sense size is less important than efficiency.[11]

Although it would be dangerous to draw conclusions from studies specific to a particular country and set of institutions, it may well be tempting to argue that size may not necessarily confer cost advantages in Hong Kong. The five largest banks are not the most profitable. Similarly the applications and use of technology may confer some benefits on larger banks whilst barring others from using this technology because of the costs involved. Differences in cost efficiency between the smaller banks in Hong Kong may well be very important in explaining the observed differences in profitability. However, this test must await the availability of bank-specific cost data for all banks in Hong Kong.

The Census Department of Hong Kong Government collects

data on aggregate cost and income flows of the banking sector as a whole. Although this information cannot cast any light on the efficiency of individual or of groups of banks, it can point towards some significant developments. Table 2.7 outlines some of these developments.

Table 2.7 Trends in costs and income sources of all banks in Hong Kong (as percentage of total category) 1981–6

	1981	1982	1983	1984	1985	1986
Income						
Net interest	64.2	65.6	64.1	61.7	58.0	54.4
Provision of services	11.1	11.4	13.8	15.7	15.9	16.2
Costs						
Salaries etc.	54.0	54.5	54.7	56.8	57.8	58.2
Rents	19.3	19.2	21.2	19.3	18.3	16.1
Profitability						
Net interest receipts						
(% of total assets)	2.07	1.55	1.17	0.95	0.83	0.72
Working profit						
(% of total assets)	1.92	1.24	0.86	0.71	0.62	0.70

Source: Census and Statistics Department of Hong Kong, *Survey of Storage, Communications, Financing, Insurance and Business Services*, various issues

Net interest receipts in Hong Kong both as a percentage of total income and as a return to total assets are declining, whilst labour costs become increasingly more important. In terms of the model developed in Figure 2.1, banks are being faced with increasing costs relating to the administration of loans (here salaries and wages) but also simultaneously by competitive pressures that reduce relatively the importance of net interest receipts as a source of income. One potential explanation for the latter is an increasing awareness of the public of alternative venues for short term riskless investment opportunities that will make the demand for deposits (or equivalently the supply of funds) more interest rate elastic. Similarly, borrowers will also be more aware of alternative sources of finance as competition increases not only for depositors but also for borrowers. In terms of Figure 2.2 the S_L curve shifts upwards but also swivels downwards to S'_L as interest elasticity increases. Similarly D'_L is more elastic than D_L all along the interest rates less than OA. The outcome is that at the profit maximizing position $MC' = MR'$

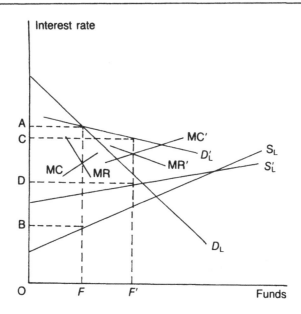

Figure 2.2 Effects of costs and demand changes on the banking firm

(from MC = MR) banks not only accept more deposits or lend more funds but also receive less gross interest receipts (from AB to CD) for every dollar they lend.

There is ample evidence of the gross interest margin in Hong Kong declining over time, compressed by the increased competition both for borrowers and depositors. The data are provided in Table 2.8. Although there are fluctuations there is a trend for a narrowing down of differentials. The best lending rate (BLR) is the rate charged on loans by the Hongkong Bank and is used as the benchmark for all other commercial loan rates.

There is plentiful anecdotal evidence over the developing competition in the Hong Kong banking market. One particular aspect of the competitive pressures relates to interest rate cartel which has been in operation since 1964. All banks in Hong Kong have to join the Hong Kong Association of Banks which is a statutory body. Amongst its other functions, the Association in consultation with the Financial Secretary fixes the interest rates paid on certain deposits. Since 1982 the agreement specified that interest rates paid on the following type of deposits had to be

Table 2.8   Interest rate spread, 1984–8

	A	B		A	B
1984			**1986**		
Q1	5.42	4.32	Q1	4.75	3.75
Q2	5.60	4.64	Q2	4.87	3.62
Q3	5.98	4.48	Q3	4.62	3.37
Q4	5.66	4.16	Q4	4.50	3.25
1985			**1987**		
Q1	5.50	4.35	Q1	4.04	2.79
Q2	5.31	4.45	Q2	4.56	3.27
Q3	4.58	3.62	Q3	4.75	3.25
Q4	4.75	3.75	Q4	4.57	3.29
			1988		
			Q1	4.26	3.50
			Q2	4.64	3.50

Source: BT Brokerage Research, *Hong Kong's Banking Sector*,
Hong Kong, September 1988
Note: A, best lending – savings deposit; B, best lending – 3
months deposit.

uniform, with certain exceptions, amongst all members: savings deposits, deposits of less than HK$0.5 million with more than 3 months maturity and fixed-term deposits with less than 15 months maturity. A number of banks were allowed to offer marginally higher rates than the ones specified in the agreement.[12]

The origin of the interest rate cartel goes back to one of Hong Kong's numerous banking crises in the 1960s when keen competition resulted in both unprofitable and potential risky practices in order to attract deposits. The interest rate agreement has survived repeated criticisms and attempts to bypass it through creative financial engineering. Its usefulness to the Government was demonstrated by the decision to link the HK dollar to the US dollar in 1983 and the 'negative interest rate' crisis of 1987.[13] The standard textbook arguments for the cartel have been used to defend it, namely that it protects the smaller banks, that it leads to orderly competition and, after 1983, that it may assist in protecting the HK dollar against speculative runs in the forex markets.

The effects of interest rate restrictions on deposits yield some unexpected results. The model outlined in Figures 2.1 and 2.2 can now be developed further in order to explore and illustrate the situation in Hong Kong. The market for funds can be divided into two sectors, one for deposits and one for loans. The interest rate ceiling on deposits introduces a constraint on the amount of loans that can be generated, and depending on the demand for deposits and loans, this may or may not be effective in the sense of changing the operations of the banks. Figure 2.3(a) shows the demand for and supply of loans and Figure 2.3(b) shows the demand for deposits by banks and supply of deposits by customers. The demand for deposits by banks will vary not only with the interest rate payable on them but also with the differential $r_0 - i_0$. For a profitable operation it is clear that $r > i$. For different levels of r, given i, the demand function in Figure 2.3(b) will shift. As interest rates receivable on loans rise, the demand for deposits by banks at all levels of i will also rise, reflecting that $D(r)$ is a derived demand from the willingness of banks to lend.[14] In order to simplify the analysis the equity base (net worth) of the banks is ignored thereby making deposits the only source of loans. In Figure 2.4 $L_0 = D_0$ so that the banks lend as much as customers wish to borrow at r_0 and accept in deposits as much as customers are willing to hold at i_0. A ceiling interest rate i^* is now imposed on the rates that banks may pay. Its effect will be explored by assuming that the ceiling is binding at $i_0 = i^*$ following an increase in the demand for loans. This is illustrated by a shift of the demand curve for loans from d_L to d'_L. The banks will be able to provide additional loans $L_1 - L_0$ only if they can attract an equal additional amount of deposits. The loan rate will rise towards r_1 shifting the demand curves for deposits from $D(r_0)$ to $D(r_1)$. As the interest ceiling is now binding the banks will not be able to attract the extra deposits and the supply curve of loans will become completely interest inelastic at L_0 (indicated by $S^*_L L_0$). Interest rates on loans may well rise to more than r_1 unless the banks use non-price-rationing methods to allocate the L_0 funds available. Similarly, the bank may attract some more deposits by changes in the quality of services including non-interest financial inducements such as free gifts for new depositors etc. As long as the interest ceiling is binding the demand for deposits by banks will become the kinked curve $ABD(r_0)$ in Figure 2.4(b).

In the case of Hong Kong it has been argued that if the ceiling was removed depositors would benefit but borrowers would suffer as rates rose. Unless a specific assumption is made about

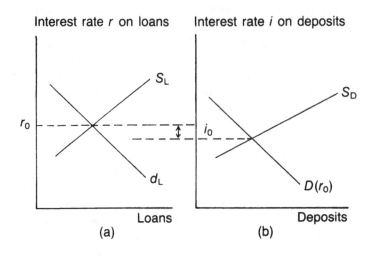

Figure 2.3 Market for loans and deposits

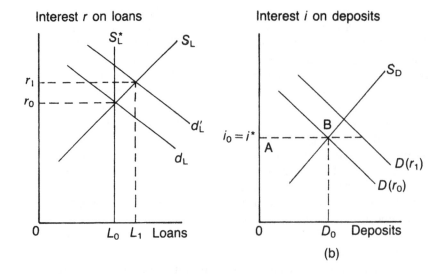

Figure 2.4 Interest rate controls

the elasticities of supply and demand involved, there is no *a priori* reason to believe that borrowers will pay more. Indeed the simple model used here predicts that borrowers would actually pay less! To illustrate this, suppose that in Figure 2.5 the fixed interest on deposits $i_0 = i^*$ is binding in the sense that there is excess demand for deposits by banks. The actual amount deposited by customers is $0D_0$, allowing the banks to lend $0L_0$ (Figure 2.5(a)). Suppose now that the ceiling is raised progressively prior to allowing the rates to float freely. At $i_1 = i^{**}$ the amount deposited by customers will increase by $D_1 - D_0$, thus shifting the supply of loans to S_L^{**}. As long as the ceiling is binding (i.e. there is excess demand of deposits by banks), the supply of loans will be a vertical curve. However, the increase in the amount of loans available will lower the interest charged from r_0 to r'. As long as $r - i > 0$ lending will continue to be profitable for the banks. The $D(r_0)$ curve will shift inwards, but as long as the initial situation is one of excess demand for deposits by the bank this will not affect the conclusions drawn.[15] If the ceiling is

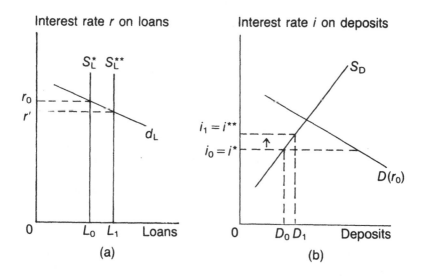

Figure 2.5 Lifting of interest rate controls

removed altogether the S_L curves in Figure 2.5(a) would become, upward sloping, indicating that banks can lend more by paying more on deposits, thereby attracting more funds which can then be lent at a higher interest. The prediction of this model can be summarized as follows:

> This [the fall in lending rates, AFF] is an important result as it contradicts the common assertion that a rise in interest rate ceilings increases loan interest rates. This assertion is based on the observation that an increase in interest rates on the bank's liabilities raises its costs. It is argued that the higher costs are passed on to borrowers through an increase in the interest rates on loans. The argument is defective because it disregards the increase in the bank's liabilities that occurs when the interest ceiling rises. The public supplies a larger amount of liabilities to the banks which causes its loans supply to shift to the right.[16]

As can be seen in Figure 2.5 the differential $r - i$ will now decline, following the rise in the ceiling and therefore the profit margin per loan will fall. Whether the total profits will decline will depend on the interest elasticities of demand and supply of loans and deposits. This conclusion has important implications for Hong Kong because one of the arguments for maintaining the IRA has been the proposition that it shields the smaller banks, and therefore their depositors, from falling profits and possible bankruptcy. This proposition is based on the expectation that, as in Figure 2.5,

$$0L_0(=0D_0)(r_0 - i_0) > 0L_1(=0D_1)(r' - i_1)$$

This would be true if either S_D was interest inelastic, so that deposits hardly increased as rates payable on them rose from i_0 to i_1, or d_L was also inelastic so that there was little or no increase in loans as the increase in the available loanable funds depressed interest rates. Given that $r_0 - i_0 > r' - i_1$ and always assuming that $r' > i_1$, total profits from loans will rise only if the percentage rise in the demand for loans is greater than the percentage fall in the interest margin.

There is some evidence in Hong Kong to suggest that the supply of deposits to the banks (or equivalently demand by the public of deposits with the banks) is sensitive to interest rate differentials and therefore unlikely to be inelastic. For example, in a particular instance during the mid-1980s, depositors appeared to be interest rate sensitive in the choice of the currency they held as they shifted out of HK dollars to foreign currency deposits and especially deposits denominated in US dollars:

> The shift in portfolio demand is a natural development when an economy moves swiftly into a low interest environment. With the Hong Kong dollars time deposit rates falling from 11½% in July 1984 to 3–4% in December 1985, depositors having reaped the benefit of higher yields, inevitably become more interest sensitive and tend to look for opportunities to protect their interest earnings.[17]

An econometric study of the demand for saving deposits using quarterly data over 1974–80 obtained own-interest elasticity of demand of about 0.30. The elasticities for time deposits were lower at about 0.16–0.17, but there was some evidence of substitutability between time and savings deposits.[18] Although this is hardly conclusive evidence, at least it points away from a completely interest inelastic demand for deposits. Similarly, demand for bank loans in Hong Kong exhibits low interest rate elasticity but no extreme or non-significant values were found.[19] The expectations that profits of banks in Hong Kong would decline if the interest agreement were abolished is based on assumptions which are not necessarily supported by evidence. In evaluating the predictions of the analysis it is important to establish whether the ceiling on the interest rate paid in Hong Kong was effective, i.e. whether banks operated along the horizontal part of their demand curve for deposits and therefore on the vertical part of the supply of loans. Furthermore, it may be necessary to measure the overall distribution of the effect of the ceiling, assuming it was binding, in view of the predominance of the Hongkong Bank in both the domestic deposit and the domestic lending scenes as the analysis at this stage does assume competition amongst the banks.

On a simpler but equally interesting level, an attempt was made to measure the effects on the total interest paid to depositors by the operation of the Interest Rate Agreement.[20] From data for the period 1978–84, the average spread earned by banks on their loans was about 4.69 per cent. This spread compared extremely favourably with an average of about 1.1 per cent earned by banks in other developed countries. The following conclusions were drawn in this study:

> Supposing HK dollar deposits subject to the IRA amount to HK$90 billion, i.e. all the saving deposits and half the time deposits at banks in HK dollars, reduction of the banks' spread by one percentage point would benefit depositors by HK$900 million.[21]

The developing competitive pressures within the banking sector have been subjecting the agreement to severe strains. Although it would be mistaken to write it off at this stage, announcements of its future demise would not be premature. Three factors are likely to predicate against its existence. First, attempts have already been made to circumvent the rules imposed by the HKAB. A number of DTCs launched the Hong Kong's equivalent of money market funds offering rates higher than those available on savings deposits. Crucially the minimum size of the funds was pitched at HK$50,000, well within the reach of the average deposit holder. These funds met with a mixed reception and did not constitute a major threat, but indicated the direction of future developments. Second, the growing sophistication of the money market and the need to develop an interest rate hedging instrument such as interest rate futures will produce additional pressures. Controlling a significant spectrum of interest rates in the important retail market of Hong Kong may become both unattainable and unprofitable. Finally, the steady but growing pressure on the dominant position of the Hongkong Bank will weaken the reasons for keeping the agreement intact. A subsidiary issue concerns the fact that since 1964 the majority of the banks that failed did so because of fraud rather than because they succumbed to competitive pressures.

Bank crises have not been uncommon in Hong Kong. For example, the Hang Seng bank, the second largest local bank, had to be rescued by the Hongkong Bank in 1965. However, the most sustained and concentrated pressure on the local banking market took place after the 1982–3 crisis which involved runs on DTCs and pressure on the HK dollar. This crisis was combined with a major scandal involving the Carrian Group which was a vehicle for property and investment deals, most of which turned out to be at best imprudent and at worst illegal.[22]

During 1983–7 six banks and a subsidiary of one of these banks had to be rescued by direct Government action primarily in terms of financial backing. In two cases involving also the subsidiary mentioned, the Government took over the banks completely. Two other banks also ran into problems during this period but they were taken over by other institutions in privately backed actions. Table 2.9 summarizes the main causes of the difficulties and the subsequent action or developments. A common characteristic of all these banks was that they were primarily family owned. Illegalities or fraud did not figure prominently as causes of their difficulties, but poor supervision by the authority and by bank auditors may well have contributed. Surprisingly enough, genuinely economic factors such as cyclical fluctuations or rapid changes in sectors, say oil or stock price movements, were minor issues in their difficulties. Overexposure to a single sector or borrower can of course be construed as an economic factor as it increases the risk element.[23] These particular factors are in stark contrast with the main causes of corporate liquidations in Hong Kong.[24] The most risky sectors in terms of numbers and frequency of liquidation are garments and electronic engineering. Indeed, in the 1970s and 1980s no bank has actually been allowed to enter into liquidation proceedings. Unlike the overall Government policy of non-intervention in the private sector, in the case of banks the Hong Kong Government has stepped in promptly and generously to provide support. The disclosed amounts for support in the cases illustrated in Table 2.9 were about HK$4 billion for three banks and an undisclosed amount for the rest. The authorities used the Exchange Fund, the account holding Hong Kong's foreign exchange reserves and accumulated fiscal surpluses, as the sources of the financial support.[25] This type of intervention drew widespread criticism at the time and revived the issue of imposing some form of deposit insurance on Hong Kong's banking system. Perhaps the most sensitive aspect of this discussion has been the role of supervisory authorities, and by extension the Government, in protecting depositors rather than shareholders when imprudence led banks into financial difficulties.

Table 2.9 Problem banks in Hong Kong, 1983–7

Cause	Bank (crisis year)					
	Hang Lung (1983)	Overseas Trust Bank (OTB) and subsidiary Hong Kong Industrial and Commercial Bank (HKICB) (1985)	Ka Wah (1985)	Win On (1985)	Union Bank (1986)	Hong Ning (1986)
Fraudulent or illegal activities	Cheque kitting	Possible breaches of Bank Ordinance Cheque kitting				

Poor supervision by Government or auditors	No early detection	No early detection by auditors	No early detection by auditors	No early detection		
Loans to family or interlinked companies		Extensive		Extensive		
Government action	Complete takeover in 1983	Complete takeover	Financial support	Financial support	Financial support	Financial support and takeover
Subsequent developments	Being sold	OTB to be HKICB sold off in 1987	Taken over in 1986 by PRC interests	Hang Seng Bank becomes major shareholder in 1986	Taken over by PRC interests in 1986	Sold off to First Pacific 1987

Source: Press reports and various issues of the *Far Eastern Economic Review*

2.3 Portfolio structure and dynamics

The simple model of the banking firm developed in Figures 2.1 and 2.2 and extended in Figures 2.3–2.5 can be used to determine the levels of loans issued, deposits accepted and interest rate charged. Of necessity, the model leaves out of the picture the allocation of funds amongst different types of loans or deposits. As liabilities can be considered equivalent to negative assets, it is possible to build up a model that examines the underlying portfolio choice and structure of a bank and also itemizes and explains holdings of individual assets. Portfolio choices are constrained by accounting identities and legal restrictions (say liquidity or reserve ratios). Mean–variance analysis of portfolio selection has been applied to banking with varying degrees of success.[26]

At the most elementary level a bank can be considered to have x_i assets and y_j liabilities. The bank's equity base EQ would then be

$$EQ = \Sigma x_i + (-\Sigma y_j)$$

It would now also follow that

$$\frac{\Sigma x_i + (-\Sigma y_j)}{EQ} = 1$$

with

$$\frac{x_i}{EQ} = w_i \qquad \frac{-y_j}{EQ} = w_j^*$$

where w_i and w_j^* are the weights of the individual assets and liabilities, and

$$\Sigma w_i + \Sigma w_j^* = 1$$

The total rate of return R of the bank's balance sheet can be defined as

$$\Sigma w_i r_i + \Sigma w_j^* r_j = R$$

where r_i and r_j are the rates of return on the assets and the liabilities respectively.

The portfolio choice can then be modelled as minimizing the risk of the bank's portfolio subject to the constraints

$$\min Z = \text{var}(R) + \lambda_1[\text{E}(R) - R^*] + \lambda_2(\Sigma w_i + \Sigma w_j^* - 1)$$

where R^* is the minimum required rate of return on the bank's equity and the λ are the Lagrangean multipliers.[27] The solution to this standard Lagrangean multiplier problem will yield an efficient banking frontier. It would now follow that, allowing for a risk-free interest rate at which borrowing or lending could take place, a 'market' portfolio for a bank could be established. The equilibrium market portfolio could then be expected to change with changes in this interest rate.

The foregoing analysis serves the simple purpose of highlighting the task facing a bank in choosing the assets–liabilities structure within the constraints imposed in order to maximize the returns (or minimize the risks) of its operations. Banks presumably respond not only to changes in expected rates of returns but also to the risk attached to specific assets in terms of the variance of returns. To the extent that banks can influence the allocation of their assets, the returns on these can be controlled. The situation may well be more complex with respect to liabilities which reflect the portfolio decisions of the personal and corporate sectors. Banks are likely to have much less direct control over these.

There have been significant changes in the composition of the assets and liabilities of banks in Hong Kong. These changes require careful consideration in order to isolate cause and effect. Furthermore, as the statistical sources available do not differentiate between local and overseas banks, a clear distinction will need to be made between assets and liabilities denominated in HK dollars and in forex. As indicated above, foreign banks are exempt from public disclosure of their balance sheets in Hong Kong and so very little can be said about them either individually or as a group. Hong Kong's rise as a banking centre has been based on its ability to operate as an offshore centre where banks could book or 'park' funds in various currencies, although primarily in US dollars. Table 2.10 shows the basic structure of the assets and liabilities of all banks in Hong Kong both local and foreign. There are four observations which can be made with regard to the structure of the balance sheet of these banks.

First, deposits from customers account for a relatively small percentage of the banks' total liabilities. The major item is deposits from other banks from abroad, 97 per cent of which are

Table 2.10 The portfolio of all banks in 1988

Liabilities				Assets			
Item	Million HK dollars	% Total		Item	Million HK dollars	% Total	
		(a)	(b)			(c)	(d)
1 Deposits from customers				1 Notes and coins	4,203		0.1
Demand	49,381	(6.3)	1.5	2 Amount due from banks and DTCs in Hong Kong	384,424		11.7
Savings	118,951	(15.2)	3.6	3 Amount due from banks abroad	1,801,393		54.8
Time	145,637	(18.6)	4.4	4 Negotiable certificates of deposit	19,776		0.6
	313,969	(40.1)	9.5				

	Amount	(a) %	(b) %
Total deposits	778,989	(100%)	23.7
3 Others			
(i) Amount due to banks abroad	2,004,095		61.0
(ii) Amount due to banks and DTCs in HK	344,449		10.4
(iii) Negotiable certificates of deposit	30,012		1.0
(iv) Other liabilities	128,849		3.9
Total liabilities	3,286,394		(100%)

	Amount	(c) %	(d) %
(iii) Building and construction	54,899	13.4	1.6
(iv) Mortgages	61,448	15.1	1.8
(v) Others	195,860	48.15	6.0
Subtotal	406,693	(100%)	12.2
6 Bank acceptances and bills of exchange	18,398		0.5
7 Floating rate notes and commercial paper	52,504		1.5
8 Treasury bills, securities and other assets	58,624		1.7
9 Other loans and assets	540,379		16.4
Total assets	3,286,394		(100%)

Source: Hong Kong Monthly Digest of Statistics
Notes: Some figures and percentages are rounded.

(a) % total = $\dfrac{\text{type of deposit}}{\text{total deposits}}$

(b) % total = $\dfrac{\text{individual item of liabilities}}{\text{total liabilities}}$

(c) % total = $\dfrac{\text{type of loans}}{\text{total loans (subtotal)}}$

(d) % total = $\dfrac{\text{individual item of assets}}{\text{total assets}}$

in foreign currency. This is not surprising given the international nature of Hong Kong's banking structure. This broad average, however, hides the fact that more than 50 per cent of the HK dollar denominated liabilities of banks are accounted for by deposits from non-bank customers. For the smaller local retail banks based in Hong Kong, client deposit base is still a major source of funds.

Second, the broad average of the loans structure aspect of the balance sheet shows the importance of inter-bank transactions. Tables 2.11 and 2.12 show the aggregate figures. The non-banking customers of banks account for a decreasing proportion of the assets of banks (Table 2.11). It would appear that banks in Hong Kong deal primarily with other banks in Hong Kong or abroad and secondarily with their non-bank clients. However, the picture changes when the loans are separated into HK dollars and forex in Table 2.12. Non-bank clients account for more than 50 per cent of the HK dollar loans. The reasons for the decrease as shown in Table 2.11 can be explained by the change in the composition of the assets of banks. As Table 2.13 shows, by 1989 almost 80 per cent of all the assets of banks were denominated in currencies other than HK dollars. As the proportion of loans to non-bank customers made in forex had been declining (Table 2.12), this also explains the decline shown in Table 2.11.

Table 2.11 Loans and advances to non-banking customers (HK$ plus forex) as a percentage of all assets (HK$ plus forex), 1980–9

1980	42.2	1985	28.4
1981	38.9	1986	23.0
1982	34.9	1987	24.1
1983	32.3	1988	26.3
1984	31.6	1989	30.2

Source: Hong Kong Monthly Digest of Statistics

Third, and equally revealing, is the distribution of loans made to non-banking customers. On a broad aggregate basis the data in Table 2.10 would indicate that a very small proportion of the assets is dedicated to client loans, reflecting that the most important activity is inter-bank lending. Within the HK dollar loans section, however, there have been some interesting

Table 2.12 Loans and advances to non-banking customers in HK dollars (or in forex) as a percentage of HK dollar assets (or forex assets), 1980–9

	HK$	Forex		HK$	Forex
1980	61.2	26.5	1985	53.8	16.9
1981	60.5	22.4	1986	52.9	13.7
1982	58.0	19.4	1987	55.0	17.5
1983	56.6	19.2	1988	59.0	18.9
1984	57.2	19.5	1989	61.5	22.5

Source: Hong Kong Monthly Digest of Statistics

Table 2.13 Proportion of all assets of banks denominated in forex, 1980–9

1980	54.8	1985	68.9
1981	56.4	1986	76.3
1982	59.7	1987	82.3
1983	65.0	1988	81.5
1984	67.7	1989	80.0

Source: Hong Kong Monthly Digest of Statistics

developments. Table 2.14 shows the distribution of bank loans for use in Hong Kong amongst the various sectors. There is still very little information available on corporate flows of funds in Hong Kong in order to appraise the role of bank loans to the corporate sector. Some of the rather inconclusive evidence is reviewed in the section in Chapter 4 on the flow of funds and the role of the stock market. In general, however, the corporate sector in Hong Kong tends to rely primarily on internal sources of finance.

As Table 2.14 shows, loans for construction, property development and mortgages account for nearly a third of bank loans and more than 40 per cent of DTC loans. The property sector of the Hong Kong economy has a reputation for high volatility, speculative activity and prices (or rents) which rank Hong Kong amongst the most expensive capitals in the world. The role of bank and DTC finance has frequently been instrumental in the rise and fall of property prices. The volatility of property prices is shown by the data in Table 2.15.

A variety of reasons contribute to this high volatility and require some explanation in view of the importance of property-related loans for the banking sector. First, the immigrant nature

Table 2.14 Sectoral allocation of HK dollar bank loans for use in Hong Kong, 1980–9

Sector	1981	1982	1983	1984	1985	1986	1987	1988	1989
1 Manufacturing	12.1	10.5	10.0	9.6	9.3	10.2	9.0	8.9	8.1
2 Construction, property development, and mortgages	25.5	34.6	31.9	30.6	29.2	27.8	27.5	29.9	34.3
	(39.9)	(41.9)	(43.4)	(47.3)	(49.4)	(47.4)	(44.8)	(46.3)	(44.1)
3 Wholesale and retail trade	NA	12.9	14.3	14.7	14.6	14.2	13.8	14.3	11.5

Source: Hong Kong Monthly Digest of Statistics
Notes: Figures in parentheses are the equivalent percentage of loans extended by DTCs and are given here for comparison and for a more complete picture. Since 1989 data on loans have been collected on an 'end usage' basis rather than on a sectoral basis. This means that prior to 1989 a loan issued to a manufacturer or retailer may well have been used to buy or construct property, but the loan would still appear under the 'manufacturing' or 'wholesale' sectors in the statistics.

of Hong Kong society has meant large and sudden influxes of people, primarily from the PRC, during periods of political crises in the large and unstable neighbour. This was particularly true during the post-war period whilst the communists consolidated their rule, and then during the period of the cultural revolution. As most of the refugees tended to be young, the demographic composition of Hong Kong changed. In the mid-1980s nearly 20 per cent of the population was in the eligible age for marriage. This, coupled with changing social habits away from communal large family life-styles, boosted demand for residential property.

Table 2.15 Price indexes of different types of property (1979 = 100), 1980–8

Year	Private domestic	Shops	Offices	Factories
1980	121	126	140	124
1981	148 (+22.3)	147 (+16.6)	174 (24.2)	164 +32.2)
1982	128 (−13.5)	117 (−20.4)	164 (−5.7)	129 (−21.3)
1983	109 (−14.8)	92 (−21.3)	98 (−40.2)	104 (−19.3)
1984	103 (−5.5)	82 (−10.8)	73 (−25.2)	94 (−9.6)
1985	113 (+9.7)	90 (+9.7)	77 (+5.4)	104 (+10.6)
1986	125 (+10.6)	104 (+15.5)	87 (+12.9)	106 (+1.9)
1987	149 (+19.5)	131 (+25.9)	110 (+26.4)	139 (+31.1)
1988	186 (+24.8)	167 (+27.5)	169 (+53.6)	199 (+43.1)

Sources: Hong Kong Monthly Digest of Statistics; Hong Kong Annual Digest of Statistics
Note: Figures are average quarterly data. The figures in parentheses denote the percentage change over the previous year.

Second, demand for private housing proved to be surprisingly interest rate inelastic in the sense that high mortgage rates coupled with high prices did not seem to create a permanent impact on the market or to make actual or potential mortgagees cautious. As an example of the wide fluctuations in the costs of buying a private home, the affordability index, i.e. the ratio of monthly repayments to median monthly household income, for an average size flat with a standard 15 year mortgage and 80 per cent financing, varied from 189 per cent in 1981 to 50 per cent in 1986. Third, the rapid expansion of Hong Kong as a manufacturing and financial centre increased demand for land and property for non-residential uses. Fourth, there is an institutional peculiarity in Hong Kong which could have added to both the high property prices and their volatility, although this is a disputed subject. The British Crown has an absolute monopoly ownership over land in Hong Kong, with some minor exceptions in the New Territories where the land was purchased from its owners. A significant portion of the state revenue is derived from regular land auctions, although the land is leased only and the freehold is never sold. The amount of land which is leased by the Government can therefore play a very significant role in determining property prices as the Government controls completely not only the supply of land but also, for planning purposes, its designated and permitted uses. The Government has been accused of pursuing policies which could have led to artificially higher prices with subsequent declines which were larger than necessary. The evidence, such as it is, is not clear as to whether there are grounds to believe that this was the case.[28] Following the Sino-British agreement of 1984, disposals of land are controlled to ensure an orderly transfer of the land endowment – a peculiar relic of colonial administration – to the new Special Autonomous Region (SAR) of Hong Kong.

The four factors outlined above indicate two forces at work. An expanding and potentially price (and interest) inelastic demand for housing and property was matched (or faced) by a potentially completely inelastic supply of land which ultimately limited the amount of usable property and construction which could be offered by the private sector. The demand for property and the supply of construction were aided and abetted by liberal bank loans which encouraged speculative activity in the sense that property buyers were frequently not end-users. This in itself could be an irrelevant consideration because speculation can be stabilizing. In the case of Hong Kong, property bought on credit could not, in a sense, be stored over indefinite periods of time, and thus led to over-reactions in the market. Perhaps the classical example of a property boom and slump in Hong Kong, including extensive involvement by banks, was the 1978–84 property cycle. The initial stages were fuelled by growing confidence in the political future of Hong Kong as China was also embarking on the post-Mao modernization campaign. Banks and DTCs provided increasing amounts of credit (see Table 2.14). The outcome was oversupply of office space which brought both prices and rentals down. A celebrated casualty was Carian Investments Ltd, a diversified property firm with debts of over HK$10 billion including debts to some leading local banks in excess of HK$1 billion. However, the Carian case was not typical in so far as later investigations brought to light extensive frauds and resulted in the longest (although inconclusive) criminal trial in Hong Kong.

The events of May–June 1989 also caused a mini-slump in the market, this time completely related to confidence. To the extent that the property market in Hong Kong has the capacity to bounce back despite rapid price movements, the banks and DTCs do not feel particularly constrained to limit their overall exposure to the property sector. This attitude is not perhaps unrelated to the fact that the equity market in Hong Kong is also dominated by companies whose main line of business is directly or indirectly related to property and development (see, for example, Chapter 4, Tables 4.2 and 4.3).

The fourth and final aspect of the composition and dynamics of the assets of banks concerns the counterpart of the declining role of non-bank customers as shown in Table 2.11, which is the increasing importance of inter-bank business. The picture can be distorted by potential double counting and by the fact that there are three different transactions involved. These are inter-bank, inter-DTC and bank–DTC. Netting out the DTCs and concentrating only on bank activities presents an interesting picture. As Table 2.16 shows, excluding a brief period in the early 1980s, banks have been net lenders to DTCs in terms of foreign currency but have depended on DTCs for HK dollar funds. This is not surprising as most DTCs are owned by banks, and one of

Table 2.16 Net loans by banks to DTCs (deposits of banks with DTCs minus deposits of DTCs with banks) (HK$ million), 1980–9

	HK dollars	Forex	Total
1980	−18,313	10,626	−7,687
1981	−24,681	13,252	−11,429
1982	−2,369	23,632	21,263
1983	−2,407	37,255	34,848
1984	−4,844	40,626	35,782
1985	−6,624	48,961	42,337
1986	2,543	62,025	64,568
1987	4,188	69,855	74,043
1988	800	36,561	37,361
1989	5,422	29,004	34,426

Source: Hong Kong Monthly Digest of Statistics
Notes: The negative HK dollar figures indicate that DTCs were actually lending to the banks.

their key functions up to 1981, when their role in the monetary sector was redefined, was to tap the market for deposits for the parent bank. After that date DTCs became progressively more dependent on banks as the importance of the foreign exchange deposits grew.

As Hong Kong does not collect official statistics on capital flows, the inter-bank, inter-DTC and bank–DTC activities can offer an insight into the inflows or outflows of funds from abroad via these transactions of the monetary sector. Table 2.17 outlines the situation for banks and Table 2.18 that for the DTCs. In both cases, and with the exception of the banks in 1985–6, these institutions were net borrowers in the sense that they accepted more deposits than the amount that they lent out to other institutions. The amounts of loans from and deposits to institutions in Hong Kong must, of course, cancel out, except for statistical errors or reporting discrepancies which in earlier years were quite considerable. This can be seen by adding together columns 1 from Tables 2.17 and 2.18 and by subtracting from them the sum of columns 5 from these two tables. The net residual from the forex borrowing and lending is, of course, inflows from abroad. The overall net borrower position of both banks and DTCs indicates, first, that there has been a continuous net inflow of funds from overseas in the period examined (with the exception of 1988–9 for the DTCs) and, second, that there has been a movement of funds from the banking and DTC

Table 2.17 Inter-bank and DTC deposits and loans by banks in HK dollars and forex (HK$ million), 1980–9

Year	Deposits from				Loans to					
	1	*2*	*3*	*4*	*5*	*6*	*7*	*8*	*9*	*10*
	Banks and DTCs in Hong Kong	Banks abroad		Total (1 + 2 + 3)	Banks and DTCs in Hong Kong	Banks abroad		Total (5 + 6 + 7)	Net position in forex (3 − 7)	Total net position (4 − 8)
	HK dollars	HK dollars	Forex		HK dollars	HK dollars	Forex			
1980	55,760	3,926	114,141	173,827	47,617	6,260	72,106	125,983	42,035	47,844
1981	88,240	6,089	164,134	258,463	74,474	6,499	112,160	193,133	51,974	65,330
1982	97,712	6,129	226,725	330,556	116,473	7,997	187,647	312,117	39,078	18,449
1983	131,736	8,870	315,006	455,611	165,135	12,881	258,707	436,723	56,299	18,888
1984	161,482	8,586	364,415	534,483	195,323	13,808	315,018	524,149	49,397	10,334
1985	183,996	13,691	450,473	648,159	225,434	24,598	419,365	669,397	31,108	−21,238
1986	276,610	19,973	811,041	1,102,651	340,886	28,255	790,042	1,159,183	20,999	−56,532
1987	321,811	24,809	1,632,839	1,979,459	398,147	25,520	1,468,283	1,891,952	164,552	87,507
1988	344,449	48,304	1,955,791	2,348,544	384,424	30,811	1,770,582	2,185,817	185,209	162,727
1989	410,255	82,077	2,259,893	2,752,225	446,508	22,042	1,957,288	2,425,838	302,605	326,387

Source: Hong Kong Monthly Digest of Statistics

Table 2.18 Inter-bank and DTC deposits and loans by DTCs in HK dollars and forex (HK$ million), 1980–9

Year	Deposits from				Loans to					
	Banks and DTCs in Hong Kong	Banks abroad		Total (1 + 2 + 3)	Banks and DTCs in Hong Kong	Banks abroad		Total (5 + 6 + 7)	Net position in forex (3 − 7)	Total net position (4 − 8)
		HK dollars	Forex			HK dollars	Forex			
	1	2	3	4	5	6	7	8	9	10
1980	31,397	623	49,338	81,358	27,787	254	23,997	52,038	25,341	29,320
1981	46,062	700	87,030	133,792	39,609	944	38,000	78,553	49,030	55,239
1982	72,778	1,056	118,597	192,431	50,636	1,047	50,636	102,319	16,278	90,112
1983	94,924	1,899	139,809	236,632	59,755	1,247	76,992	137,994	62,817	98,638
1984	107,191	1,586	141,869	250,646	71,347	1,035	84,500	156,882	57,369	93,764
1985	124,371	1,392	185,957	311,720	82,110	894	117,165	200,169	68,792	111,551
1986	150,118	1,675	152,992	304,785	85,577	1,013	115,017	201,607	37,975	103,178

sectors to the non-banking sectors. This is another way of quantifying Hong Kong's position as an important international banking centre. Banks from overseas sent over funds to Hong Kong for on-lending in Asia's money markets. It is important to note, however, that this net transfer of funds represented a relatively small percentage of the total assets or of loans by both banks and DTCs. Table 2.19 shows an example of this by taking the net position of column 10 from Table 2.17 and expressing it as a percentage of total assets or loans for banks. A similar estimate obtained by taking the net forex position of both banks and DTCs and then expressing it as a percentage of their combined total assets is shown in column 3 of Table 2.19. In all cases illustrated the percentages involved were relatively small.

Table 2.19 Net inter-institutional position of all banks (columns 1 and 2) and net forex position of all banks and DTCs (column 3) as percentage of assets, 1980–9

	1	2	3
	As % of total bank assets	As % of total bank loans	As % of total assets (banks + DTCs)
1980	16.0	38.4	15.4
1981	15.7	40.3	15.9
1982	3.0	8.8	12.4
1983	2.3	7.4	10.6
1984	1.1	3.6	8.4
1985	−1.9	−6.7	6.4
1986	−3.3	−14.4	2.7
1987	3.1	13.1	5.8
1988	4.9	18.7	4.9
1989	8.4	27.8	6.8

Source: Hong Kong Monthly Digest of Statistics
Note: The negative figures indicate a net borrower position by banks.

On the liability side of the balance sheets of the banks, the major development has been the rapid rise in importance of forex deposits. Table 2.20 demonstrates the relevant data. This rise generated considerable discussion and anxiety in Hong Kong as it was considered evidence of the flight from the local currency. Taking all the monetary sector together, the proportion of HK dollar deposits to total deposits almost halved between 1980 and

1988. There were no significant changes in the decline in comparing the figures for banks and those for the DTCs. The primary denomination of the foreign currency deposits has always been the US dollar. The main break appears in 1982 and this is easily explained by the abolition of a 15 per cent withholding tax on interest receivable from forex deposits. The 1983 HK dollar crisis arising from the Sino-British negotiation over the future of Hong Kong, which also led to the stabilization of the HK dollar and its link-up to the US dollar, restored confidence in the local currency and this is reflected in the relatively stable share of forex deposits.

Table 2.20 Deposits in forex and HK dollars as a percentage of total deposits (end of year figures), 1980–9

Year	All banks and DTCs		Banks		DTCs (L + R)	
	HK dollars	Forex	HK dollars	Forex	HK dollars	Forex
1980	86.3	13.7	87.8	12.2	83.1	16.9
1981	82.1	17.9	82.2	17.8	82.0	18.0
1982	58.2	41.8	57.7	43.3	64.7	35.3
1983	53.3	46.7	52.0	48.0	59.6	40.4
1984	54.4	45.5	53.4	46.6	59.8	40.2
1985	49.2	50.8	47.4	52.6	59.7	40.2
1986	44.5	55.5	43.4	56.6	53.5	46.4
1987	44.0	56.0	43.4	56.6	50.1	49.9
1988	41.0	58.9	40.3	59.6	49.2	50.7
1989	38.4	61.5	38.1	61.8	42.1	57.8

Source: Honk Kong Monthly Digest of Statistics
Note: L + R, licensed plus registered DTCs.

There are further considerations to be taken into account, however, in explaining the growth of forex deposits and in particular that of the interest paid to HK dollar deposits compared with those available to other forex assets. During 1981–3 Hong Kong depositors received increasingly negative returns on their deposits and the experience was repeated for 1986–8. There is no doubt that the IRA did not help the situation by limiting competition on the retail side. Table 2.21 gives an approximation of the negative returns on bank deposits.

A study by the Hongkong Bank of the behaviour and growth of forex deposits over 1983–5 pointed to three specific factors which contributed to their rapid rise but which also explained why there was no cause for alarm.[29] First, the relative decline

Table 2.21 Spread of real interest rate on bank deposits, 1981–8

Year	Savings deposits	3 month deposits
1981	+1.7 to +5.2	+4.2 to +7.7
1982	−2.7 to −6.9	−0.2 to −4.2
1983	−0.3 to −4.8	−1.8 to +1.7
1984	−5.5 to +2.0	−4.5 to +3.5
1985	−2.1 to +1.1	−1.1 to +2.6
1986	−2.3 to −3.3	−1.05 to −2.05
1987	−2.9 to −5.1	−1.1 to −3.9
1988	−3.4 to −7.4	−2.2 to −6.9

Source: Hong Kong Monthly Digest of Statistics
Note: The real interest rate spread is calculated as the difference between the annual spread of interest rates offered minus the annual percentage change of the Hang Seng CPI. The figures for 1981–6 are based on the Hang Seng 1979–80 = 100. Those for 1987 are on the basis of 1984–5 = 100 and hence are not strictly comparable.

since 1983 of the US dollar and therefore of the HK dollar against other major currencies has inflated the total value of non-US dollar deposits when these are measured in HK dollars. Therefore, for example, although non-US dollar forex deposits accounted for about 20 per cent of the total, the 'valuation effect' of the decline of the US dollar (and HK dollar) accounted for nearly 14 per cent of the total rise in foreign currency deposits for the latter half of 1985. Furthermore, there is the problem of swap deposits which at present are classified under foreign currency deposits but are ultimately payable in HK dollars. As both the outright foreign currency deposits and the swap deposits are not classified in the statistics in terms of specific currencies, there is considerable difficulty in adjusting the data to arrive at a more realistic picture:

> an approximate adjustment is possible on two simplifying but quite reasonable assumptions or procedures. One is to treat the trade-weighted exchange rate index as if it had not changed during 1980–6. This will remove most, if not all, 'valuation effect'. The other is to treat swap deposits as a constant fraction of customers' deposits . . . . By adjusting for such swap deposits the alleged distorting effect due to inappropriate classification will also be largely eliminated.[30]

The result of this adjustment still yielded a rising trend in both deposits and loans, thereby confirming that this change was real and not the outcome of simple accounting or valuation conventions

Second, the shift to foreign currency deposits may have been influenced not just by the real returns but by the sheer variation in the nominal return available to depositors in Hong Kong over some of these time periods. Therefore, for example, within 2 years (1984–5) depositors were faced with a maximum of 11 per cent to a minimum of 1.75 per cent returns on their savings deposits, or an 84 per cent potential fall in the nominal yield. Comparisons with the equivalent real US dollar rates are less easy to make, not least because the differences should refer to the expected rather than the actual inflation rates. None the less, real Eurodollar rates during 1984–9 were consistently positive compared with the predominantly negative real HK dollar rates available to depositors. Switching into US dollars must have always carried an implicit risk premium or discount depending on the expectations as to the viability of the link of the HK dollar to the US dollar and the direction of the HK dollar–US dollar exchange rate if the link was severed. This premium-discount effect cannot be underestimated, as the Hong Kong Government found to its cost when from December 1987 to February 1988 it had to threaten the introduction of negative interest rates in order to force depositors away from HK dollar deposits and relieve the pressure on the pegged exchange rate. On this occasion the switch of deposits was in favour of the HK dollar, but the implicit risk effect must have played a role on previous occasions. Finally, the Hongkong Bank study pointed out that the rapid rise in forex deposits was another sign of Hong Kong's arrival as an international financial centre. This was coupled with a stable HK dollar demand function (at least in terms of nominal GDP velocity measurements) and a rising share of loans made in foreign currencies rather than in HK dollars.[31]

Another important development in the liabilities side of the balance sheets of banks has been the rise of negotiable certificates of deposit (NCDs). Although still accounting for a very small percentage of total liabilities their growth has been spectacular. In 1980 total NCDs issued by banks in both Hong Kong dollars and forex accounted for 0.7 per cent of total liabilities, rising to about 1.0 per cent in 1987. Total NCDs held by banks (issued both by other banks and DTCs) as a percentage of assets also rose from 0.07 per cent in 1980 to 0.4 per cent in 1987. For reasons to be explored in greater detail in Chapter 3 the NCDs have remained primarily an inter-bank and inter-institutional market, thus ensuring some breadth but hardly any depth in their trading.

2.4 The demand for bank loans: an exercise in estimation

The declining role of loans to the non-banking sector is not necessarily a cause for concern as it reflects choices both on the part of corporate and personal borrowers and on the part of banks. But given the absence of any kind of consistent data for corporate flows of funds and for disposable personal income in Hong Kong, an investigation which throws some light on the factors determining demand for loans also helps to explain some aspects of the financial behaviour of the corporate and personal sectors. Another aspect of lending to the personal and corporate sector is, of course, its potential impact on the growth of the stock of money. For example, the ratio of total loans in HK dollars by banks and DTCs remained remarkably stable as a proportion of HK dollar M3 at about 1.02 times (i.e. 102 per cent) with a standard deviation of about 11 per cent over an 8 year period (1981–8).

There is very little that has been published on demand estimation for bank loans by the personal or the corporate sector.[32] Indeed, the standard theory of finance offers very little help in the treatment of bank loans. Bank loans can be classified as negative assets in the firm's portfolio. They are different from bonds not only in terms of their maturity but also because they are not marketable. Standard textbooks of finance hardly mention bank loans in the context of the financial and portfolio decisions of firms.[33] The situation is no better with respect to the demand for loans from the personal sector. Although life-cycle and permanent income models allow implicitly for borrowing, there are few direct studies on the factors determining personal bank borrowing. Mortgage loans are a different proposition because of the length of time and the different risk factors involved.[34] One of the recent models examining the borrowing behaviour of industrial and commercial companies was the study by Moore and Threadgold.[35] Their basic premise and building block was that firms used bank loans as working capital:

> Whenever wages or raw material prices rise, current
> production costs increase so that company demand for
> working capital will increase unless product prices are raised
> simultaneously. In the absence of instantaneous replacement,
> cost pricing companies must finance their increased working
> capital needs by increasing their short-term borrowing or by
> running down their liquid assets.

It now follows that changes in current costs such as wages, imported inputs, tax payments and the actual level of inventories (rather than its change) will all affect the volume of lending. Moore and Threadgold tested a model that used the changes in the level of borrowing rather than the level of loans as the dependent variable. Their reason for doing so was that it was 'only increase in costs that must be financed by additional credit because existing levels will be fully financed out of current sales proceeds'. However, this is hardly a convincing argument. Firms, for example, may wish to maintain a certain amount of loans as a proportion of their total liabilities or liquid assets. This may well be particularly true with revolving credit or unused overdraft facilities.

Moore and Threadgold fitted a simple unweighted lagged model using wages, import bills for manufacturing inputs, tax payments and the level of interest rate and inventories. The effect of possible 'round tripping' was also explored. Their results indicated a low interest elasticity of demand of loans but the importance of wages as a key component of working capital costs in explaining borrowing behaviour. Cuthbertson[36] also discussed similar models but the results on the role of interest rates are not unequivocal.

The models used here partially follow Moore and Threadgold's approach. However, since the total bank loans definition used for Hong Kong includes loans to the personal sector as well as to trading, commercial and industrial companies it was important to formulate an approach that could be justified on aggregate terms. Sectoral demand functions were relatively easier to construct and justify.

For both corporate and personal borrowers the BLR was used as a proxy for the cost of borrowing. As already indicated this is the prime rate charged to blue chip customers by the two note-issuing banks. It has no formal standing in the loans market other than as an overall indicator. Wages would reflect costs to firms and incomes to consumers, particularly in Hong Kong where there are no data for personal disposable income. In either case the link with borrowing would be positive. Finally aggregate demand in terms of either exports or retail sales would influence business borrowing. In the case of personal loans the causality, at least in the case of retail sales, could well run the other way. However, lagged exports and retail sales may also stand as proxies for personal income and again influence the level of borrowing. The general form of the model fitted to the aggregate data thus had the form

$$L_t = a + b(\text{BLR}_{t-i}) + c(E_{t-i})\ d(W_{t-i}) \tag{2.1}$$

where L, BLR, E and W stand respectively for loans, best lending rate, exports and wage index. As retail sales are correlated with exports they were used as an alternative proxy for aggregate demand or income. As already indicated the inclusion of personal loans in an aggregate which covered primarily loan to commerce and industry was justified in terms of obtaining a generalized estimate of demand for bank loans. Loans for the purchases of houses were omitted as were loans to the construction and property sector. This was primarily because mortgage loans involved very long-term decisions and because the construction sector in Hong Kong is notorious for its instability and dependence on expectations easily swayed by political rather than purely economic events. Aspects of this have already been explored in Section 2.3. This left personal loans being used either for the purchase of consumer durable goods or as working capital. To a considerable extent the variables used to explain the demand for loans by the corporate and business sector could therefore be used to explain demand by the personal sector as well.

A supply function of loans could be written as

$$\text{SL} = f(\text{BLR, LA, } Y) \tag{2.2}$$

where BLR is the best lending rate, LA are liquid assets as specified by the monetary authorities and Y is some scale factor, such as GNP or a proxy for aggregate demand. This variable could also represent the willingness of the public to hold bank deposits as part of their wealth. To the extent that BLR and aggregate demand in the form of exports appear in the demand functions for loans, this would give rise to problems with identification of the demand function for loans.

A number of studies simply ignore the problem and proceed as if the demand function is identified.[37] At a simpler level, if there are institutional or other reasons to believe that the supply of loans is perfectly interest elastic, then we can proceed to the estimation of demand. In the case of Hong Kong the issue is complicated by two considerations. First, throughout the period under examination the interest rate payable on deposits (or at least on certain types of deposits) has been fixed under the IRA. This did not, of course, limit the level of the BLR but it did limit its movement and frequency of changes. Indeed, it can be taken as given that changes of the deposit rate were automatically reflected in the BLR as well. It would now follow that BLR would not necessarily reflect market clearing levels of interest rates. Second, banks in Hong Kong were never constrained by liquidity ratios prescribed by the authorities. Actual ratios were always in excess of the minimum requirements. Although the reported ratios include the effects of 'window-dressing', the endogenous nature of most of the liquid assets meant that if banks needed any assets they simply generated them via their normal lending processes. The liquidity ratio rules in Hong Kong were not meant to act as constraints on credit creation but to provide minimum insurance cover for depositors.

There are a number of possibilities that can now be explored in the context of Hong Kong. Figure 2.6 reproduces Figure 2.3. The demand for deposits by banks is a function of the interest payable on loans. The differential $r - i$ shows the profit margin per dollar lent. The interest on deposits is now fixed at i^*. The banks can expand their loans by acquiring more equity, i.e. they can issue new shares, by accepting a lower profit margin or if demand for deposits by the public increases (S_D shifts to S_D'). A condition for identifying d_L in Figure 2.6(a) would now be a continuous increase in the demand for deposits by the public over a time period. This would also shift S_L in Figure 2.6(a) and trace and out d_L. However, this very simple model assumes that the interest rate agreement controlling the level of i^* is not binding.

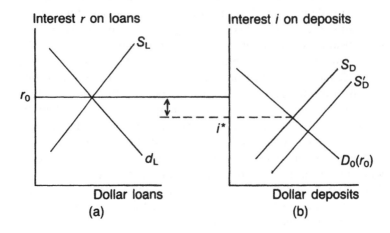

Figure 2.6 Demand for loans and deposits

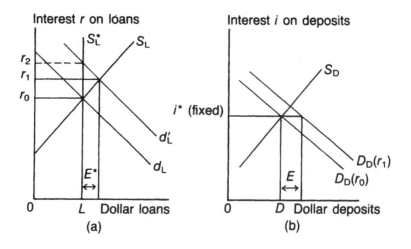

Figure 2.7 Identifying demand for loans

Figure 2.7 shows the case of a binding fixed i^*. As long as the demand for deposits is not rising (i.e. S_D shifting to the right), any increase in the demand for loans (d_L shifting to the right) will result in an inelastic S_L. Specifically, in Figure 2.7 as d_L shifts to d'_L interest on loans increases to r_1 from r_0, thus shifting $D_D(r_0)$ to $D_D(r_1)$ in Figure 2.7(b). There is now an excess demand for loans which is matched by the excess demand E for deposits in Figure 2.7(b). As the banks cannot lend more than $0L(=0D)$ interest on loans will be pushed to r_2 along the fixed supply curve S^*_L.

As there has never been any evidence of credit rationing in Hong Kong, it can safely be assumed that the IRA was never binding in the sense of giving rise to an interest inelastic supply of loans. It is therefore very likely that the supply of loans in Hong Kong is demand determined. Figure 2.8 outlines the more extreme version of this hypothesis in terms of a perfectly elastic supply of deposits at the fixed interest i^* and an equally elastic supply of loans at r_0. At a given r_0 and i^* the amount of loans is purely demand determined. As the fixed interest rate varied, curve $i^* S_D$ shifted and, given the link between i^* and r, so did curve $r_0 S_L$, thus tracing out d_L. However, even this extreme version is not necessary for explaining the situation in Hong Kong as long as there is no reason to believe that IRA resulted in interest inelastic S_L functions or that the liquidity ratio rules constrained bank lending in any way.

A number of regressions were run for nominal and real values of loans for both aggregate and sectoral data using quarterly data over 1978(i)–1986(ii).[38] The equation used was based on equation (2.1) and its variations in lagged and in logarithmic forms. The following symbols were used: L_t, loans in million HK dollars; BLR_t = best lending rate (per annum); W_t, wage index for industrial workers (1981(i) = 100); S_t, index of retail sales in value terms (1981(i) = 100); X_t, exports in million HK dollars (current prices), seasonally adjusted. In the results of the equation LM denotes the Lagrangean multiplier test for auto-correlation at the appropriate degree of freedom, here set at 3, CHOW is the Chow test of stability and the 't test' values appear under the coefficients. For the rest of the tests for ease of comparison the appropriate χ^2 or F-test critical 5 per cent values are given in parentheses.

A sample of representative results is given in Table 2.20. In general, models I–IV appear well specified although, significantly, the interest elasticity of demand for loans is very low. All the variables have the predicted signs and are significant except for retail sales. The models are also in general stable in terms of the Chow test. It must be pointed out, however, that in most cases the models proved to be extremely sensitive to the length of the sample time period. Examination of the data showed that the BLR was most volatile of the variables. Given the lagged relationship used it is important to note that the BLR began to rise at the start of 1979 until it reached its highest level, at 20 per cent, in October 1981. From then on it declined for the rest of the sample period. As the total sum of loans increased continuously throughout this period, a sample period that covers 1978(iii) onwards will yield first a positive and then a negative partial correlation between BLR and loans. If the sample period (allowing for at least two lags) starts in 1980(iii) then the correlation is negative and the overall fit improves. This explains

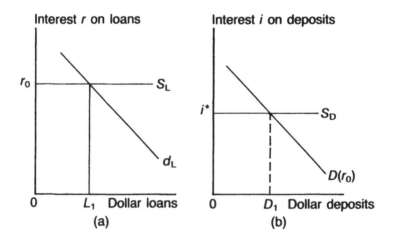

Figure 2.8   Identifying demand for loans

why the best fit was obtained with the data from 1980 onwards which are shown here.

The linking of the HK dollar to the US dollar after 1983(iii) does not seem to have affected the stability of the models. Following the linking of the exchange rate in October 1983, domestic interest rates became temporarily more volatile in terms of the number of changes of the BLR in any single year. Significantly, however, as Table 2.23 shows, the amplitude of the changes of the BLR did not increase after 1983. The spread of the inter-bank bank rate is also given for comparison. There is therefore no evidence that interest rate movements became more volatile in terms of either the number or the amplitude of changes after 1983.

However, in order to test whether the surge in the number of changes and the temporary increase in amplitude after 1983

Table 2.22 Estimation results

Model I: Total Loans 1980(iii)–1986(ii)

$$L_t = -29,011.95 - 1,081.53BLR_{t-2} + 117,876.24W_{t-2} + 2.67X_{t-2}$$
$$(-3.14) \quad (-3.81) \quad (13.12) \quad (3.75)$$

$R^2 = 0.99$, DW = 2.09, SSR = 0.217 $\times 10^9$, $N = 24$, LM (3rd) $\chi^2 = 3.73$ (at 5%, 7.81), CHOW(4 obs), $F(4, 16) = 1.77$ (at 5%, 3.11)

Model II: Total loans 1980(iii)–1986(ii)

$$\log L_t = 10.24 - 0.07 \log BLR_{t-2} + 1.28 \log W_{t-2} + 0.15 \log X_{t-2}$$
$$(17.91) \ (-2.23) \quad (11.45) \quad (2.37)$$

$R^2 = 0.98$, DW = 1.80, SSR = 0.02, $N = 24$, LM (3rd) $\chi^2 = 1.27$ (at 5% = 7.81), CHOW(4 obs), $F(4, 16) - 0.63$ (at 5%, 3.01)

Model III: Total loans 1981(ii)–1986(ii)

$$L_t = -5,566.42 - 932.25BLR_{t-1} + 80,067.78W_{t-1} + 101.58S_{t-1}$$
$$(-0.32) \quad (-2.33) \quad (3.92) \quad (0.79)$$

$R^2 = 0.98$, DW = 1.08, SSR = 0.10 $\times 10^9$, $N = 21$, LM (3rd) $\chi^2 = 6.40$ (at 5%, 7.81), CHOW(4 obs), $F(4, 13) = 4.11$ (5%, 3.18)

Model IV: Total loans 1981(iii)–1986(ii)

$$\log L_t = 10.76 - 0.10 \log BLR_{t-1} + 0.99 \log W_{t-2} + 0.15 \log S_{t-2}$$
$$(21.101) \quad (-3.39) \quad (5.70) \quad (1.31)$$

$R^2 = 0.98$, DW = 1.80, SSR = 59.12, $N = 20$, LM (3rd) $\chi^2 = 9.54$ (at 5%, 7.81), CHOW(4 obs), $F(4, 12) = 1.70$ (at 5%, 3.26)

Table 2.23 Behaviour of the BLR and inter-bank overnight rate, 1978–88

Year	No. of changes of BLR	Average size of change (percentage points of BLR)	Standard deviation of change of BLR	Spread of highest–lowest difference of inter-bank overnight rate (%)
1980	11	0.27	1.26	15.50
1981	6	−0.16	1.21	13.00
1982	6	−0.91	0.34	10.75
1983	8	0.62	1.51	28.00
1984	16	−0.15	1.36	47.87
1985	9	−0.55	0.64	11.50
1986	3	−0.16	0.84	14.75
1987	10	−0.01	0.86	8.75
1988	9	+0.55	0.19	9.62

Source: Hong Kong Monthly Digest of Statistics
Note: The changes in the BLR are those which occurred during the calendar year. The percentage point change refers to the previously effective BLR. The average size of change indicates that, for example, each time the BLR changed in 1980 it increased on average by about a quarter of a percentage point whilst in 1985 it fell on average by about half a percentage point.

affected the stability of the estimates, an extended version of the Chow test plus a χ^2 forecast test was run. Models I, II and III were re-estimated, omitting the observations for 1984(i)–1986(ii) for the purpose of the stability test, i.e. the period following the stabilization which took place in 1983(iv). The sample period was 1979(ii)–1986(ii) for models I and II and 1981(ii)–1986(iii) for model III. The results were as follows (d.o.f., degrees of freedom):

Model I CHOW (10 obs), $F(10, 15) = 0.94$ (at 5% 2.54)
Forecast χ^2 (10 d.o.f.) = 13.99 (at 5% 18.31)

Model II CHOW (10 obs), $F(10, 15) = 0.94$ (at 5% 2.54)
Forecast χ^2 (10 d.o.f.) = 13.99 (at 5% 18.31)

Model III CHOW (10 obs), $F(10, 7) = 2.96$ (at 5% 3.64)
Forecast χ^2 (10 d.o.f.) = 10.75 (at 5% 18.31)

All these 'extended' models gave reasonably good fits with coefficients with appropriate signs. Models I and II are effectively being tested over two different sample periods, although, for reasons already explained, tests using data before 1980(iii) tended to give poorer results with the BLR being non-significant. In neither case is there any sign of instability. There is no evidence that the greater volatility of interest rates had any effect on the stability of the relationships calculated. One explanation may be the fact that interest rates do not seem to be an important factor in demand for loans. Hence their greater variability could not be expected to have much influence on the stability of the estimates.

A selection of results for disaggregate models is given in Table 2.24. In general the results are reasonably convincing, with the exception that the interest rate coefficient for the equation for exports–imports is not significant.

Table 2.24 Results of regression analysis of sectoral demand for bank loans

Model IV: Loans LM_t to the manufacturing sector 1981(iii)–1986(ii)

$$LM_t = 16,083.82 - 325.68BLR_{t-1} + 0.49X_{t-2}$$
$$\quad\;\;(9.44)\qquad\;\;(-4.71)\qquad\quad(4.35)$$

$R^2 = 0.85$, DW = 1.87, SSR = 0.11×10^8, $N = 20$, LM (2nd) $\chi^2 = 0.1$ (at 5% 5.99), CHOW(4 obs), $F(4, 13) = 1.72$ (at 5% 3.18)

Model V: Loans $LXIM_t$ for the finance of import and export trade 1981(i)–1986(ii)

$$LXIM_t = 12,644.32 - 26.26BLR_t + 0.68X_{t-1}$$
$$\qquad\;\;(7.92)\qquad(-0.41)\qquad(6.52)$$

$R^2 = 0.82$, DW = 1.74, SSR = 0.11×10^8, $N = 22$, LM (3rd) $\chi^2 = 0.14$ (at 5% 7.81), CHOW(4 obs), $F(4, 15) = 2.33$ (at 5% 3.06)

Model VI: Loans LWR_t for the financing of wholesale and retail trade 1982(i)–1986(ii)

$$LWR_t = -2,642.0 - 444.79BLR_{t-1} + 206.99S_{t-1}$$
$$\quad\;\;(-0.62)\qquad(-3.74)\qquad\quad(9.74)$$

$R^2 = 0.94$, DW – 1.90, SSR = 0.20×10^8, $N = 18$, LM (2nd) $\chi^2 = 3.98$ (at 5% 5.99), CHOW(4 obs), $F(4, 11) = 1.16$ (at 5% 3.36)

When the results for the aggregate and disaggregate models are taken together, the picture which emerges is that of a stable demand function for bank loans with a low but statistically significant interest elasticity of demand. Additional tests using real rather than nominal versions of these models did not improve on these results, with the real BLR coefficient turning out to be non-significant. The relatively low influence of interest rates in both nominal and real terms can perhaps also be explained by the low levels of inflation experienced by Hong Kong. Indeed, between 1978 and 1980 the real BLR was effectively negative.[39] However, it is important to point out that most borrowers would not have paid the BLR but perhaps several points above it. The low interest elasticity of demand for loans is also reflected in studies for the demand for bank deposits in Hong Kong as well as in demand for loans studies in the UK.[40] The absence of a developed non-equity capital market in Hong Kong might have presented businessmen with few or no alternative sources of medium-term capital other than bank loans. Similarly, there are no equivalent savings and loans associations or building societies in Hong Kong other than commercial banks to provide house buyers with alternative sources of funds. In this case the absence of specific mortgage-oriented institutions cannot be used as a valid argument for the observed low interest elasticities as loans for property-related purposes were excluded from the estimates. However, the example is indicative of the potential lack of substitute sources of finance in some key areas. The foregoing considerations, did not preclude banks from competing for clients on the basis of keen interest rate margins. It could be argued that marketing strategies to attract borrowers on the basis of services only would be unlikely to succeed, thus forcing banks to consider very carefully the rates offered in view of the potential low sensitivity of borrowers to interest rates. In the extreme case banks might have had to cut interest rates significantly in order to generate additional demand for loans. A relatively captive retail base where the IRA limited competition might have made the situation relatively easier for the bank in acquiring funds. As there are no official public data for the maturity structure of either loans or deposits, it is very difficult even to guess the exact reasoning behind the pricing of loans where information is available through the publicity material provided by banks.

2.5 The developing environment

The bank market in Hong Kong presents an interesting picture characterized by the rapidly eroding division between local and foreign banks. The local banking market is dominated by the Hongkong Bank group but this dominance is being challenged by the Bank of China group. The rest of the local market is being altered by continuous purchases and takeovers by foreign banks. The truly local, i.e. Chinese, banks have now shrunk to nine, with only four of them being independent. The relevance of maintaining a legal and regulatory distinction between local and foreign banks is therefore increasingly questionable. In any case the market share of local banks, other than those of the Hongkong Bank group are individually so small as to make them irrelevant in terms of their own 'local' importance. The non-local side of the market contains an increasing number of foreign banks. The overall potential of the truly local retail market in Hong Kong is ultimately limited by the rate of growth of personal incomes and of the GDP. Market shares are likely to be hotly contested, but the potential growth in banking business must lie more with the international side and the role of Hong Kong as an offshore centre. There are a number of developments which clearly point that way.

Starting from a micro approach, the dominant bank in the market, Hongkong Bank, has been busy internationalizing its base with acquisitions in the USA (Marine Midland) and the UK (partial holdings in the Midland Bank). This might in a sense present a special case in view of the uncertainties over the group's position after 1997 but also because of the serious threat posited by the aggressive expansion of the Bank of China group.[41]

The role of price competition in terms of interest rate margins on both loans and deposits is likely to increase. The IRA covers the basic retail side of deposits. Banks have bypassed this restriction by setting up their own DTCs which are excluded from pure retail operations but have no restrictions on the interest rate offered either. Furthermore, as indicated in Table 2.8 the interest rate margin spreads have been reduced with interest income also declining as a source of revenue for banks. The growing trend of securitization will add to this pressure as it is impossible to fix interest on freely traded paper. Perhaps the strongest element still propping up the cartel is the desire of the Hong Kong Government to carry on using interest rates in order to maintain the HK dollar–US dollar link. This aspect of the debate is reviewed in Chapter 6. However, once interest-rate-based competition develops in the HK dollar market this will inevitably lead to an internationalization of the HK dollar itself, something which the Hong Kong Government resisted until 1989 when it changed its stance and allowed international issues of bonds denominated in HK dollars to be made in Hong Kong. The growth of forex deposits and the net borrower position of the banking sector in terms of inter-institutional foreign transactions point in that direction. A freer and competitive HK dollar denominated paper market will simply complement and fit in with the existing forex denominated markets.

Foreign banks in Hong Kong draw funds from parent institutions abroad and similarly channel funds from all over Asia to the much less controlled and much more secretive banking sector of Hong Kong.[42] As the authorities in Hong Kong do not collect comprehensive statistics of capital flows it is difficult to quantify the importance of Hong Kong other than on a piecemeal basis. One study offers a summary of the situation in 1985:

> At the end of 1985 Hong Kong's total foreign currency external claims amounted to US$ 97 billion whereas its total foreign currency liabilities to banks abroad was US$ 81 billion. Of the external claims about 80% of the total were foreign currency loans to banks outside Hong Kong with the remaining 20% directed to non-bank customers all over the world. Four countries, namely Singapore, United Kingdom, Japan and the United States collectively accounted for 50% of Hong Kong's total foreign currency loans to banks abroad in 1985. On the other hand, claims on nonbank customers outside Hong Kong were largely directed to South Korea, Panama, Indonesia and Liberia. Transactions with the People's Republic of China (PRC) have become increasingly significant over the past five years. At the end of 1985, Hong Kong's total claims on PRC amounted to US$ 1.8 billion up from US$ 47.8 million in 1981.[43]

The situation in 1988 had not changed. Banks in Hong Kong had HK$1,845 billion claims against banks outside Hong Kong plus HK$382 billion against non-bank clients, a total of HK$2,227 billion. The figures include both HK dollar and forex funds, although the forex funds, predominantly US dollars, account for more than 95 per cent of the total. Claims against Hong Kong banks from banks outside Hong Kong stood at

HK$2,000 billion leaving a net lending position of HK$227 billion. The major borrowers were Japan with 66 per cent of total loans followed by Singapore with 8.4 per cent. Similarly, the major creditors were Japanese banks with 65 per cent of funds lent to Hong Kong. Indeed, Japanese banks were overall net lenders to Hong Kong. The major non-bank customers for 1988 were Japanese and PRC clients.

The role of the Japanese banks was touched on in Section 2.1 of this chapter, as was Japan's role in Hong Kong's external trade in Chapter 1, Section 1.2. The figures quoted above make it obvious that Hong Kong's development as an offshore banking centre owes a great deal to the direct involvement of Japanese banks. The liberalization of Japan's financial markets was thought to present a serious threat to Hong Kong's developing offshore activities as business could have shifted to Tokyo. The evidence so far indicates the contrary, with Hong Kong increasing its share of offshore lending of the global total from 10.5 per cent in 1980 to 22.8 per cent in 1987 with Japan still holding about 5 per cent.[44] Even more remarkably the two centres, Hong Kong and Tokyo, appear to be developing a symbiotic relationship with active inter-bank flows exploiting primarily the still partially regulated interest rates in Japan and the freer ones available in offshore markets:

> The Japan Offshore Market (JOM) was established in December 1986 . . . at the end of December 1987 (it) . . . accounted for 5% of the BIS area bank's external assets . . . . Outstanding lending from Hong Kong has grown from US$ 38 billion at end 1980 to US$ 266 billion at end 1987. Most of the growth has occurred since September 1986. The dominant feature of the past fifteen months has been interbank lending to Japan which grew from US$ 27 billion at end September 1986 to US$ 125 billion at end 1987; this followed the opening of the JOM. Borrowing by Japanese non-banks increased to US$ 21 billion at end 1987 well in excess of borrowing by non-banks in any other country. Prior to the opening of JOM, Hong Kong's most important interbank business had been with the UK and Singapore.[45]

The links between Hong Kong and other offshore centres are strong but not as rapidly developing as those with Japan. Thus, for example, the sum total lent to Hong Kong in 1988 by the Cayman Islands, Bahrain, the Bahamas and the Netherlands Antilles stood at 2.6 per cent of the total, with 4 per cent of the total of the sum lent to them. Even Singapore's potential threat to Hong Kong as the major Asiadollar trading centre seems to have been less important than first thought. Singapore's share of the offshore market expanded during 1980–7, but the link with Japan's newly established offshore market was not as close as that between Japan and Hong Kong. Thus, for example, between September 1986 and September 1987 total inter-bank lending from Singapore grew by US$34 billion compared with US$81 billion for Hong Kong. For comparison Table 2.25 shows the sizes of six major offshore centres, with Hong Kong maintaining a respectable third position.

Table 2.25 Major offshore market size (US$ billion), 1984–8

	Onshore and offshore separated system				Onshore and offshore combined system	
	Japan	USA	Singapore	Bahrain	London	Hong Kong
1984	–	2,276	1,281	627	6,717	1,137
1985	–	2,605	1,554	568	7,508	1,435
1986	937	2,982	2,006	557	8,764	2,114
1987	2,388	2,549	2,449	635	10,241	3,360
1988	4,142	2,870	2,695	632	9,993	3,859
		(Nov 1988)	(Oct 1988)	(Jun 1988)	(Sep 1988)	(Aug 1988)

Source: H. Kitagawa, 'The role of Hong Kong vs Tokyo as an international financial market centre in Asia', paper presented to the Hong Kong Capital Markets Conference, International Research Institute, Hong Kong, April 1989

The role of the PRC in Hong Kong's bank market can be seen in two different contexts. The BOC group will continue to consolidate and expand its position, but by no means unopposed. Indeed its official role, if any, after 1997 has been left undefined and is likely to remain so. Its willingness to shoulder potential loss-making responsibilities has already been tested both in the rescue of failing banks by PRC-linked groups and, as will be recounted in Chapter 5, in the rescue of the index futures market in Hong Kong after the 1987 stock market crash. The second aspect of the PRC's role can be seen in terms of using Hong Kong not only as a potential source of funds but also as a training ground for the future bankers who will have to run China's developing financial and banking system. However, the BOC group's situation still remains delicate in balancing commercial with political considerations. Following the Beijing massacre in June 1989 there was a run on the BOC group banks with massive withdrawals of deposits both as a precautionary measure and a protest move. The authorities were firm in discouraging this action but the run had an unexpected side benefit. In order to meet the HK dollar claims made on the group, the Bank of China sold large amounts of US dollars in the market in order to obtain HK dollar funds. This helped to prop up the exchange rate for the HK dollar at a time when there was also panic buying of US dollars.

But perhaps the ultimate test of any industry to survive is to observe its reactions under competition and change. Following the bank crises of 1982–6 the authorities made a determined attempt to revamp the regulatory system. The outcome of their efforts was the 1986 Banking Ordinance which not only consolidated previously diverse legislation but brought Hong Kong's standards to an international level. The quick adoption and adherence to the Basle capital adequacy ratios was also a good example of the willingness of the system to show itself in the best possible light. These developments are explored in detail in Chapter 6.

The response of Hong Kong's banking and financial markets to 'financial technological innovations' has been most encouraging. One study of the subject classified financial innovation under four broad categories: applications of electronics and telecommunications to finance, the creation of new markets, the creation of new products, new organizational forms of banking or new techniques of bank management and finally structural changes primarily in terms of cross-invasions between financial intermediaries. In terms of these categories:

> While [Hong Kong] cannot claim originality for any of the listed innovations, it has been quite good at absorbing them. In respect of the applications of technology for example, over 80% of the innovations are now significantly present in Hong Kong. For other categories the average 'absorption rate' is about 50%.[46]

In terms of size and growth Hong Kong's bank sector is

undoubtedly the most important of all the financial sectors. Its importance will continue to grow, but will have to be further assessed in terms of the development of the non-equity capital markets and the forex markets. All recent evidence from other countries with developed financial and banking systems is pointing to the rapid erosion between what were once traditional banking markets and all other financial activities. The growth of securitization put an end to this division and the entrance of banks into equity markets further eroded these traditional distinctions. The capacity of the system in Hong Kong to withstand political shocks was also put to a test in May–June 1989 and it passed it with flying colours. Hong Kong's position as an international banking centre is linked to the developments in the PRC, but as explained and illustrated in Chapter 1 the relationship is complex and involves two-way links. To the extent that the international financial community makes use of Hong Kong's expertise and its regulation-free and liberal environment as an offshore base, then the China factor is of less importance than the capacity of Hong Kong to continue to provide these services and maintain the attractiveness of its environment.

Chapter three

Deposit-taking companies and the capital market

3.1 Introduction

Hong Kong has experienced the emergence of financial inter-mediaries as a response to a variety of causes, both economic and non-economic. The whole group of institutions which constitutes the merchant banking side of the bank market emerged partially as a response to official regulations. One of the major banking crises in Hong Kong occurred in 1965 and was related to real estate loans, inadequate liquidity provisions and panic runs on banks. The subsequent rescue operation involved the Hongkong Bank's buying the Hang Seng Bank, a fundamentally sound bank which was caught out in the general panic. As part of the rescue package the Government announced a complete ban on the issuing of new banking licences, a moratorium which lasted until 1972. One more licence was issued between 1972 and 1975 and the moratorium was reimposed until 1978.[1]

A direct result of this barring of entry into the local bank market was the generation of a rapid process of disintermediation. Finance houses exploiting a potential legal loophole (or rather being allowed to interpret loosely the then relevant banking ordinance) were already accepting deposits and offering banking services to their customers. Being effectively outside official control their activities expanded very rapidly with their numbers rising to about 2,000 in the 1970s. There are no official statistics on the size and operations of these institutions, but it is generally assumed that although they were small they were willing and able to finance all types of activities from mortgages to hire purchase loans and forex transactions. Foreign banks refused access to the

Hong Kong market began to use these finance houses as an indirect form of entry and soon became the most important force behind them. This unregulated rise of non-bank financial intermediaries, collectively known as deposit-taking companies (DTCs), produced three interrelated problems for the authorities.

First, the finance houses competed for deposits with banks on a basis which the banks considered unfair. As the finance houses did not have to meet the liquidity requirements imposed on banks nor were they under the umbrella of the Interest Rate Agreement (IRA) already in force in 1964, they could, and did, offer higher interest rates on deposits. Second, the unregulated pattern of their growth led to fears over the security of depositors in the event of a crisis. Finally, the tight links that these houses had developed with trading companies could have led to a domino effect in the event of a crisis, or even in the event of the sudden imposition of a tighter regulatory system.[2] The outcome of these concerns was the Deposit Taking Companies Ordinance 1976 which required registration of all DTCs, imposed a minimum capital requirement and prohibited them from accepting deposits of less than HK$50,000. This was the first step taken in Hong Kong to organize a tiered system of financial intermediaries. The outcome of this Ordinance was an immediate drop in the number of DTCs, as the smallest of them could not meet these requirements. This was followed by a gradual rise in their numbers as foreign banks started up their own DTCs as a way of bypassing the licence moratorium still in force. The number of registered DTCs rose from 179 in 1976 to 350 in 1981. In 1981 the Government attempted to limit this increase by registering companies only when they were at least 50 per cent owned by an adequately supervised bank. But the supervisory authorities were further concerned with two related developments. First, by 1981 it had become obvious that DTCs were used by parent banks to gather deposits unhindered by the IRA. Second, the deposit base of banks was being eroded by DTCs; the latter's share of total deposits had risen from about 15 per cent in 1978 to over 36 per cent in 1981. The situation was clearly anomalous with foreign banks maintaining an 'unofficial', presence in Hong Kong through largely unregulated subsidiaries, and with local banks enthusiastically competing with each other for deposits behind the back of their own association! But undoubtedly most pressing was the fear that the IRA was being rapidly eroded from its position as the key monetary instrument of the Hong Kong Government.

The outcome of these considerations was the introduction of the three-tier system in 1981, and as amended in 1986, which largely shaped the development of Hong Kong's financial market in the 1980s. The first tier consisted of licensed banks, both local and foreign, which could carry out the whole gamut of banking business. The second tier consisted of licensed DTCs (LDTCs), whose functions and operations rested primarily with the wholesale market and which were expected to take large deposits outside the scope of the IRA but were not to do any retail banking business. Finally, the third tier consisted of registered DTCs (RDTCs) which would carry out the rest of the functions of finance houses which could not take short-term deposits.

As amended by the 1986 Banking Ordinance the requirements imposed on DTCs were as follows:

(1) RDTCs must have a paid up capital not less than HK$10 million and cannot accept deposits of less than 3 months or less than HK$100,000 or an equivalent amount in foreign currency. An amendment to the 1986 Banking Ordinance now requires that an RDTC must be 50 per cent or more owned by a bank.
(2) LDTCs must have originally been licensed as RDTCs and at the time of the application must have issued share capital of not less than HK$100 million and paid up capital of HK$75 million. Unlike the RDTCs, an LDTC can accept deposits of less than 3 months but cannot open savings accounts. The minimum deposits acceptable on deposit are HK$0.5 million or an equivalent amount in foreign currency.

The history and regulatory development of the RDTCs and LDTCs has been described in some detail because their role as financial intermediaries sprang directly from attempts to bypass regulations. Hong Kong's experience was not unique in this respect as witnessed by the attempts in the UK to restrict bank lending by an assortment of special deposits, corsets and other instruments, all of which were repeatedly circumvented by processes of disintermediation, by financial engineering or simply by discovering loopholes in the regulations.

3.2 Morphology of the deposit-taking companies market

As Table 3.1 indicates, the overall number of DTCs fluctuated, but since the creation of the three-tier system it has been continuously declining. The attrition rate has been particularly high amongst the RDTCs.

Table 3.1 Numbers of LDTCs and RDTCs in Hong Kong (end of year), 1980–8

Year	LDTC	RDTC
1980		302
1981		350
1982	18	343
1983	30	319
1984	33	311
1985	36	277
1986	38	254
1987	35	232
1988	35	216

Source: *Hong Kong Monthly Digest of Statistics*; Commissioner for Banking, Hong Kong, *Annual Reports*

Note: Before 1981 there was no distinction between LDTCs and RDTCs.

The structure of ownership and the size distribution of DTCs casts an interesting light on the dynamics of this particular sector of the market. As Table 3.2 indicates, in terms of numbers foreign banks are the predominant owners of both LDTCs and RDTCs. Indeed the number of foreign-owned LDTCs and RDTCs is greater than that indicated in Table 3.2 as a number of local banks are, in turn, owned by foreign banks. Taking the RDTCs alone, Japanese banks owned twenty-seven, two less than the US owned at twenty-nine. It is also obvious that amongst the RDTCs there is a preponderance of small institutions in terms of assets which may also explain the high attrition rate.

The Commissioner of Banking has released a set of data which allows an even more detailed breakdown of the ownership of RDTCs and of the relative concentration amongst the different classes. Table 3.3 supplies the details.

Estimates by the Commissioner of Banking showed that in 1987 RDTCs owned by foreign banks accounted for more than 50 per cent of all the deposits held by RDTCs and indeed for almost 85 per cent of all the assets. The RDTCs owned by Hong Kong

Table 3.2 Morphology of DTCs, 1986–8

LDTCs	1986	1987	1988
1 Subsidiaries of licensed banks			
Local	3	3	3
Foreign	14	12	11
2 Subsidiaries of foreign banks			
not licensed in Hong Kong	9	8	8
3 Bank related	10	10	11
4 Others	2	2	2
	—	—	—
Total	38	35	35
5 With assets of			
HK$6 billion and over	6	6	6
HK$3–6 billion	6	5	4
HK$3 billion and less	21	20	22
	—	—	—
Total (excludes LDTCs not incorporated in			
Hong Kong (5 in 1986, 4 in 1987 and 3 in 1988)	33	31	32
RDTCs			
1 Subsidiaries of licensed banks			
Local	35	34	33
Foreign	84	81	76
2 Subsidiaries of foreign banks			
not licensed in Hong Kong	51	52	49
3 Bank related	17	18	21
4 Others	67	47	37
	—	—	—
Total	254	232	216
5 With assets of			
HK$10 billion and over	5	7	2
HK$1–10 billion	49	53	53
Less than HK$1 billion	194	166	159
	—	—	—
Total (excluding 6 RDTCs not incorporated in			
Hong Kong for 1986–7, and 2 for 1988)	248	226	214

Source: Commissioner of Banking, Hong Kong, *Annual Reports*

non-banking interests had a mixed portfolio of business, some specializing in mortgages and others in share financing. The ones owned by foreign non-banking interests specialized primarily in the securities business. Those owned by banks, and particularly those in Table 3.3, Section 3, were predominantly involved in offshore forex lending and less so in securities. This was primarily true for the twenty-two of these RDTCs owned by Japanese banks.[3] A survey carried out by the Commissioner of Banking covering all DTCs found that twenty-seven of the LDTCs and

Table 3.3 Ownership and size in terms of deposits of RDTCs (May 1987)

1 Owned by banks licensed in Hong Kong with deposits of
(HK$ million)

Over 200	6
51–200	10
11–50	11
Less than 10	9
	—
	36

2 Owned by foreign banks licensed in Hong Kong with deposits of
(HK$ million)

Over 1,000	4
501–1,000	7
51–500	16
11–50	18
Less than 10	44
	—
	89

3 Owned by foreign banks not licensed in Hong Kong with deposits of
(HK$ million)

Over 200	4
51–200	15
11–50	25
Less than 10	21
	—
	65

4 Owned by Hong Kong interests not related to banks with deposits of
(HK$ million)

Over 100	2
11–100	11
Less than 10	9
	—
	22

5 Owned by overseas interests not related to banks with deposits of
(HK$ million)

Over 100	7
51–100	3
11–50	12
Less than 10	11
	—
	33

Source: Commissioner of Banking, 'RDTC – the current position', Consultative Paper 2, mimeo, Hong Kong, 1987

Table 3.4 Ranking of LDTCs and RDTCs in terms of assets and net profit (in US$ million converted from HK dollars at current rates of exchange), 1981–6

DTC	1981		1982		1983		1984		1985		1986	
	A	NP	A	NP	A	NP	A	NP	A	NP	A	NP
Wardley	1	2	1	1	1	4	1	7	1	6	1	5
Hang Seng Finance	2	3	2	2	3	1	5	1	10	4	8	7
Wayfoong Credit	3	4	4	3	NA	NA	NA	NA	*	2	*	6
LBI Finance (HK)	4	9	7	11	6	7	*	*	NA	NA	*	*
Yasuda Trust	5	*	8	*	5	*	8	14	9	10	14	14
LTCB Asia	12	11	3	9	2	5	2	5	4	5	2	11
Chase Manhattan (Asia)	*	*	5	4	16	2	*	6	*	9	*	*
Mitsui Trust Finance (HK)	9	*	9	*	4	*	3	17	2	15	3	*
Mitsui Finance Asia	NA	NA	NA	NA	10	14	4	*	6	*	4	*
Sumitomo Trust Finance (HK)	17	*	17	16	14	13	7	16	3	7	6	*
Sanwa International	*	*	*	*	*	16	12	11	5	17	9	*
Sumitomo Finance (Asia)	*	*	13	19	7	8	6	9	11	16	12	15

fifty-nine of the RDTCs were involved in securities-related business during 1987. The majority of these DTCs acted as principals and wholesalers primarily in debt securities, with a smaller number (about eleven) acting in the non-debt securities market.[4]

Table 3.4 gives an approximate indication of the relative concentration of market power amongst the DTCs over a 6 year period. Of a total of nearly 300 institutions about ten appear fairly consistently in the top positions. Despite the fact that those figures are based on a selective sample, i.e. DTCs that are involved in merchant banking activities only and not in hire purchase, leasing or mortgages, the predominance of the Hongkong Bank group is once again evident. Wardley, Hang Seng Finance and Wayfoong Credit are all subsidiaries of the Hongkong Bank. The presence of Japanese-owned DTCs is also obvious and of increasing importance.

Table 3.5 Share of LTDCs and RDTCs in total deposits and assets of banks plus all DTCs, 1980–8

	% total assets		% total deposits		% of HK dollar deposits of all DTCs
	LTDC	RDTC	LDTC	RDTC	
1980	NA	NA	NA	NA	31.4
1981	NA	NA	NA	NA	36.0
1982	NA	NA	3.9	14.3	20.3
1983	NA	NA	5.3	11.3	18.7
1984	8.3	20.5	5.2	11.3	18.2
1985	8.9	20.3	4.8	9.8	17.9
1986	5.8	15.2	4.1	6.6	12.9
1987	5.1	14.2	4.0	4.7	10.0
1988	3.7	7.3	3.6	4.2	9.4

Source: *Hong Kong Monthly Digest of Statistics*; Commissioner of Banking, Hong Kong Consultative papers 2 and 3; Commissioner of Banking, *Annual Reports*
Note: Totals include deposits or assets of all banks and DTCs in both HK dollars and foreign currencies.

In summary, the RDTC market presents a picture of a declining number of institutions, primarily owned by foreign banks, with a large number of very small RDTCs in terms of the size of deposits held (ninety-four out of the 245 surveyed in Table 3.3 had less than HK$10 million in deposits). These institutions appeared to have two primary functions: to act as financial intermediaries for the parent banks particularly in offshore business, and to carry out diverse types of merchant banking activities of which securities dealing is one. However, it is important to keep clearly in focus the role of the DTCs as financial intermediaries, as the creation of the three-tier system effectively abolished any cost or interest rate advantage that they may have had. As Table 3.5 indicates, the share of LDTCs and RDTCs in the total assets and deposits of the whole banking system has been declining and it is likely to continue to do so.

3.3 Portfolio structure and dynamics

Some aspects of the assets and liabilities distribution of DTCs has already been explored in Chapter 2, Section 2.3, dealing with inter-institutional deposits. It was pointed out that the original dependence of banks on DTCs as their sources of deposits was quickly eliminated after 1982 with the introduction of the three-tier system. However, as Table 2.16 indicates, in terms of HK dollar funds, up to mid-1980 DTCs were still net lenders to banks, with banks providing a net amount of forex denominated deposits. That DTCs supplied parent banks with HK dollar deposits was not surprising, given the existence of the IRA. However, this source of funds is not as comparatively cheap as it was before 1981 because now all DTCs have to maintain liquidity and capital adequacy ratios as well as being restricted as to the minimum size of deposits that they can accept, thus excluding them from the retail market.

Table 3.6 summarizes the portfolio structure of all DTCs in 1988. The official statistics do not differentiate between licensed and registered DTCs and so disaggregate figures are not available.

Given the wholesale and merchant banking type of activities that DTCs have been associated with from their inception, the structure of their assets and liabilities does not hold great surprises. Compared with the portfolios of banks as shown in Table 2.10, DTCs hold proportionally more certificates of deposit (CDs), floating-rate notes (FRNs) and treasury bills (TBs). DTCs have been intimately linked with the rise of the debt market in Hong Kong in terms of their support and development of negotiable instruments. Thus, for example, in 1981 they held about 3.4 per cent of their assets in the form of negotiable CDs

Table 3.6 Assets and liabilities of DTCs (HK$ million), 1988

	Liabilities			Assets	
	% Total			% Total	
	(a)	(b)		(c)	(d)
1 Deposits in HK$	32,775	49.2	1 Notes and coin	7	

(ii)	Amount due to banks abroad	128,011	31.0	
(iii)	NCDs	4,098	1.0	
(iv)	Other liabilities	96,545	23.4	
Total liabilities		**411,582**	**(100%)**	

5	Loans and advances for use in Hong Kong			
(i)	Manufacturing	2,807	5.6	0.7
(ii)	Wholesale and retail trade	1,461	3.0	0.2
(iii)	Mortgages	19,122	38.4	4.6
(iv)	Building, construction	3,965	8.0	0.9
(v)	Others	22,439	45.0	5.4
		49,794	(100.0)	11.8
6	Banks acceptances and bills of exchange	1,001		0.2
7	Floating rate notes and commercial paper	37,432		9.0
8	Treasury bills and securities and other assets	25,689		6.2
9	Others, loans and assets	80,454		19.5
Total assets		**411,582**		**(100%)**

Source: *Hong Kong Monthly Digest of Statistics*

Notes: Percentages and figures are rounded and are approximate.

(a) % total = type of deposit / total deposits

(b) % total = individual item of liabilities / total liabilities

(c) % total = type of loans / total loans (subtotal)

(d) % total = individual item of assets / total assets

(NCDs), less than 0.4 per cent in bank acceptances (BAs) and bills of exchange (BEs), about 2 per cent in FRNs and commercial paper (CP) and 1.9 per cent in TBs. The equivalent percentages for 1988 were 3.2 per cent (NCDs), 0.2 per cent (BAs and BEs), 9 per cent (FRNs and CP) and 6.2 per cent (TBs).

If the term 'merchant banking' was to be applied to Hong Kong then, in a sense, all DTCs are potential merchant banks but by no means all DTCs are involved in merchant banking activities. A typical merchant bank offering a complete range of services and products, for example, would be involved in the marketing and market-making of debt instruments, would lead or participate in the syndication of loans, would operate in an advisory function and finally would be involved in equity issuing and marketing activities (placing, underwriting etc.) as well as wider issues of corporate finance. Some of the equity-linked activities of DTCs are examined in chapters 4 and 5, particularly their investment management and unit trust functions. The role of the DTCs in the debt market, although very important, cannot be separated from that of banks for the very simple reason that the majority of the DTCs are their subsidiaries. Furthermore, although in relative terms debt instruments may figure more prominently in the balance sheets of DTCs, in absolute terms the situation is reversed except for FRNs. Table 3.7 shows some of the relevant data in aggregate terms, i.e. without trying to net out any inter-institutional holdings.

Table 3.7 Comparative holdings of debt instruments: banks and DTCs (HK$ million), 1988

	NCD		BAs and BEs		FRNs and CP	
	HK$	Forex	HK$	Forex	HK$	Forex
Banks	8,642	11,133	1,335	17,063	8,499	44,005
DTCs	4,118	9,279	61	941	2,805	34,627

Source: Hong Kong Monthly Digest of Statistics
Note: Figures for NCDs include those issued by banks both inside and outside Hong Kong and by DTCs.

3.4 The development of the debt market

It has been claimed that before 1984 there was no debt or capital market other than equity in Hong Kong. Indeed, a Capital Market Association was not formed until 1985, but with more than seventy members it signified its growing importance. The relative underdevelopment of the Hong Kong debt market can be attributed to and explained by a number of factors. First, the prominence of the active but highly volatile equity market had given firms relatively easy access to funds. Similarly investors, particularly the smaller private ones, had grown accustomed to investing in shares rather than debt instruments. This, in a sense, had created both a demand and supply deficiency which initially could only be bridged by institutional initiatives. Second, as an outcome of deliberate fiscal policy there has been virtually no government debt issued in Hong Kong. As Chapter 6 will show, the public sector in Hong Kong since 1977 had a deficit on two occasions only – in the fiscal years 1983 and 1984. As a result the Hong Kong Government had until 1989 only one issue of bonds outstanding at HK$1 billion, quoted in the Stock Exchange but hardly ever traded.[5] The absence of government debt has meant that the market has never had a benchmark instrument on which to base comparisons and assess relative yields and risk. Given the importance of the government bond markets in the USA and the gilts market in the UK, this is perhaps one of the key contributory factors in the underdevelopment of Hong Kong's debt markets. Third, the linking of the HK dollar to the US dollar since 1983 had made the Hong Kong Government very wary of any development in the interest rate front which could directly or indirectly threaten this link. For example, in the mid-1980s the Government refused permission to the World Bank to launch an HK dollar denominated issue of its bonds giving as reasons its unwillingness to see the HK dollar becoming an 'international investment currency'. Since then the Government's attitude has shifted considerably, allowing foreign institutions with significant HK dollar business to issue HK dollar debt and reversing its decision on the World Bank issue.[6] An additional factor hindering the development of the short-term side of the market must have been the IRA. Any attempt to introduce tradeable paper which would result in higher interest rate yields on maturities covered by the agreement met with either the resistance or suspicion of the authorities. A good example of this was the attempt by DTCs to introduce a Hong Kong version of money market funds at sufficiently small denominations to tap the retail market. These funds were not tradeable, but were the first step to a short-term market of instruments other than CDs or bank deposits. Investor response was lukewarm and these funds never really took off. Fourth, the taxation treatment of privately issued debt compared with bank issued paper has been anomalous in Hong Kong, with the former bearing tax whilst the latter did not. This meant that corporate lenders would have to offer higher yields to investors to attract them, thus making this form of lending quite expensive. Similarly corporate holders of HK dollar denominated debt had to pay corporation tax on interest receivable but not on interest earned on non-HK dollar assets. This also created a further disincentive for institutional holders of debt. This unfavourable tax treatment was abolished in 1989. Fifth, and finally, the October 1987 stock market crash and in particular the severe problems with the Hang Seng Stock Index futures markets postponed the introduction of an interest rates futures contract for Hong Kong. The trading of an instrument that would have allowed the existing and actively traded money market and inter-bank market funds and deposits to be arbitraged may well have given a boost to the longer-maturity sectors. It has been a common and obvious enough observation to make on the existence of large gaps in the time spectrum of interest rates in Hong Kong, gaps which undoubtedly hindered arbitraging and the development of further types of debt.[7]

Table 3.8 presents the details for the amounts and numbers of debt instruments issued in Hong Kong. It is perhaps indicative of the developing stage of Hong Kong's capital markets that no single or consistent source of statistics is yet available. For ease of comparison and in order to offer another estimate of the size and number of issues involved in the capital market, Table 3.9 gives a different set of estimates. The discrepancies between the totals in these two tables are significant in at least two years, 1987 and 1988. Some of the discrepancies can be explained by the inclusion or exclusion of certain issues, although the sources are not clear on this and neither could the data be cross-checked against other information. However, Table 3.9 is interesting to the extent that

Table 3.8 HK dollar capital markets: distribution and totals issued (HK$ million), 1982–8

Year	FLRCDs		FRCDs		CP and bonds		FRNs		RUFs		Total	
	No.	HK$	No.	HK$	No.	HK$	No.	HK$	No.	HK$	No.	HK$
1982	NA	NA	1	40	NA	NA	NA	NA	NA	NA	–	–
1983	NA	100	0	0	2	850	0	0	NA	NA	–	–
1984	13	1,950	3	260	6	2,100	1	500	0	0	23	4,810
1985	11	1,510	47	5,410	15	8,100	4	1,760	0	0	77	16,780
1986	6	1,200	78	10,101	9	3,755	7	3,850	9	4,485	109	23,391
1987	6	1,299	32	3,856	4	1,740	1	400	4	3,450	47	10,745
1988	5	850	40	3,455	5	2,291	0	0	6	6,950	56	13,546
Totals	41	6,909	201	23,122	41	18,836	13	6,510	19	14,885	312	69,272

Sources: Asian Finance, January 1988, December 1988; Chinese Banks' Association, *Hong Kong's Banking System*, p. 65; D.P.M. Chan, 'Hong Kong bond market', *The Securities Bulletin*, Stock Exchange of Hong Kong, No. 14, June 1987, pp. 32–3

Notes: NA signifies that there are no available figures for that year rather than that no issues were made; total figures are therefore approximate and the sums of rows and columns do not add up.
FLRCD, floating-rate certificate of deposit; RUF, Revolving Underwriting Facility.

Table 3.9 HK dollar capital markets: types of instruments and institutions, 1984–8

Instrument	1984		1985		1986		1987		1988	
	No.	HK$	No.	HK$	No.	HK$	No.	HK$	No.	HK$
Financial institutions										
FLRCDs	7	1,425	6	1,000	7	1,350	9	1,999	6	1,050
FRCDs	3	260	36	5,300	85	10,926	33	3,816	36	2,741
RUFs	3	1,050	5	860	–	–	2	600	–	–
FRN	–	–	1	360	–	–	–	–	–	–
Others	–	–	–	–	–	–	3	1,650	3	1,300
Total	13	2,735	48	7,520	92	12,276	47	8,065	45	5,091
Commercial institutions										
Bonds	–	–	3	1,500	2	1,180	–	–	2	591
FRN	1	500	1	200	5	4,100	1	400	–	–
RUFs	3	1,350	15	8,000	9	4,485	6	4,590	4	4,910
TLCs	–	–	2	2,390	1	1,450	3	2,768	6	4,086
Others	–	–	–	–	–	–	1	500	2	3,500
Total	4	1,850	21	12,090	17	11,215	11	8,258	14	13,087
Grand Total	17	4,585	69	19,610	109	23,491	58	16,323	59	18,178

Source: K.M. Hurst, 'A review and prospects for Hong Kong capital markets, *Securities Bulletin, Stock Exchange of Hong Kong* No. 33, January 1989, p. 21
Note: TLC, transferable loan certificates.

it classifies the issues in terms of the institutions which made them (i.e. financial or commercial) as well as in terms of the type of papers sold.

The first issue of CP in Hong Kong was undertaken in 1979 by the Mass Transit Railway (MTR), a Government-controlled institution. The same body issued the first HK dollar FRNs in 1984. Given its quasi-sovereign status it is not surprising that the MTR has always been in the forefront of financial innovation in Hong Kong and has also been a key borrower in the market. However, the modest beginnings of the CP market were swiftly overtaken by the rise of CDs, which were hardly new to Hong Kong but which accelerated into prominence in the mid-1980s. Because of the unfavourable taxation treatment CP issues have not yet developed an active secondary market. Furthermore, since CPs are issued under revolving underwritten facilities (RUFs), it is worth noting that at present only about 37 per cent of the facilities are used.

The development of the fixed rate CDs (FRCDs) in Hong Kong is both illustrative and instructive as to the problems and opportunities of the developing debt market. The market developed primarily along a placement orientation.[8] In other words it was dominated by investors who intended to hold the papers to maturity. This restricted the liquidity of the market and reduced secondary activity. A corollary of this was that the market was dominated by exceptionally high quality paper with over 90 per cent of outstanding issues rated at single A or better. Equally, however, the average size of issue tended to be quite small and by some estimates nearly 50 per cent of all issues were locked away until maturity with another 45 per cent also ending up with firm holders within the 3 months following the issue.[9] Table 3.10 shows a composite picture of the average size and distribution of FRCD holdings in Hong Kong.

The dominance of banks is obvious and this particular characteristic of the market will be raised again later. Compared with Eurobonds the market is still very small indeed. When CP is excluded, on average over 1986–8 the HK dollar denominated issues amounted to about 1.5 per cent of the total Eurodollar issues in the world Eurodollar market. If the rest of the Eurocurrency issues were to be included, the market is shown to be very small indeed in value terms. Finally, the transaction cost

Table 3.10 Average size and allocation of FRCDs in Hong Kong, 1985–8

	1985	1986	1987	1988
Size (% of total)				
Below HK$100 million	25	32	32	37
HK$100 million	35	37	43	49
Above HK$100 million	40	31	25	14
Holders (% of total)				
Pension funds	22.0	8.3	24.3	20.0
Local banks	17.0	10.5	7.5	5.4
PRC banks	4.0	4.5	5.0	22.0
Other banks/DTCs	35.0	40.0	38.0	17.0
Bank-asset swaps	7.0	26.0	7.0	–
Individuals	7.6	5.0	8.0	5.6
Corporate	0.6	2.0	0.4	7.0
Insurance companies	2.7	1.5	1.0	8.0
Others	4.1	2.2	8.8	15.0

Source: Compiled from various tables in the references in notes 8 and 9. The allocation figures are based on the experience of the Manufacturers Hanover Asia who were leading arrangers and underwriters in the period 1985–8 surveyed

of the HK dollar FRCDs in terms of the bid–ask spread is comparable with that of the Eurodollar market, but as indicated this does not compensate for the relative illiquidity of the market. This is compounded by the absence of a reasonably large number of market-makers. All these characteristics which shaped the market brought their influence to bear in the crash which occurred in March 1987.

In the three years preceding March 1987 the relative fall of market interest rates in Hong Kong caused a number of corporate borrowers to switch from floating to fixed interest rate finance. Banks were instrumental in this process through corresponding arrangements of swaps facilitated by the issuing of FRCDs. As long as interest rates continued to fall banks were willing to carry on issuing CDs and holding them in the expectation that they could be resold in a very active secondary market for a capital gain. Almost all CDs issued during this 1985–7 period were swap driven. As the market had been oversupplied with CDs, the discounts which borrowers had to offer on the issuing prices deepened. Banks started exposing themselves to greater risks by financing their holdings of CDs by borrowing in the inter-bank market. As long as the interbank rates were less than the yield on the CDs an effectively artifical demand could be created based almost exclusively on banks. There was a further problem in that the majority of the bank-held CDs had maturities longer than the average inter-bank loan which financed them, thus leading to an additional maturity mismatch as well as a potentially volatile market.[10] When interest rates began to rise in early 1987 and expectations about potential CD capital gains disappeared, there was a scramble to unload bank-held CDs. By April 1987 the market came to a virtual standstill, with new issues falling by more than 60 per cent from the high level of 1986. The fixed-rate CD market found it difficult to recover, with the consequence that a rather unbalanced situation developed. Whilst investors wished to hold FRCDs there were very few new issues. In addition, a growing number of issues were maturing in the early 1990s, thus worsening the shortage. The outcome of that was an increase in innovative issues attempting to tap this market such as 'bull and bear' bonds or 'gold linked' bonds. The floating-rate certificate of deposit (FLRCD) market was never as popular as the FRCD market and hence suffered less, not forgetting the fact that yields there were linked to current market rates. Perhaps the most important lesson that this particular crisis illustrated was that the absence of a wider retail and non-bank based market is essential for the development of a broad and deep market. The data in Table 3.11 outline this aspect of the market. In 1980 the public, primarily institutional investors, held most of the NCDs of issued by banks and DTCs. By 1986, with the exception of CDs in forex, most of the paper was held by banks and DTCs. The market had thus developed along rather incestuous lines, being primarily inter-bank and inter-DTC and therefore subject to volatility as it lacked breadth, i.e a large value of orders, and depth, i.e. a large number of orders to buy or sell above or below the current market price.

The Corporate Bond market has been perhaps the least developed part of the Hong Kong debt market. At the beginning of 1989 only nine bonds were quoted in the Stock Exchange. One of these was the only Hong Kong Government issue, one by MTR, two by Banque Indosuez, three by Paribas Investment (Asia) and only two by non-bank companies (Hong Kong Land and Hutchinson Whampoa). Three factors have been indicated as the reasons for this absence of issues and activities.[11] The first concerns taxation on interest receivable on non-bank HK dollar bonds. The second has been the absence of a Hong Kong based independent rating authority which would allow some risk assessment. This was felt to be particularly pertinent given the absence of Government debt which could be used as a benchmark. Finally, the existing bond issues traded thinly because it was difficult to arrange transactions of less than HK$100,000 to HK$0.5 million or more than HK$20 million. This excluded both the smaller private investors and the larger institutional buyers from the market.

Table 3.11 Holdings of NCDs (per cent), 1980–6

	1980		1986	
	HK$	Forex	HK$	Forex
Bank issued (HK)				
Banks	12.6	4.6	40.0	29.7
DTC	42.5	24.8	31.2	23.0
Public	44.9	70.6	28.8	47.3
DTC issued (HK)				
Banks	1.3	33.0	30.6	5.7
DTCs	35.0	35.9	31.6	8.0
Public	63.7	31.3	38.8	86.3

Source: Chinese Banks' Association, *Hong Kong's Banking System*, Hong Kong, 1988, p. 67

As illustrated in Chapter 2, the banking market in Hong Kong was quick to adopt and use financial engineering products. This is also true for the capital market where, despite the limited number of instruments, a larger number of innovations were adopted including bull and bear bonds, transferable loan certificates, gold linked CDs, etc.[12]

3.5 The developing situation

The most obvious observation which can made in examining the trends in the market area occupied by the DTCs is that their numbers and share of both HK dollar denominated and all other deposits are declining and are likely to continue to do so. This has been the outcome of both competitive pressures and the effects of the changes in the regulatory system. The remaining

DTCs in the market are responding in a number of ways, primarily through diversification of their activities away from the standard 'banking and deposit' type of business. It is perhaps indicative of the relatively strong financial position of the DTCs that the imposition of the capital adequacy rule under the 1986 Banking Ordinance caused them very little difficulty.[13]

The authorities have been concerned enough to set in motion a discussion and a review of the possible directions in which the DTC sector could develop. The Office of the Commissioner of Banking outlined six basic options open to the industry varying from no change from the status quo to the creation of limited service banks. Other variations included changes in the minimum size and maturity of deposits which could be accepted as well as in the capital adequacy rules applicable to DTCs.[14]

In 1989 the Government introduced further reforms in the structure of DTCs.[15] The three tier system still remains except that now the names and the capital requirements of the DTCs will change. From now on LDTCs will be called 'restricted licence banks'. This was a change that LDTCs had been pursuing in order to establish firmly their claims to be banking institutions. The name was particularly important to DTC subsidiaries of banks which could not use the word 'bank' in their title. In recognition of their status as restricted banks the minimum share capital was raised from HK$100 million to HK$150 million with a 2 year transitional period. The RDTCs will now be called just DTCs, but their minimum share capital was also raised from HK$10 million to HK$25 million, also with a 2 year transitional period to comply. No further changes were made on the type of deposits that these two newly styled institutions could accept, and their remit is still firmly in the wholesale market.

The authorities saw these changes in the light of strengthening the capital base of the existing institutions and acknowledging their position, or at least that of the LDTCs, as leading merchant banks in the region. This is a position which has been confirmed by both surveys and the growth of Hong Kong LDTCs and their active participation in equity and debt finance. Table 3.12 shows the results of one of these surveys with Hong Kong institutions consistently occupying top places.

With yet another formal restructuring of the DTC sector and the raising of the minimum capital requirements the authorities

Table 3.12 The ranking of Hong Kong's DTCs amongst the top five merchant banks in Southeast Asia (ranking based on assets), 1982–5

DTC	1982	1983	1984	1985
Wardley	1	1	1	1
LTCB Asia	4	3	3	5
Hang Seng Finance	3	4	–	–
Mitsui Trust Finance	–	5	4	3
Mitsui Finance Asia	–	–	5	–
Sumitomo Trust	–	–	–	4
Wayfoong Credit	5	–	–	–

Source: *Asian Finance*, February 1984, March 1985, March 1986, March 1987
Note: The list includes merchant banks only from Hong Kong, Singapore, Malaysia, Indonesia, Thailand and the Philippines.

are clearly pointing the way towards a two-tier system in the not too distant future:

> Since DTCs were first authorised in 1976 the supervisory standards applied have moved closer to those to which banks are subject. Since the Banking Ordinance 1986, those standards have effectively been the same. While this has worked to the advantage of the more substantial DTCs, it has caused other companies critically to assess whether they should be in the deposit-taking business. This was an important factor behind the secular decline in the number of RDTCs which continued during the year. This trend points to the emergence, in time, of a two-tier system. As yet it would be premature to predict when.[16]

The upheavals that the debt market has gone through also point in that direction since any further developments must rely on LDTCs, now restricted licensed banks, which have the size and the ability to lead and make markets.

The development of the DTC sector has been yet another proof of the vitality of the financial market in Hong Kong, even when the helping hand of the authorities was necessary to bring forward changes.

Chapter four

The Stock Exchange

4.1 Introduction

In early 1989 the Stock Exchange of Hong Kong listed 468 securities spread over 301 companies. As a financial institution and market the Hong Kong Stock Exchange has perhaps attracted a disproportionate amount of interest, i.e. disproportionate as to its actual rather than its perceived importance and potential weaknesses. There are now enough myths and misconceptions about this market to warrant a monograph rather than a chapter. There is no doubt, however, that in the light of the available statistical and other empirical evidence the market emerges considerably better than a cursory examination of press coverage would suggest.

The first stock exchange was established in Hong Kong in 1891, changed its name from the Association of Stockbrokers in Hong Kong to the Hong Kong Stock Exchange in 1914. A second exchange was established in 1921 but it merged with the first in 1947. The late 1960s and early 1970s saw a spectacular growth in the share market activity in Hong Kong with the establishment of three more exchanges in addition to the Hong Kong Stock Exchange, namely the Far East (1969), the Kam Ngan (1971) and the Kowloon (1973). The general regulatory laxity led to a proliferation of both listed companies and brokers, nearly 300 and 1,000 respectively by the end of 1973. Market activity flourished, with the Hang Seng Index (HSI) (see Section 4.3) reaching a record high of 1,774 in March 1973. When the inevitable bubble burst, the HSI fell from a high of 1,775 in March 1973 to 437 in December and then to an all-time low of

150 at the end of 1974. The outcome of this speculative bubble was a number of regulatory measures including the establishment of a Securities Commission. There was also a move to establish the framework under which the four exchanges, and their diverse rules and practices, would be unified. This scheme came to fruition in April 1986 when the unified stock exchange, The Stock Exchange of Hong Kong (SEHK) opened for business.[1]

The unification of the exchanges had an undoubted effect on turnover although the bull market of 1986–7 makes it quite difficult to separate its effects. Table 4.1 shows the total turnover.

Table 4.1 Value of turnover in the stock market(s) (HK$ million), 1980–8

1980	95,670	1985	75,821
1981	105,970	1986	123,128
1982	46,221	1987	371,406
1983	37,166	1988	199,480
1984	48,808		

Sources: Stock Exchange of Hong Kong, *1st Anniversary Report*, 1987, p. 162; *1988 Factbook*, 1989, p. 42
Note: The figures for 1986 (April) onwards refer to the unified exchange; before that date they refer to the turnover of the four exchanges.

Since the stock market is a market just like any other, it can be analysed in terms of its dynamics, degree of competition, concentration and efficiency. In the following section we attempt to quantify certain characteristics of the SEHK. Particular attention is paid to the time period leading up to the October 1987 crash because the post-crash period was atypical in a number of ways not least because of the precipitous drop in turnover. This would have made any numerical calculations or samples biased as to their accuracy and representativeness. Furthermore, the stock market underwent a number of reorganizations (perhaps better termed convulsions) following the decision of the then leadership of the exchange to close it for trading for 4 days (20–23 October 1987). The decision was related to the exceptionally large long positions in the stock index futures market which, with share prices crashing, were certain to lead to large-scale defaults. The relevant and related developments in the futures market are described in Chapter 5, Section 5.2.

The decision to close the market was highly controversial and led to widespread scepticism and doubts as to the claims that the SEHK was to become the leading regional market after Tokyo. The situation did not improve with the arrest of the former chairman of the exchange on bribery charges in January 1988. The Government's reaction to this crisis of confidence in the institution rather than in the market itself was not particularly commendable. Observers criticized the absence of leadership but welcomed the setting up of an investigatory committee under Ian Hay-Davison. The committee's report made a large number of recommendations on the structure and organization of both the securities and the futures markets and on the functions of the Office of the Commissioner for Securities. Most of the recommendations were implemented including a complete revamping of the regulatory bodies.[2]

4.2 Quantifying the characteristics of the market

A crucial characteristic of any financial assets market, which also helps to determine other important aspects of its operations, is its breadth and depth. Breadth refers to the existence of a substantial volume of bid and ask orders. A broad market should generate a relatively small bid–ask spread because a broad market will provide dealers with a larger number of transactions on which to generate income. Similarly, the wider the trading of a particular share amongst brokers, the greater will be the effect of competition as reflected in the spread. Depth of a market refers to the existence of orders to buy and sell above and below the current market prices. The result of depth is that excess demand or supply will have a smaller effect on the changes in prices. A shallow market will tend to result in large price fluctuations. The excess demand or supply for the shares will generate large price changes precisely because there are no orders above or below the current market price to cushion it.[3]

Market activity in the SEHK is concentrated in a relatively narrow group of shares in terms both of sectoral distribution and the individual structures. For a start, the property sector dominates the capitalization of the Hong Kong equity market. From that it follows that for the majority of the shares the market is narrow or thin, i.e. a small volume of orders to buy or sell. Also the market is likely to be shallow as well, thus partially explaining the volatility of Hong Kong stock market prices. All these, however, are empirically testable propositions. Share trading activity in the market is dominated by a relatively small group of shares in terms of both sectoral distribution and the actual shares themselves. As indicated, the property sector dominates the market capitalization and overall turnover (Table 4.2).

Table 4.2 Sectoral distribution of market capitalization and turnover (per cent of total), 1986–8

Sector	1986		1987		1988	
	MC	TO	MC	TO	MC	TO
Finance (36)	16.9	NA	16.3	13.5	13.7	10.7
Utilities (9)	18.9	NA	17.4	9.8	17.2	7.6
Properties (101)	24.8	NA	26.1	37.4	28.4	39.0
Consolidated enterprises (77)	30.9	NA	29.6	23.9	29.4	27.6
Industrials (64)	5.3	NA	6.3	12.3	6.6	11.2
Hotels (12)	2.7	NA	4.0	2.8	4.2	3.9
Others (5)	0.1	NA	0.05	0.08	0.1	0.1

Sources: Stock Exchange of Hong Kong, *1987 Factbook*, 1988; *1988 Factbook*, 1989
Note: Percentages are slightly rounded; numbers in parentheses denote the number of listed companies in 1988.
MC, market capitalization; TO, turnover.

Property firms figure prominently in the list of the top twenty companies in terms of market capitalization (Table 4.3). It is worth noting also that interlinked share holdings or companies belonging to the same group, but trading separately, concentrate the market shares even further. Thus, for example, Hang Seng Bank is a subsidiary of Hongkong Bank, Swire Pacific maintains large holdings in Cathay Pacific as does Jardine Matheson in Hong Kong Land (and vice versa) and Dairy Farm International, and last but not least Cheung Kong, Hutchinson Whampoa, Cavendish International and Hong Kong Electric are all closely interrelated companies.

A sample period of trading activity between February and July 1987, i.e. 6 months coming up to the October 1987 crash, yielded some interesting insights into the trading patterns of the market.[4] Table 4.4 shows a fairly typical distribution of turnover in terms of both the number of securities involved and the range of values traded. Given that the total turnover in July 1987 stood at

Table 4.3 Market capitalization: top twenty firms (percentage of total market), 1988

1	Hong Kong Telecom	9.16
2	Hongkong Bank	5.78
3	Swire Pacific	4.89
4	Cathay Pacific Airways	4.59
5	Hutchinson Whampoa	4.49
6	Hong Kong Land	4.03[a]
7	Hang Seng Bank	3.41
8	China Light	3.24
9	Sun Hung Kai Properties	3.21[a]
10	Cheung Kong (Holdings)	3.05[a]
11	New World Development	2.69[a]
12	Wharf (Holdings)	2.61
13	Hong Kong Electric	2.22
14	Cavendish International	1.59[a]
15	Jardine Matheson Holdings	1.56
16	World International Holdings	1.54[a]
17	Henderson Land	1.50[a]
18	Dairy Farm International	1.34
19	Hong Kong and China Gas	1.32
20	New Town (NT) Properties	1.32[a]
		63.54

Source: Stock Exchange of Hong Kong, *1988 Factbook*, 1989
Note: [a] Primarily a property-related company.

Table 4.4 Distribution of turnover in terms of number of securities and value of transactions (July 1987)

Turnover (HK$ million)	No. of securities	Percentage of total securities traded
Less than 1	36	13.7
1–10	72	27.3
10–50	56	21.3
50–100	28	10.7
100–500	48	18.2
Over 500	23	8.8
Total	263	100.0

Source: Securities Bulletin, Stock Exchange of Hong Kong, August 1987
Note: The figures exclude shares suspended or not traded, warrants, debt securities and unit trusts.

HK$34,978 million, it can be deduced that most transactions covered a small number of shares which were actively traded in terms of both value and volume, thereby leaving about three quarters of the shares to be traded in a market of low value and volume. Table 4.5 produces some additional evidence by examining the trading activities of the top twenty shares in terms of market capitalization.

In the first 18 months of the operations of the unified stock exchange (April 1986 to August 1987), the top twenty most active shares accounted consistently for more than 60 per cent of the

Table 4.5 Share activity of the top twenty shares in terms of market capitalization, February–July 1987

Shares ranked in order of market capitalization (percentage in parentheses), July 1987	No. of times shares appear in top 20 most active shares (value)	No. of times shares appear in top 20 most active shares (volume)	Rank of share in terms of market capitalization in Feb 1987
1 Hongkong Bank (7.68)	6	6	1
2 Swire Pacific (6.23)	5	2	4
3 Hutchinson Whampoa (6.0)	5	2	2
4 Hong Kong Telephone[a] (4.43)	4	–	3
5 Hang Seng Bank (4.30)	5	–	10
6 Cheung Kong (4.23)	6	2	9
7 China Light & Power (4.22)	5	–	6
8 Sun Hung Kai Prop. (3.67)	5	–	12
9 Cathay Pacific Airways (3.26)	6	4	8
10 Hong Kong Land (3.20)	6	6	7
11 New World Development (2.60)	6	3	13
12 Wharf Holdings (2.54)	5	3	11
13 Hong Kong Electric (2.32)	6	5	5
14 Cavendish (2.08)	1	1	[b]
15 Jardine Matheson (2.01)	6	–	14
16 Henderson Land (1.81)	4	4	19
17 Jardine Strategic (1.54)	1	–	[c]
18 Hang Lung (1.53)	2	–	18
19 Hong Kong and China Gas (1.50)	–	–	17
20 World International (1.44)	2	5	16
Percentage of total market	66.6		

Source: Securities Bulletin, Stock Exchange of Hong Kong, various issues
Notes: [a] Hong Kong Telephone is now Hong Kong Telecom.
[b] Started trading in July 1987.
[c] Jardine Securities became a subsidiary of Jardine Strategic Holdings in February 1987.

value of turnover and easily for 65 per cent of the market capitalization. As Table 4.5 shows, over a 6 month period in 1987 at least a third of these shares appeared in the top twenty in terms of value of turnover, although there was a much lower correlation in terms of volume of trade. Significantly, over the same 6 month period the 'membership' of the top twenty shares in terms of market capitalization remained virtually unchanged, although the ranking varied. The figures in Table 4.5 are not strictly comparable with those in Table 4.2, however, as the introduction of Hong Kong Telecom in 1988 changed the ranking. Significantly, though, as Table 4.5 shows, over the same 6 month period four shares (Hongkong Bank, Swire Pacific, Hutchinson Whampoa and Hong Kong Telephone) continuously hold the top four positions in terms of market capitalization. These top four shares accounted for nearly a quarter of the local market capitalization. The single largest share of the market over April 1986 to July 1987 was that of Hongkong Bank with 9.74 per cent in April 1986. Furthermore, of these top twenty shares only seven appeared in the list of twenty shares whose prices showed the largest rise or fall over February–July 1987. Six of these made only one appearance, and one appeared three times. This is perhaps indirect evidence that active trading tends to prevent wide fluctuations, although in the case of Hong Kong this is only a comparative evaluation. This overall picture of concentration of market activity in a small number of stock is further confirmed by the data in Table 4.6.

Table 4.6 Turnover in terms of volume of shares traded (per cent of total turnover), 1979–86

	Dec 1979	Mar 1986	Dec 1986
10 most active stocks	40	40.3	41.2
30 most active stocks	77.4	74.9	67.7
50 most active stocks	90.5	89.0	81.6

Source: D. Chan, 'Is Hong Kong Stock Market Approaching Maturity', *Chinese General Chamber of Commerce Bulletin*, No. 2: 35–7, 1987.

As already indicated the breadth of a market is measured by the volume of bids and offers, and by extension, by the bid–ask spread. The performance of the Hong Kong market does not compare unfavourably with that of New York where between 1978 and 1982 over 60 per cent of the quoted spreads were US$0.25 or less.[5] However, this figure is meaningless unless it can be compared with a mid-point price such as the closing price. Taking the two weeks of 1–16 October 1987 and using the ten most active shares as the sample, we obtain the following spread between bid and offered prices in Hong Kong:

| Average | 9 cents (HK) | Average | 1.04% closing price |
| Standard deviation | 7.9 cents (HK) | Standard deviation | 0.62% closing price |

Similar samples for less actively traded shares or blue chip stocks which did not appear in the ten most active shares did not reveal any significant differences. It is important to note that, although in absolute terms the spread varied between nearly 17 and 2 cents, it was never more than about 1.5 per cent of the closing price and could fall to less than 0.5 per cent. This percentage compares well with spreads in both New York and London. A post-Big Bang survey for London has shown that as a result of the increased competition the spreads narrowed:

> In the most frequent traded securities (Alpha Stocks) it [the spread] has remained almost unchanged at 0.75 per cent. In the less frequently traded Betas and Gammas it has fallen fractionally – from 3.37 per cent to 2.95 per cent by June this year.[6]

Another aspect of quantifying the quality of the SEHK are estimates of the price continuity of transactions, i.e. the percentage of trades that have been made sequentially either at the same price or with a minimum price variation. The evidence for New York over 1978–82 indicates a factor of price continuity of over 80 per cent, using an eighth of a dollar as the maximum price change.[7] Although random observations taken over two trading weeks (1–16 October 1987) for several Hong Kong stocks indicated frequent price changes from trade to trade, the changes were very small in proportion to prices and no systematic pattern depending on whether the transactions were for board, odd, special or direct lots was observed. However, the question of price continuity in the SEHK is still open.[8]

Trading costs are another important aspect of market efficiency as they can reduce returns to investors and therefore lead to fewer transactions and a less liquid market. The minimum commission charged by brokers in Hong Kong has remained unchanged for nearly 20 years at 0.25 per cent of the contract value. There are now two additional levies related to the SEHK itself and to stamp duty payable. Hong Kong's total costs of trading securities compare favourably with those in the rest of the region and other markets (Table 4.7).

Table 4.7 Average comparative costs of trading securities (per cent of total contract value), 1988

Australia	2.00	Japan	1.23
USA	1.62	Singapore	1.08
Canada	1.47	Hong Kong	0.61
FRG	1.33	Taiwan	0.30

Source: Securities Bulletin, Stock Exchange of Hong Kong No. 29, September 1988, p. 35

In summary, trading in Hong Kong's stock market is confined to a small number of shares which account for a large percentage of the overall value and volume of the market's activity. Not surprisingly these shares also account for most of the market's capitalization. It also follows that the majority of the shares are traded infrequently in terms of both value and volume. Sample observations, however, indicate that this lack of breadth in the market is not necessarily reflected in very wide spreads, at least in comparison with other markets. Furthermore, trading costs are comparatively lower than in other centres, thus adding to the competitive edge of the SEHK in attracting overseas business and maintaining a higher volume of transactions to the extent that this is influenced by costs.

4.3 Measuring market activities: stock indexes

At present there are three main stock indexes in Hong Kong. The oldest and most widely used is the Hang Seng Index (HSI) compiled by HSI Services Ltd, a subsidiary of the Hang Seng Bank which in turn belongs to the Hongkong Bank. The HSI was first published in 1969 based on 31 July 1964 as its starting point (HSI = 100). The index is based on the prices of thirty-three leading stocks. In 1983 four subindexes were introduced in addition to the main HSI, namely Commerce and industry, Finance, Properties and Utilities. The index was then rebased on 13 January with HSI = 975.47, but for the subindexes only; the aggregate index remained based on 1964 as 100. Given the long run of the index it is not surprising that it has always been the key market indicator and that the stock futures contract is based on it.

The second main index is the Hong Kong Index (HKI) compiled by the SEHK. The index is based on forty-nine leading stocks and includes another sixteen shares in addition to the thirty-three constituent shares of the HSI. It has six subindexes, namely Finance, Utilities, Properties, Consolidated enterprises, Industrials and Hotels. The HKI and its subindexes are based on 2 April 1986 as 1,000.

The third and most recent index, the All Ordinaries, was introduced by the SEHK on 1 February 1989 and, like the HKI, is based on 2 April 1986 as 1,000. The new index covers the prices of all the ordinary stocks in the SEHK. In view of the importance of the indexes in both measuring and reflecting the level of activity in the market, their underlying structure and weighting are important considerations in appraising their accuracy and representativeness.[9]

The HSI is a Laspeyere type index using the market capitalization of its constituent shares as weights:

$$HSI = \frac{\text{aggregate market value at currrent market prices}}{\text{aggregate market value at base market price}} \times 100$$

The criteria for choosing the constituent shares are threefold. First, the company must have Hong Kong as its principal operational base, second it must satisfy a minimum average monthly market value for a specified period, usually in the last 12 months, and finally must satisfy a minimum aggregate monthly turnover value for a specified period, usually the last 24 months. Additional subjective criteria are employed, such as the past and current financial earnings' and growth record of the company and the prospects of the sector.[10] The constituent stocks represent about 75 per cent of market capitalization (based on the average of the last 12 months) and over 70 per cent of turnover (based on the average of the previous 24 months).

Table 4.8 shows the constituent shares of the HSI just before the October 1987 crash with their weights in the index, dollar sensitivity and index elasticity calculations. It is important to stress that the composition of the HSI is changed frequently. The most up-to-date version is shown in Section 4.4 (Table 4.12) where the risks and returns of the shares quoted on the SEHK are discussed.

The elasticity estimates in Table 4.8 are point elasticities derived using the formula of

$$\frac{\text{market capitalization of shares } S_{it}}{\text{base value of HSI} \times \text{HSI}} \qquad (4.1)$$

where S_{it} is the market value of the ith share at period t, the base value of the HSI is in millions of HK dollars and the HSI is in points at t. Given that,

$$\text{HSI} = \sum_{i=1}^{33} P_{it} Q_{it} \Big/ \sum_{i=1}^{33} P_i^o Q_i^o = B \qquad (4.2)$$

where P_{it} and Q_{it} are the price and issued amount respectively of the ith share in period t, and the superscript o denotes the base period value B of the index at 31 July 1964.

As HSI Services Ltd does not release the actual value of B in millions of HK dollars, it has to be approximated by using the daily index value in points and the capitalization of the existing constituent shares at that day. Although, as indicated, there have been numerous changes in the components of the HSI since 1964, no attempt has been made either to rebase or re-estimate it on a consistent basis.[11] The index is in fact calculated on an 'chain link' basis:

$$\text{HSI}t = \left[\frac{\text{MV}_t}{\text{MV}_{t-1}} \right] \text{HSI}_{t-1}$$

where HSI_t and HSI_{t-1} are the closing values of the index at t and $t-1$ and MV_t and MV_{t-1} are the closing market values of the constituent shares at t and $t-1$, with MV_{t-1} adjusted as necessary for capital changes or changes in constituent stock.[12]

Table 4.8 HSI components: individual weights in the index, HK dollar index sensitivity and index elasticity (as at 30 September 1987)

Share	Weight	HK Dollar sensitivity	Index elasticity
Finance			
Bank of East Asia	1.0	1.0	0.008
Hang Seng Bank	5.6	4.2	0.05
Hongkong Bank	10.3	37.0	0.10
Jardine Strategic	1.9	5.2	0.02
Properties			
Cheung Kong	5.2	15.6	0.05
Hang Lung Development	2.2	8.9	0.02
Henderson Land	2.5	11.3	0.02
Hongkong Land	4.3	18.0	0.04
Hongkong Realty & Trust (A)	0.5	2.8	0.004
Hysan Development	1.1	30.8	0.01
New World Development	3.5	8.8	0.03
Sung Hung Kai Properties	4.4	8.4	0.04
Tai Cheung Properties	0.4	3.0	0.004
Utilities			
China Light & Power	5.8	7.4	0.06
Hong Kong & China Gas	2.0	3.5	0.02
Hong Kong Electric Holdings	3.2	11.8	0.03
Hong Kong Telephone	7.7	16.6	0.08
Kowloon Motor Bus	0.8	2.4	0.008
Trading			
Hutchinson Whampoa	8.2	20.9	0.08
Jardine Matheson Holdings	2.8	4.5	0.02
Swire Pacific (A)	5.5	7.4	0.05
Wharf Holdings	3.6	13.3	0.03
World International	2.0	16.0	0.02
Industrial and Others			
Cathay Pacific Airways	5.0	22.4	0.05
Cavendish International Holdings	2.6	18.9	0.02
Dairy Farm International Holdings	1.6	10.1	0.01
Green Island Cement	0.4	0.7	0.001
Hong Kong Aircraft Engineering	0.6	1.3	0.006
Winsor Industrial	0.7	1.8	0.007
Hong Kong TV Broadcasts	1.4	3.2	0.01
Hotels			
Hongkong and Shanghai Hotels	1.3	0.7	0.01
Mandarin Oriental International	0.8	4.7	0.007
Miramar Hotel	0.8	3.5	0.008

Notes: All calculations refer to the capitalized value of the constituent stocks at closing prices on 30 September 1987.

HK dollar sensitivity refers to the number of points that the HSI will change for a change of HK$1 in the price of a constituent stock.

Index elasticity refers to the percentage change in the HSI for a 1 per cent change in the price of a constituent stock.

The elasticity formula in (4.1) is easily derived from equation (4.2) by using

$$E = \frac{\Delta \text{HSI}_t}{\Delta P_{it}} \frac{P_{it}}{\text{HSI}_t}$$

and since

$$\frac{\partial \text{HSI}_t}{\partial P_t} = \frac{Q_{it}}{B}$$

then

$$E = \frac{Q_{it} P_{it}}{B \, \text{HSI}_t}$$

These estimates must be used and interpreted carefully, however, because it is almost certain that $\partial P_{it}/\partial P_{jt} \neq 0$ for $i \neq j$. The bias in general must be positive especially for important stocks since $\partial P_{it}/\partial P_{jt} > 0$, $i \neq j$.

It would be tempting to interpret or use the data of Table 4.8 as a rough indicator of the 'manipulability' of the HSI, especially in conjunction with trading in the HSI stock futures contracts. Leaving aside the fact that these are point estimates for one specific time period only, it is also worth keeping in mind the elasticity calculations which are not influenced by the units of measurement. For example, the largest dollar sensitivity after the Hongkong Bank is exhibited by Hysan Development. The reason for this is simply because Hysan had the next largest *number* of issued shares after Hongkong Bank. Furthermore, at the date of these estimates the price of Hongkong Bank shares was nearly seven times higher than those of Hysan, a fact which is reflected in the elasticity values. In other words a change of HK$1 in the price of Hysan represented almost a doubling of the price of the share, with consequent effects on its market capitalization, whereas it reflected about a 10 per cent change for the Hongkong Bank. This illustrates the degree of care with which these figures must be interpreted. However, there is some evidence that in view of the relative stability of the market capitalization share of constituent stocks the dollar sensitivity index, and by extension the index elasticity, might be stable enough over short periods of time to allow their use as a basis for calculations to move the index via concentrated trading. The only item missing from the

Table 4.9 Constituents of the HKI, April 1988

Share	Weight	HK dollar sensitivity	Share	Weight	HK dollar sensitivity
Finance			*Consolidated enterprises*		
Bank of East Asia	0.70	0.72	Cathay Pacific	4.86	11.62
Hang Seng Bank	4.35	2.79	Cavendish International	2.29	11.76
Hongkong Bank	8.16	21.10	Dairy Farm International	1.34	5.26
Jardine Strategic	1.54	2.74	Hong Kong TVB	1.52	1.70
Sung Hung Kai	0.24	2.28	Hutchinson Whampoa	6.02	12.26
			Jardine Matheson Holdings		

Properties		
Cheung Kong	3.86	8.91
Great Eagle	0.49	3.36
Hang Lung	1.44	4.64
Henderson Land	1.83	5.88
Hong Kong Land	4.95	10.14
Hong Kong Realty (A)	0.41	1.49
Hopewell	1.24	5.83
Hsiu Chong	0.17	1.01
Hysan	0.93	17.57
New Town Properties	1.64	4.63
New World	2.75	4.59
Sino Land	0.77	25.05
Sung Hung Kai Properties	3.64	5.85
Tai Cheung	0.34	1.56

Green Island Cement	0.35	0.41
HAECO	0.53	0.75
Johnson Electric	0.55	1.24
Nan Fung	0.78	1.40
Paul Y Holdings	0.10	0.86
San Miguel	0.31	0.75
Winsor	0.51	1.06
Hotels		
Harbour Centre	0.45	0.85
Hong Kong Hotels	0.98	4.00
Mandarin Oriental	0.65	2.49
Miramar	0.80	1.87
Regal Hotels	0.42	2.37

Source: Securities Bulletin, Stock Exchange of Hong Kong No. 25, May 1988, p. 18
Note: The weight is the market capitalization weight of the share in the total of the index. HK dollar sensitivity refers to the changes in points of the HKI each time the price of a constituent share changes by HK$1.

equation is the cost of such a movement which will, of course, depend on the price elasticity of demand for the key stocks. This raises a host of related issues such as the extent to which the demand curves for stocks slope downwards and the degree of price interdependence, which is here assumed to be zero. The capital asset pricing model (CAPM) approach to asset pricing produces a horizontal, or almost horizontal, demand curve for shares. To the extent that stocks have some close substitutes in other financial assets, then their underlying value is not dependent on the supply of these assets.[13] These considerations, which involve testable propositions, have some bearing on whether the sensitivity and elasticity calculation can be of any use in determining the trades necessary to move the HSI or otherwise influence the market.

By comparison the structure and movements of the HKI and All Ordinaries are less controversial not only because they are not involved in the specifications of futures contracts but also because of their relative recent inception and use compared with the HSI.

As already indicated the HKI contains forty-nine shares chosen on similar principles to those for the HSI but with one additional condition, that the share must have been quoted for at least 2 years. This condition can be waived under certain circumstances. The numerical construction of the index is identical with that of the HSI, i.e. it is market capitalization weighted. There are similar provisions for adjustments following capital changes in the constituent shares, rights issues, splits etc. The index reflects more than 80 per cent of the market's capitalization and 70 per cent of the turnover. Table 4.9 shows the constituent shares of the HKI in April 1988, their weights and HK dollar sensitivity.[14] The All Ordinaries index is also based on the market capitalization weights of the underlying shares traded on the SEHK.[15] Overseas companies which have a listing in the SEHK are excluded, except those who although registered overseas are generally accepted as local. The justification for the introduction of yet one more index was based on the need to offer investors a more broadly based instrument to measure performance. Although the relationship with the HSI is very close the percentage changes in the three indexes can diverge.[16] Therefore, for example, for two different sample periods the three indexes exhibited the changes shown in Table 4.10.

Table 4.10 Comparison of percentage changes of the three stock indexes

Index	1 Feb 1988 to 29 Apr 1988	1 Feb 1988 to 30 Sep 1988
HSI	10.37	3.51
HKI	11.34	4.26
All Ordinaries	14.22	7.55

Sources: Securities Bulletin, Stock Exchange of Hong Kong No. 25, May 1988, p. 17; No. 30, October 1988, p. 22

4.4 Risk and returns in the Hong Kong stock market

As the data and the analysis in Section 4.3 have indicated, the concentration of activity in a small number of shares has implications for the returns of the individual shares or for groups of them. There are three issues to consider here: first, the relative returns of a broad classification of shares in the market in terms of their dividend yields and price-to-earnings (PE) ratios, second, the sectoral returns in relation to risk and, finally, the cross-relationships between returns of different shares and different sectors. Table 4.11 shows the overall market and sectoral dividend yields and the PE ratios of the constituent of the HKI. A cursory examination of these figures does indicate differences in the performance of these sectors. The Hong Kong stock market had always had the reputation of being driven by capital gains rather than dividends. Investors in the market were assumed to prefer to trade rather than to buy and hold. This is partially reflected in the relatively low dividend yield figures, which in most cases failed even to match the current rate of inflation. Equally Hong Kong had the reputation of a relatively inexpensive market in which to buy in terms of its comparatively low PE ratios. However, given the impossible task of a meaningful and consistent comparison of PE ratios across different exchanges, first impressions gained from simple numerical data may well be misleading, unless allowance is made for the risk factors involved. Table 4.12 reproduces the estimated characteristic line equations for the constituent shares of the HSI derived as

$$\Delta \log P_{it} = \alpha + \beta \Delta \log \mathrm{HSI}_t$$

where $P_i, i = 1, \ldots, 33$, are the daily share prices over $t = 26$ weeks.

113

Table 4.11 Dividend yields and average price-to-earnings ratios of HKI constituents (year end), 1982–8

Year	All HKI		Finance		Utilities		Properties		Consolidated enterprises		Industrial		Hotels	
	DY	PE	DY	PE	DY	PE	DY	PE	DY	PE	DY	PE	DY	PE
1982	7.90	6.21	6.12	8.62	5.75	10.30	12.38	3.85	6.53	5.46	10.06	7.47	7.10	12.06
1983	6.32	7.53	6.31	8.49	5.80	9.32	7.39	5.77	5.00	6.93	12.15	6.52	7.11	11.99
1984	5.99	11.13	4.87	10.81	4.84	11.04	3.79	16.32	10.64	8.77	7.51	7.83	3.93	18.55
1985	3.50	16.73	4.75	11.91	3.53	16.63	2.51	24.62	3.02	17.66	5.81	9.81	4.25	25.50
1986	2.92	19.13	3.82	14.18	2.72	19.39	2.72	20.50	2.51	22.77	3.63	20.46	3.59	20.17
1987	4.44	12.32	4.48	12.28	3.37	15.85	4.57	10.24	4.91	12.57	7.23	9.17	4.14	16.64
1988	4.34	12.12	4.86	10.74	4.81	12.93	4.13	11.78	3.85	12.86	5.44	8.63	3.95	16.60

Sources: Stock Exchange of Hong Kong, *Factbook 1987*, 1988, p. 50; *Factbook 1988*, 1989, p. 52
Note: DY, dividend yield; PE, price-to-earnings ratio.

Table 4.12 Beta values of HSI stocks (daily data for 26 weeks)

Stock	α	β	R^2
Bank of East Asia	0.0006	0.5830	0.2787
Cathay Pacific Airways	−0.0002	0.5956	0.3769
Cavendish International Holdings[a]	0.0004	1.0263	0.3148
Cheung Kong[a]	0.0003	1.4717	0.7780
China Light & Power	−0.0010	0.8246	0.3787
Dairy Farm International Holdings	0.0015	0.4551	0.0960
Great Eagle[a]	−	−	−
Hang Lung Development[a]	−0.0003	1.2960	0.5952
Hang Seng Bank	0.0001	0.6335	0.3574
Henderson Land[a]	0.0004	1.4629	0.6764
Hong Kong Aircraft Engineering	0.0022	0.6340	0.1220
Hongkong Electric Holdings	−0.0004	0.7347	0.5470
Hong Kong & China Gas	0.0005	0.5121	0.2018
Hongkong Land[a]	0.0004	1.1758	0.6137
Hongkong and Shanghai Banking Corp	0.0002	0.8821	0.5441
Hongkong and Shanghai Hotels	0.0010	0.3928	0.0825
Hong Kong Telecom	−0.0012	1.0259	0.4764
Hopewell Holdings[a]	−	−	−
Hutchison Whampoa	−0.0004	1.4389	0.7603
Hysan Development[a]	0.0014	1.2846	0.3948
Jardine Matheson Holdings	0.0017	1.0197	0.4664
Jardine Strategic Holdings	0.0017	0.9944	0.3210
Kowloon Motor Bus	−0.0006	0.6777	0.3625
Lai Sun Garment (International)	−	−	−
Mandarin Oriental International	0.0011	0.8004	0.2004
Miramar Hotel	0.0030	0.7103	0.0806
New World Development[a]	−0.0001	1.2696	0.6632
Sun Hung Kai Properties[a]	−0.0002	1.4349	0.7089
Swire Pacific (A)	0.0001	0.9419	0.5731
Hong Kong TV Broadcasts	−	−	−
Wharf (Holdings)	0.0011	1.0502	0.5721
Winsor Industrial	0.0011	0.7313	0.1696
World International[a]	0.0005	1 0207	0.5291

Source: HSI Services Ltd, Weekly Hong Kong Stock Market Statistics
Notes: Regression period, 30 September 1988–30 March 1989; $n = 120$.
[a] Property related companies

Not surprisingly the dominant property sector shares end up with beta values greater than one, indicating the greater returns volatility of that sector. At the same time, however, there is some evidence that the property sector also exhibits systematically greater returns than the rest of the sectors. For example, during 1987 (1986 year-end to start of 1987) the HKI declined by 8.10 per cent with properties exhibiting the lowest decline of −2.98 per cent against the highest decline of −16.16 per cent shown by industrials.[17] Similar figures for 1988 show the HKI rising by

17.69 per cent with properties yet again the highest with a rise of 37.87 per cent.

The returns R of a share i over period t can be described by the relationship to the market return R_{mt} and a residual factor e_{it}:

$$R_{it} = a_{it} + b_i R_{mt} + e_{it} \qquad (4.3)$$

where a_{it} indicates the expected returns even when the market return as a whole is zero. The sectoral return R_{st} is then a weighted average of the returns of the constituent shares:

$$R_{st} = \sum_{}^{n} w_i R_{it} \qquad (4.4)$$

where w_i is the proportion of the holdings of share i out of the n shares in that particular sector. It would now follow that:

$$R_{st} = \sum_{}^{n} w_i a_{it} + \sum_{}^{n} w_i b_i R_{mt} + \sum_{}^{n} w_i e_{it} \qquad (4.5)$$

with variance of

$$\text{var}(R_{st})^2 = \left(\sum_{}^{n} w_i b_i \right)^2 \text{var}(R_{mt}) + \sum w_i^2 \, \text{var}(e_{it}) \qquad (4.6)$$

given the standard assumption $E(e_i e_j) = 0$, $i \neq j$, and $E(e_{it}R_{mt}) = 0$. The first term on the right-hand side of (4.6) is the market-related risk and the second term is the sector-specific risk, which can be diversified away by including more shares in the sample.

Equations (4.3)–(4.6) were used by Mok in a study to estimate the relationship between risk and return in the different sectors covered by the HKI and HSI.[18] Mok used the movements of the HKI as the 'market return' since its coverage is wider than that of the HSI. However, the sectoral indexes are those of the HSI. The data covered the daily index levels over a 12 month period (April 1986 to March 1987). This period was subdivided into three 4 month periods characterized respectively by 'quiet trading and consolidation, enthusiastic trading and (an) experience of shock from the demotion of China's party leader Hu Yaobang'.

The results from the estimation are given in Table 4.13. Column 6 provides the returns-to-risk ratio in terms of the total mean return of holding shares of firms in a particular sector divided by the variance of those returns against total market risk (column 2/column 4). This is the relevant risk factor to consider since the residual sector-specific risk can be reduced by including more shares in the portfolio.

Table 4.13 Sectoral returns and risk, Stock Exchange of Hong Kong, 1986–7

Sector	Mean return	Full variance	Market-related risk	Sector-specific risk	Return-to-risk ratio
1	2	3	4	5	6
HKI	0.2326	1.4087	–	–	–
HSFIN	0.1682	1.5218	1.0387	0.4831	0.1619
HSUTI	0.1795	1.4653	1.1714	0.2939	0.1532
HSCOM	0.2341	1.6626	1.4642	0.1981	0.1599
HSPRO	0.2928	2.1533	1.8766	0.2767	0.1560

Source: H.M.K. Mok, 'Stationarity of returns and risk of sectoral indices in Hong Kong's stock market', Working Paper 19, Department of Business and Management, City Polytechnic of Hong Kong, August 1987

Notes: HKI, Hong Kong Index; HSFIN, HSI Finance; HSUTI, HSI Utilities; HSCOM, HSI Commerce; HSPRO, HSI Properties.
Full period, April 1986–March 1987.
Column 4, which shows the market-related risk, incorporates both the market risk and its sensitivity to the market return. Column 5 is var(e_i). It follows that column 3 = column 4 + column 5.

The property sector yielded the highest returns and highest risk during the second period examined. Equally, however, the returns from property in the other two periods were associated with higher risk in terms of both the total returns variance and the returns-to-risk ratio. This is also confirmed from the results for the whole period shown in Table 4.13. In general the results for all sectors are consistent with the standard prediction of financial theory of an inverse relationship between yield and risk. However, these results must be appraised against evidence of instability in the coefficients of the sectoral regression estimations of equation (4.5). All the sectoral coefficients $w_i b_i$ are significant, but Chow tests on the four sectoral equations also proved significant indicating that the sectoral returns as estimated were not stable over time.

The sectoral approach to the behaviour of returns in the Hong Kong market can be taken a step further by applying more sophisticated statistical techniques which attempt to extract greater differentiating details or clarification from the data. For example, the larger quoted companies in Hong Kong tend to belong to conglomerates usually under the leadership or influence of families or tycoons. Such companies may straddle a number of sectors which makes the strict 'sectoral' approach to returns a little narrow. Thus, for example, Li Ka Shing, perhaps the richest and best known Hong Kong tycoon, controls a group of companies which cover property (Cheung Kong), utilities (Hong Kong Electric), cement (Green Island Cement) and diversified trading (Hutchinson Whampoa) including supermarkets, docks and terminals, telecommunications etc.

Mok, Lam and Cheung re-examined critically the sectoral groupings approach to returns and found some revealing trends and developments.[19] Using a version of equation (4.3), they first established the rates of return of forty-eight out of forty-nine constituent stocks of the HKI. One share was left out as its trading record did not cover the whole sample period from 2 January 1984 to 30 December 1988. The changes in the HKI were used as the market return proxy with the residual e_{it} being the estimate of the individual shares' return which was not explained by market movements. The correlation coefficients of these residuals were estimated and clustered together so as to group those shares with the greatest degree of similarity. Not surprisingly, shares of firms in the same sectors or industries clustered together, but so did shares belonging to the same family group.[20] Principal component analysis of the residual (stock specific) returns yielded similar results. Eight factors were chosen with eigenvalues ranging from 2.99 for the first component to 1.34 for the eighth. For the forty-eight companies the first factor explained $(2.99/48) \times 100 = 6.2$ per cent of the variation with a cumulative 31.3 per cent for all the eight factors. As, on average, market movements accounted for 42 per cent of the movements in the individual returns of shares, this meant that the analysis could explain about 60 per cent of the stock return variations.[21] The companies were then arranged in groups by choosing only those which had a factor loading greater than 0.3 (in absolute terms, disregarding the sign). The results were very similar to those of the correlation cluster analysis. Companies under family influence or interlocking directorships grouped together, with each of the eight factors relating fairly clearly to family or industry group. Mok *et al.* conclude that the possible explanation for the principal components results is as follows:

the interlocking-control companies appear closely interdependent at the accounting level (and) . . . the tendency of the market traders to classify the trading of stocks in the same family as a collective group.[22]

This study casts an interesting light on the dynamics and interrelationship of stock returns in the market in Hong Kong. The implications for the portfolio structure of investors in Hong Kong shares is fairly obvious since diversification amongst different sectors or industries may not be as important as diversification amongst different family groups.

The development and the greater maturity of the market may be expected to dilute the effect of family groupings. The extent that cultural aspects influence company structures and finance (i.e. tightly knit Chinese families, including nepotism amongst family groups) must eventually be countermanded by the growing financial needs of these companies. In order to maintain majority shareholdings families will have to turn to their own resources and in the end this may be a self-limiting process. There is no evidence, however, of the market effect on share prices diminishing in Hong Kong, which would indicate that the individual characteristics of stocks are not necessarily increasing in importance in determining their returns.[23]

The picture which emerges from these investigations does not contradict the initial impressions sketched in Section 4.2. The market is dominated by a small group of shares which themselves are clustered together in terms of returns. The returns-to-risk performance of the market is as predicted by standard financial analysis with the property sector playing a dominant role.

4.5 Flow of funds and the role of the stock market

There are scarcely any data for the flow of funds in the Hong Kong economy. This makes it difficult to appraise and put in perspective the role of the equity market in raising capital for firms and to assign relative importance to it. In general, firms can be expected to draw financial resources either internally (retained earnings) or externally (issue of new equity and borrowing including receiving credit). A sample of approximately thirty-three firms which were constituent components of the HSI was examined over a 5 year period (1983–7). Use was made of their individual annual reports in order to extract information concerning the sources of their funds. A summary of the results is shown in Table 4.14. However, the data have to be interpreted with care and they are purely indicative for a number of reasons. First, the companies examined were constituents of the HSI in 1987 but not necessarily in the previous years. This meant that there were gaps in the data for each year.[24] Second, the figures for debt finance are arrived at by taking the differences in the amount of debt outstanding in any single year. Thus, for example if company X had HK$100 million of debt in its accounts in 1983 and HK$200 million in 1984, this implies that during 1984 it had raised HK$100 million in credit. Of course, this approach does not indicate the importance of loans as part of the cash flow of the firm. The same company might have booked up HK$1 billion of bank loan in the middle of the financial year which it then paid off just before the end, leaving only a balance of HK$200 million. Third, retained earnings cover a multitude of practices. These are post-tax profits which firms did not distribute. In some of the accounts these appear as reserves; in other they are classifed under different headings. Furthermore, no attempt was made to add back to those figures provisions made for depreciation. There are a number of reasons for doing this. One, which is rather controversial, is that depreciation could be deemed to be payment for capital used as opposed to provisions made for capital to be replaced. Furthermore, the amount set aside for depreciation is governed primarily by the ruling provisions of tax laws rather than determined by the firm's own internal appraisal. Fourth, the role of debt finance in these corporate flows was distorted by the presence of banks in the sample. Banks maintain large hidden reserves which distort the retained earnings figures. It is also difficult to appraise the role of bank loan finance in their activities, given the large but very short-term nature of the inter-bank loans market. For this reason banks were excluded from the sample. In addition to this complication the property sector repaid a significant proportion of its loans during this period. Indeed, in a number of years (1983, 1985) that sector had a negative sum total of funds raised indicating that its balance sheet was effectively shrinking through selling assets and then using the proceeds to repay loans. Fifth, equity issues refer to the sales of new shares in the market which result in the raising of additional capital. It follows that share splits, bonds issues and capital restructuring which did not result in additional funds accruing to the firms were not included in the calculations.

Table 4.14 Sources of finance for selected HSI constituents (sum total raised in million HK dollars), 1983–7

	Total	Debt	Ratained earnings	New equity
1 Commercial and industrial	43,976.5	16,978.4 (38.6)	15,340.6 (34.8)	11,657.7 (26.5)
2 Properties	11,657.7	−22,773.2 (−195.3)	9,254.1 (79.3)	25,176.8 (215.9)
3 Utilities	13,712.0	2,654.6 (19.3)	6,729.0 (49.0)	4,328.4 (31.5)
4 Total	69,346.4	−3,140.2 (−4.5)	31,323.7 (45.1)	41,162.9 (59.3)

Source: see text including the caveats
Notes: Figures and percentages are rounded.
Numbers in parentheses are the percentage of the total for each sector as appropriate.

Table 4.14 shows the main sources of corporate finance for the three sectors. The property sector was a net repayer of loans. Not surprisingly retained earnings are quite important for all sectors including utilities. In their case some of the firms (electricity, public transport etc.) operate under the so-called 'schemes of control'. These are rules which determine the pricing policies of utilities in relation to set returns on their capital. Under these schemes a portion of the firms' earnings has to be transferred to reserves and used for investment if the firm earns more than the permitted return on its capital. The basic broad pattern apparent in these figures is the importance of loans and the relative unimportance of new equity. The overall gearing ratio of the firms in each sector, defined as the ratio of long-term loans to market capitalization, gave fairly uniform results. The yearly average for all sectors stood at 25.1 per cent with commercial and industrial at 28.4 per cent, property at 30.9 per cent and utilities at 12.6 per cent. These figures are not, of course, comparable with any of the data in Table 4.14 which are flow figures as opposed to the gearing figures which are stock figures. A study which examined the debt-to-asset ratio of firms in Hong Kong produced some interesting results which can be used in conjunction with the broad data in Table 4.14. Ip and Hopewell[25] calculated the book values of the (debt-to-total asset) ratio for an average of 123 firms over 1970–84, fifteen annual observations in all. The firms were separated into eight broad categories. In general the debt-to-asset ratio rises from a low of 0.34 in the early 1970s to 0.46 in 1984. The calculated ratio of long-term liabilities to total assets also rose during the period under examination from nearly zero to 8 per cent. Finally, an analysis indicated that the differences in the mean debt ratios of firms in the eight broad categories were statistically significant in 12 of the 15 years examined. This does confirm the proposition that the financial structure may well be determined by the characteristics of the industry. In the sample examined in that study, the banking and finance and shipping and godown (storage) sectors tended to have higher ratios. A survey of some relevance to the issue here was undertaken by Tai who examined the attitudes and practices of managers in Hong Kong towards debt.[26] Tai concluded that financial directors of firms in Hong Kong aimed at ratios of long-term debt to total capitalization between the ranges of 0–20 per cent and 46–50 per cent, although these were not actual but target ratios.

On the related issue of dividend policy the evidence is relatively sketchy with some of the major firms in Hong Kong favouring constant payout ratios.[27] Companies within industries tended to adopt similar payout rates thus establishing an 'industry norm' for dividend policy.

There is very little evidence from Hong Kong to link bankruptcy to debt (or liquidation to use the more accurate legal term which refers to corporate rather than personal financial distress). A macroeconometric model developed by Freris and Ho explained the number of corporate liquidations in Hong Kong over 1968–84 primarily in terms of the changes in exports (an aggregate demand proxy) and in interest rates and wages (cost proxies).[28] The picture is somewhat complicated by the fact that the highest risk groups (garments manufacturing, electronics, imports and exports, restaurants and land investment) are not, in general, well represented in the listed companies in the SEHK, and neither is there enough public information available on their balance sheets to allow any meaningful studies to be made of their financial policies and their eventual demise.

These admittedly sketchy data allow an intriguing glimpse of the financial structures of Hong Kong firms, and in particular of the role of equity and loan financing. As indicated at the beginning of this chapter, the absence of flow of funds data for Hong Kong does not permit any firm conclusions to be drawn at present other than the relative importance of loans and retained earnings in the corporate financial decisions of listed firms.

The role of the capital market in raising funds is of course crucial in providing liquidity for the equity raised and price discovery for investors. The market can be used by existing firms to raise additional capital, or by new firms to obtain quotations for their shares and to raise new capital. The related questions of the pricing and dynamics of initial public offerings (IPOs) will be examined in Section 4.6 which also covers the measurement of the market efficiency.

Table 4.15 Estimates of capital raised by new issues in the stock market(s) of Hong Kong (HK$ million, current prices), 1975–88

1975		–	1,236.4	1,236.4	–	1,394	
1976	1,223.3	1,223	886.9	486.9	–	1,957	
1977	1,299.1	1,299	1,356.0	1,206.0	–	1,514	
1978	607.11	610	663.2	663.2	–	684	
1979	1,056.0	1,060	1,060.0	1,060.0	–	1,418	
1980	5,547.9	5,550	5,861.8	5,861.8	–	5,589	5.500
1981	9,789.0	9,790	19,773.8	9,773.8	9,103.8	10,073	9.800
1982	1,676.8	1,680	2,061.4	1,777.5	1,157.2	–	1.700
1983	1,666.3	1,670	1,526.1	–	1,513.6	–	1.100
1984	2,462.7	2,460	3,542.8	–	1,705.4	–	2.500
1985	2,464.7	2,460	–	–	3,568.5	–	2.500
1986	8,894.8	12,500	–	–	–	–	11.100
1987	31,206.71	–	–	–	–	–	44.300
1988	6,423.27	–	–	–	–	–	

Sources: 1, Stock Exchange of Hong Kong, *Annual Year Book*, 1988, p. 94.
2, *Hong Kong Economic Journal Monthly* No. 119
3, R.H. Scott et al., *Hong Kong's Financial Institutions and Markets*, Hong Kong: Oxford University Press, 1986, p. 66
4, D. Lethbridge (ed.), *The Business Environment in Hong Kong*, Oxford: Oxford University Press, 1984 [2nd edn], p. 157
5, A. Rowley, *Asian Stock Markets*, Hong Kong: Far Eastern Economic Review, 1987, p. 148
6, T.Y. Cheng, *The Economy of Hong Kong*, Hong Kong: Far Eastern Publications, 1982, p. 269
7, Jardine Fleming estimates quoted in *South China Morning Post*, 26 October 1987; the figures for 1987 are for 8.5 months
Note: Sources 1, 2 and 6 offer no details whether bonds and convertibles are included; sources 3 and 4 include all equity and debt, source 5 includes equity only.

There are a number of sources estimating the sums raised in the stock markets in Hong Kong via the issue of new equity, rights, placings or public offers. The data are outlined in Table 4.15. Figures on the size of private sector investment of Hong Kong and the role of equity financing are shown in Table 4.16. The discrepancies in the figures in Table 4.15 are quite considerable. Presumably those of column 1 are the most reliable as they emanate from the Stock Exchange itself. Table 4.16 puts the sums raised by equity issues in some perspective by expressing them as a percentage of the gross capital expenditures in Hong Kong. It is rather interesting to note that, despite the fact that equity issues represent such a small part of the total sources of funds for companies, in some years they account for a considerable percentage of investment expenditures. Again, it is important to stress that the figures in Table 4.16 do not necessarily imply that the equity raised was actually used for investment in the type of capital assets indicated.

Table 4.16 Gross private domestic capital formation (in million HK dollars) and stock exchange financing, 1976–87

Year	GPDCF	SEF (% GPDCF)
1976	11,021	11.0
1977	14,606	8.7
1978	17,978	3.4
1979	27,370	3.8
1980	38,825	14.3
1981	47,205	20.7
1982	46,352	3.6
1983	39,719	4.2
1984	44,397	5.5
1985	46,416	5.3
1986	57,218	15.5
1987	75,856	41.1

Sources: *Hong Kong Annual Digest of Statistics*, various issues; Table 4.15, column 1.
Notes: GPDCF is gross domestic capital formation minus Government expenditure on buildings, construction, plant, machinery and equipment; this adjustment is necessary as the Hong Kong Government and public corporations do not raise capital in the Stock Exchange, with the possible exceptions of joint schemes such as the Cross Harbour Tunnel.
SEF, stock exchange financing.

The role of the equity markets in corporate finance has been an issue of concern in Hong Kong. There was serious discussion in setting up a 'second market' along the lines of either an over the counter (OTC) or unlisted securities market (USM). There was also concern over the supply of venture capital in the context of enabling smaller or riskier firms to tap the market.[29] The October 1987 crash and the subsequent events leading to the SRC Report on the reform of the equity market have placed these issues in a secondary order of priority. The development of the market as an efficient, transparent and well-regulated market is, in a sense, inseparable from the degree by which the market can be used by large and small firms to tap investors' funds.

Very little is known about the dynamics of corporate investment expenditures in Hong Kong, and even less or nothing about the influence of developments in the equity markets on these decisions. There are analytical reasons for believing that variation in stock prices do affect corporate investment decisions. For example, stock index movements are deemed to be reasonably good leading indicators and can therefore influence, if not the size, at least the timing of investment.[30] Even more directly, changes in stock prices change the opportunity cost of investment projects and thus can influence investment decisions. For example, there is some evidence that exogenous events whose only direct effect is to change share prices have a smaller indirect effect on corporate investment in Japan and the FRG compared with the UK or the USA.[31] There are a number of reasons for these conclusions based on both institutional and economic factors. For example, takeovers are relatively more frequent in the UK and the USA than in the FRG or Japan. Employees have a comparatively greater say in corporate decision-making in the FRG and Japan. Finally, managers in the UK and the USA have their remuneration linked to share prices (option schemes etc.) far more so than their Japanese or German counterparts and hence are more willing to maximize share prices via investment-related decisions. The only, and extremely tentative, conclusions which can be drawn from the little evidence there is for Hong Kong can be summarized along the following lines. Equity issues can account, at least in pure financial terms, for a substantial proportion of gross private domestic capital formation (Table 4.16), but as the sums raised fluctuate widely from year to year (Table 4.15) they may influence investment negatively. At this juncture, however, there is no evidence to determine the direction of the effect. Given also the family-dominated structure of major firms in the stock market and the fact that share prices tend to move in a manner which suggest group and/or industry influences, then it would be surprising if fluctuation in share prices did not affect the investment decisions of these firms.

On the institutional side, the market for the managing and underwriting of new issues, rights, placings etc. as well as takeovers and acquisitions is dominated by a small number of merchant banks (DTCs). As has been indicated in Chapter 3, DTC activities extend not only to the certificate of deposit and debt market side but also to corporate finance. In addition to acting in a purely advisory role, merchant banks also underwrite new issues and manage the floating or quotation of firms in the stock exchange. Table 4.17 shows some comparative data for 1980–5. However, the situation has been changing rapidly with the rise of the Japanese DTCs which have entered the market quite aggressively and are challenging the existing leaders.

Table 4.17 Merchant banking activities in Hong Kong 1980–5

Merchant banks	No. of takeovers and mergers	No. of rights issues	No. of new issues
Wardley	39 (27.0)	38 (41.3)	17 (32.6)
Schroders Asia	38 (26.3)	14 (15.2)	13 (25.0)
Jardine Fleming	13 (9.0)	12 (13.0)	17 (32.6)
Total	144	92	52

Source: South China Morning Post, 6 February 1986
Note: Figures in parentheses are the percentages of the total numbers of cases.

4.6 Analysis of the efficiency of the Hong Kong stock market

The various tests, techniques and approaches to measuring or appraising market efficiency, are an important part of the 'tool kit' of the financial analyst and economist. One of the classic textbooks of finance defined market efficiency in the following succinct and brief manner:[32]

> A (perfectly) efficient market is one in which every security's price equals its investment value at all times. In an efficient market a set of information is fully and immediately reflected in prices. But what information? A popular taxonomy is the following:

Form of efficiency	Information which is fully reflected in security prices
Strong	All currently known
Semi-strong	All publicly available
Weak	Previous prices of securities

Unlike the state of research (or lack of it), for most of the financial markets in Hong Kong there are a fair number of studies examining or testing for the degree of efficiency in the stock market.[33] Eleven of these studies are surveyed here. Three of the studies test for the weak form of efficiency, five for the semi-strong and three for the strong form, although these are rather broad and perhaps arbitrary classifications.

In markets which are efficient in the weak sense, past prices provide no information about future prices. The semi-strong version requires that all publicly available information is fully reflected in the security prices. Therefore, for example, professional investment advice would be useless in the long run in a semi-strong market. For a strongly efficient market *all* information, not just that which is publicly available, is always fully reflected in the prices of securities. This form would effectively rule out insider trading. Aspects of testing for strong efficiency can overlap with those of a semi-strong market. For example if an investment advisor did have 'insider' information which was made available to his clients or to a share tip newsletter, then the advice would not be exclusive any more.

Tests concerning the prices of newly issued shares otherwise known as IPOs examine whether the information available to the market is disseminated and incorporated quickly enough in the prices to eliminate excess returns. Although this is not necessarily a direct test of any form of strong, semi-strong or weak efficiency, it does permit an investigation of the speed of adjustment of the market to new situations and is therefore classified as a test of semi-strong efficiency.

The first study by Law used daily price data randomly chosen over a 3 month period from a set of prices covering January 1978 to December 1979.[34] The sample actually chosen was September–November 1979. Fifty-six shares with continuous trading record over this sample period were examined, of which twenty-five were constituents of the HSI. A number of tests were applied seeking to establish whether the market exhibited the weak form of efficiency.

The first was a random walk test using serial correlation coefficients from the logarithmic expression

$$U_t = \log P_t - \log P_{t-1}$$

where U_t is the difference between the prices of shares in periods t and $t - 1$. Five successive daily changes in prices were calculated for each stock after allowing for adjustments for share splits, rights issues etc. Five serial correlation coefficients of these price changes were then calculated and tested at various significance levels for the null hypothesis. Of the fifty-six stocks, thirty-nine were found to have at least one out of their five coefficients significantly different from zero at the 90 per cent level. Twenty stocks had coefficients significant at 95 per cent. Therefore there was substantial evidence that price changes over roughly a week would provide guidance for future price changes, i.e. a refutation of the weak form of market efficiency.

Another test used the non-parametric runs approach. A run is defined as an unbroken sequence of positive, negative or zero changes in stock prices. The observed changes are then compared with the theoretical distribution in order to test for their independence. Tests for thirteen stocks rejected the null hypothesis at the 90 per cent, 95 per cent or 99 per cent levels with four at the 95 per cent level. Four criteria based on these tests were then used to classify whether stock prices were non-random. On the basis of these criteria thirty-two out of the fifty-six stocks exhibited non-random price behaviour, and nineteen of these passed more than two of the four conditions. Thirteen of these non-random stocks were constituents of the HSI. Altogether these thirty-two stocks accounted for 65 per cent of the total market capitalization for the sample period. There was therefore enough evidence to refute the weak efficient hypothesis for the Hong Kong market during these 3 months in 1979.

Wong and Kwong[35] conducted a similar series of tests for the weak form hypothesis using data for twenty-eight out of the thirty-three actively traded constituent stocks of the HSI. The sample period covered January 1977 to December 1980, an overall average of more than 900 trading days. Prices of stocks were adjusted for dividends, splits, rights issues etc. Serial correlation tests for daily price changes were run for lags of 1–30 days. The coefficients calculated were then divided into three broad lag groups of 1–10, 11–20 and 21–30 days. These yielded significant coefficients at 95 per cent for only 17.9 per cent of the total for the first group, and 7.5 per cent and 5 per cent respectively for the other two groups. There were considerable variations in sign, size and significance amongst these coefficients depending on the length of the lag. Thus, for example, for a one period lag 53.6 per cent of the coefficients were significant at the 95 per cent level. Taking the 280 coefficients (twenty-eight stocks over ten lags), twenty-two stocks had at least one coefficient significantly different from zero at the 95 per cent level. The runs test was also estimated for these price changes, with ten out of the twenty-eight yielding significant results. Further qualitative analysis of the runs test, using the percentage differences between the actual and expected number of runs, produced some interesting results. The largest percentage difference in daily runs was 22.3 per cent, whilst those for similar studies using US and UK data were −10.4 per cent and 18.2 per cent respectively. The study by Law outlined above also yielded a 24.7 per cent difference. The average percentage, however, stood at −4 per cent compared with −2.1 per cent in Law's study for Hong Kong and −3.3 per cent and −10.8 per cent for US and UK studies. The authors concluded that for the runs tests:

> These results indicate a somewhat uncertain position. In general, the evidence seems to support the weak form efficient market hypothesis. Yet in individual cases there are significant discrepancies that suggest that some nonrandom patterns are present in stock price changes.[36]

Wong and Kwong conclude that, in comparison with other

studies for the USA and UK, their own serial correlation tests do not support the weak form of market efficiency but the runs tests do. Since the latter contain individual cases of significant discrepancies from non-random patterns, the overall conclusion must be that the Hong Kong stock market does not exhibit signs or symptoms consistent with a weak efficient form.

The unification of the stock exchange in 1986 generated a larger centralized market where information to all the participants was made instantaneously available through screen trading. Therefore it could have been expected that the overall efficiency of the market might have improved. A study by Chan *et al.* tested for this hypothesis by using a 'before and after unification' methodology.[37] Daily price data for all the 260 shares traded between September 1985 and August 1986 were used. The time period was separated into before unification (September 1985 to March 1986) and after unification (April–August 1986). Shares were classified into four groups depending on the volume of their trading: top fourteen, middle ten, bottom ten and a random group. A separate category contained hybrids such as bonds, warrants etc. Three standard efficiency tests were then applied: the serial correlation test of the daily price changes, the runs test and a time series regression to test for the existence of a time trend. A simple criterion of efficiency was established on the basis of any single share failing any one of the three tests in either period at the 95 per cent confidence level. It was then shown that 36 per cent of shares in group 1, 30 per cent in group 2, 55 per cent in group 3 and 30 per cent in group 4 failed this criterion. The authors summarized their finds as follows:

> From the above results it is difficult to claim that the Hong Kong stock market is efficient even in the weak form. Moreover the suspicion that efficiency increases with trading volume is given some support from this study since the results suggest a higher proportion of non-random behaviour amongst the more thinly traded shares. If we consider the regression of price changes on time we find that for a majority of securities the coefficient of determination increased from period 1 to period 2. This suggests contrary perhaps to expectation, that efficiency did not improve after unification.[38]

It is important to note that the criterion of trading volume used by the authors in choosing and classifying the shares in categories did not necessarily introduce a bias. As shown in Table 4.5, shares with a high volume also tended to have a high value of trading. Chan *et al.* also point out that there was evidence of consistent patterns of dependence between different stocks. This might not be surprising in view of the findings concerning the 'group behaviour' of shares outlined in Section 4.4. Although the evidence against the weak form of efficiency is quite clear, it may well turn out that the pattern of interrelationships between stocks is considerably more complex than was first thought.

Mui and Law tested for the semi-strong efficiency of the Hong Kong stock market by examining the relation between changes in interest rates and stock prices.[39] The data used were the nine sectoral indexes, the main index of the Far East Exchange and the changes in the best lending rate (BLR) between 1 January 1979 and 31 December 1981. As there were twenty-one changes in the interest rate, this yielded 210 usable observations, i.e. the reactions of the ten indexes to the twenty-one changes. The underlying hypothesis was that a semi-strong efficient market would quickly incorporate all publicly available information relevant to stock price formation. Since expectations also play an important role in price information, the tests involved a simple fourfold classification of the expectations of and reactions to changes in interest rates. Thus, for example, if prices of stock rose before interest rates declined, this was deemed to be a right expectation with a right reaction. Therefore right or wrong expectations could be followed by right or wrong reactions. Several hypotheses were tested. The simplest involved the proposition that in an efficient market a rise in interest rates would be followed immediately the next day by a fall in stock prices. Another involved the proposition that, given Hong Kong's close links with the USA, the greater the divergence between local and US interest rates, the greater the probability that the market would guess, and react correctly to, the next interest rate movement. Overall the results of the seven tests undertaken yielded a mixed picture. Approximately half the hypotheses (or their variations) were supported by the evidence. There was therefore only partial positive evidence for the proposition that the market was efficient in the semi-strong sense.

The behaviour of stock prices before and after takeover announcements and activities may provide an indirect test of market efficiency. Takeovers generate new information to which the market adjusts. Movement of stock prices before the announcement of takeovers may indicate the activities of insider trading and hence constitute a test for the strong form of efficiency. The speed with which the market incorporate new information also constitutes a test for semi-strong efficiency. Law and AuYeung[40] used data from eleven takeovers in Hong Kong during 1980. The prices of the stock involved were observed for 30 days before the announcement and 30 days after. The rate of return R_{it} for each stock was calculated as a function of the market rate R_{mt}:

$$R_{it} = \alpha + \beta R_{mt} + e_t \qquad i = 1, \ldots, n$$

where e_t is a random error.

These estimates were then used to calculate the 'abnormal rate' of return AR_{it} defined as $AR_{it} = R_{it} - (\hat{\alpha} + \hat{\beta} R_{mt})$, where the circumflex indicates estimates. The rate of return here was calculated as the percentage change in the daily closing prices, and the market rate was proxied by the percentage change in the HSI. The abnormal rate of return, which is the residual of the equation, was used as part of the test of the market efficiency. These residuals indicated the return over and above that justified by the overall market return. Of the eleven stocks, eight experienced positive abnormal rates of return on the first day after the takeover announcement. This abnormal rate declined rapidly in the succeeding second and third days of trading thus indicating that the market adjusted speedily to the news. However, a test of the cumulative abnormal returns for 10, 20 and 30 days before the announcement found that for all eleven shares there were positive abnormal returns 10 days before. In five of those cases the abnormal returns ranged from 10.6 to 40.9 per cent. This could constitute evidence for potential insider dealing and therefore refutation of the strong efficient hypothesis.

Hong Kong's stock market has frequently been accused of being manipulated and dominated by rumours and actions of people with insider information. The Securities Ordinance in Hong Kong did not classify insider trading as an offence, although this was subsequently amended and penalities were imposed. In the past market participants caught using insider information were only castigated in public of being 'culpable' of the offence. This slightly unusual provision in the law led to one very prominent member of Hong Kong's business community, the chairman and controller of Cheung Kong, Wharf Holdings, Cavendish International, Hong Kong Electric etc., being found culpable of insider dealing. As the transgression is not an offence in Hong Kong law, it was hotly denied and contested, and the sums of money involved were small enough to make the whole incident somewhat absurd in the eyes of the financial community. It has been pointed out that for a number of reasons the Hong Kong market would be a rather difficult market in which to use insider information repeatedly and profitably. First, as indicated in Section 4.2, the market is generally shallow and narrow. As Tables 4.4, 4.5 and 4.6 indicate, most of the trading is concentrated in a small number of blue chip stocks. Any unusual price movement or deal would result in instant reaction in this part of the market. The institution of computer screen trading in April 1986 has also ensured that all current stock market information is available to all traders and outsiders who can subscribe to the wire service. Second, as shown in Section 4.4, most prices of the more important stocks tend to move together in fairly predictable patterns determined by groupings (family type companies) and industry. Family members who exercise substantial control over shareholdings in their companies would find it difficult to hide their own activities or avoid abrupt price changes if sizeable parcels of shares were being bought or sold. Finally, and again based on the evidence of Section 4.2, insider information on shares other than the constituents of the HSI may prove expensive or impossible to use profitably. Market activity in second- or third-line shares is sufficiently thin to guarantee very large price changes when any attempt is made to do anything out of the ordinary. None the less rumours of insider dealing frequently arise in the press or circulate amongst the financial community. These rumours cannot easily be brushed aside, as the evidence against insider dealing in Hong Kong is deductive rather than positive. If these arguments do not constitute evidence against the existence of insider dealing in Hong Kong, they may indicate that its extent and the possible harm may be limited. The question still remains as to who actually loses in insider dealing, or how to define in legal and economic terms exactly what 'inside' information is.

The behaviour of prices during and after IPOs of shares in Hong Kong has been examined in three studies. The underlying assumption here is that in semi-strong efficient markets any overpricing or underpricing of new shares will quickly be eliminated. Shares will not earn excess returns after adjusting for the market trend and risk. Since new issues tend to be underpriced, an efficient market will eliminate any excess returns quickly, possibly within 1 or 2 trading days. The initial price change will reflect the differences between the issuer's fixed offering price in relation to the market's initial valuation of shares. This can be termed the primary market valuation effect. In the secondary market, however, there are no initially fixed prices and the traders are free to determine the valuation of the share. If the Hong Kong stock market is efficient in the semi-strong sense then all the available information will be incorporated in the prices established in the secondary market. Changes in the prices of newly issued shares will continue to occur later on, but, if the market is efficient, these changes are as likely to be positive as negative and so there will be no consistent excess returns. It is important, however, to differentiate clearly between the primary effect, i.e. the excess returns made on the initial fixed price, and the secondary returns when the shares trade freely following the first trade on the first day that the issue becomes available to the public. The secondary return can be measured, for example, on the basis of the first freely traded price or the closing price of the first day of trading.

Dawson and Hiraki have undertaken a number of studies of IPOs in Hong Kong, Japan, Singapore and Malaysia. The results of their tests give a qualified positive answer to the question whether Hong Kong's stock market is efficient in the semi-strong sense when tested against the performance of the price of IPOs. However, their findings are somewhat suspect because of their estimation procedures.

Dawson and Hiraki[41] examined the IPO prices of thirty-one stocks in Hong Kong between January 1979 and the end of 1984. The first-day trade yielded a primary average return of 10.9 per cent compared to 51.9 per cent for the Japanese shares. The returns were calculated on the difference between the IPO price and the closing price and were not adjusted for the overall movement in the market (market adjusted). For a different sample period (1978–84) covering twenty-one IPOs, the primary average return was 13.8 per cent. This again compared favourably with primary average returns of 39.4 per cent for Singapore and 166.6 per cent for Malaysia for a sample of IPOs over the same period.[42] All these returns were calculated on the difference between the IPO and the closing price and were market adjusted. These results were extended by observing the market-adjusted secondary returns, i.e. the returns following the first trading of the IPO. The returns here were calculated on the basis of the closing price of the first day. For the same sample of twenty-one IPOs over 1978–83 and using daily, weekly and monthly intervals to calculate returns, Dawson found that the observed returns were all not statistically different from zero and hence excess returns were not available to buyers of shares in the secondary market.[43] A similar study by Dawson using data for thirty-four IPOs made in Hong Kong from 1979 to 1985 confirmed, but with some reservations, the other findings regarding secondary returns.[44] The time periods used to calculate the returns on the closing price of the first day were days 2–5, 1–2 weeks, and 1–6,. 1–9 and 1–12 months, fourteen periods altogether. The author concluded that:

> In general the results of four separate calculations correspond to those expected in an efficient market, but there are a few exceptions. The initial market price was reasonably close on average to future prices, after adjustments for market trends at selected observation points over the periods from 2 weeks through to 6 months.[45]

The adjustment for market return in IPOs is essential in order to differentiate the returns on the offer price from the overall market trend. It is also important to allow for the systematic risk inherent in the returns, i.e. the beta factor. This was not done in any of these studies because of the difficulties in obtaining other than proxy values of the betas for stocks who have no trading history. Therefore subtracting the market return is only an approximation. Thus these results are indicative rather than conclusive.

An interesting attempt to test the efficiency of the Hong Kong market in the strong form was also undertaken by Dawson.[46] A series of stock recommendations made by Sun Hung Kai, one of the major securities firms in Hong Kong, was used. The hypothesis here was that if the market was efficient in the strong sense, i.e. prices incorporated *all* the available information, then these recommendations would not outperform the market. Since the Sun Hung Kai advice is available only to its clients, then the test can be construed to be a test for the strong form of efficiency, although this stretches the definition a little too far.

Dawson used 654 reviews of shares made between August 1974 and October 1980. Three hundred share tips were classified as 'buy' (195), 'buy on weakness' (fifteen), 'hold' (forty-five) and 'not buy' (forty-five). No recommendations at all were made for the other 354 cases. The test consisted of a comparison of the prices of the stocks 1 day, 1–12 weeks, 6 months and 1 year later with their price the day *before* the recommendation was made. Pre-recommendation price movements over 1–12 weeks were also calculated to allow for any trends. In addition, the change in prices was tested against the null hypothesis The results were quite unequivocal even when the price changes were adjusted for market trends by using the Far East Stock Exchange Index:

> The results . . . show the stock recommendations under study were reliable. The stocks with a buy recommendation gained in value; those with a negative recommendation lost value initially and trailed the other group for most of the subsequent observations. The buy group also outperformed stocks receiving a 'buy on weakness' or 'hold' designation. The market did not adjust quickly to the recommendations. The stock with favorable recommendations rose gradually over the following year, and those with negative recommendations continued their pre-recommendation decline for another month . . . . If the Hong Kong market is efficient in the semi-strong sense, we would expect the price to change soon after the recommendations became public, making it difficult for investors to profit from recommendations. (Data) . . . show no rapid price changes at the time of recommendation. Instead, especially, for the 'buy' group, the price change is gradual.[47]

Further refinement of these tests included an adjustment for risk in order to eliminate the possibility that the persistent excess returns simply reflected higher risk. A portfolio beta was calculated by using all the 195 'buy' recommendation shares. The betas calculated over eight different time periods were all statistically significant and, with one exception, less than 1. Overall, therefore, the shares were no more risky than a representative market portfolio. Finally these 195 stocks were separated into two groups one which included the constituents of the widely followed HSI and another with the rest. The performance of the two groups was then compared. The hypothesis here was that stocks such as the constituents of the HSI would be more accurately priced thus making it difficult for the stocks recommended by Sung Hung Kai to outperform the market. After adjusting for market changes, the returns of the two groups did differ significantly, with the non-HSI group performing better. This would be further supporting evidence that, acting on the Sun Hung Kai recommendations for the less closely followed stocks, excess return could be earned on a consistent basis. The study therefore rejected the proposition that the Hong Kong Stock market was efficient at either the strong or semi-strong sense. An extension of this study covering roughly one more year did not contradict the initial findings.[48] It must be noted, however, that the strong efficient form hypothesis requires that information which is *not* publicly available should be reflected in the stock prices. It is debatable whether a recommendation by a leading stockbroking firm to its private clients is not publicly available information despite the fact that it cannot be purchased directly from a news-stand.

Finally, we must mention a study which, although it does not purport to test for market efficiency, does have indirect implications. Ho tested the reactions of three stock indexes – HSI, the Far East Index and the Kam Ngan Index – to changes in M1 and M2 money stock between January 1975 and December 1979.[49] The hypothesis tested was that, as the stock of money changed, portfolios would be adjusted with increases in the stock of money leading to decreasing interest rates and rising stock prices, and vice versa. The results indicated that movements of M2 led stock price changes whilst there was no discernible relationship between changes in M1 and stock prices. This can be construed as evidence supporting the proposition that the Hong Kong market is not semi-strong efficient in so far as stock prices do not react instantly to changes in publicly available information. There is a snag in this interpretation in that any announcement or expectations effects are lost, as the changes in money stock are announced well after they have taken place and are thus not useful in either the formation of expectations or the making of forecasts.

The overall conclusions from these studies are summarized in Table 4.18. A question mark denotes either uncertain or debatable evidence. A simple count of the Yes and No answers would yield an overall No answer to the efficiency question. However, there are a number of considerations which will need to be taken into account. For a start, there is no inherent contradiction in some tests yielding positive answers and others yielding negative answers for the same form of efficiency. Markets change over time or respond at the same time in different ways to different circumstances. Second, these studies are not necessarily a good guide for the current performance of the Hong Kong market. In particular, both the methodology and some of the data used may not be accurate. This, of course, may cut both ways in that more sophisticated tests may reconfirm the market's inefficiency. The unification of the stock exchange, the entrance into the market of large international broking firms, the rise of unit trusts and other institutional investors in the middle to late 1980s, and finally the introduction of stock index futures have changed both the speed and the overall responsiveness of the market to changes. Some of the evidence outlined here, especially that concerning the effect of unification, points towards an inefficient market. In other areas, however, which are admittedly tangential to the question of efficiency, the evidence points elsewhere. For example, the introduction of the highly successful HSI stock futures did not have any discernible effect on the volatility of the underlying equity market. The evidence for this is reviewed extensively in Chapter 5, Section 5.2. For an equity market which is potentially open to manipulation, this evidence is quite significant. Furthermore Hong Kong shares with other Asian stock markets some common characteristics regarding seasonality effects, except that these characteristics sometimes run contrary to those of the well-documented US share market. Table 4.19 summarizes the research findings of Ho *et al.* who used data from eight Asian countries (Japan, Hong Kong,

Taiwan, Korea, Philippines, Thailand, Singapore and Malaysia), Australia, New Zealand and, for comparison purposes, the USA and the UK. The period covered 1975–87 using daily stock indexes.[50]

Table 4.18 The evidence for market efficiency in Hong Kong

Type of data/situation influencing stock prices	Weak	Semi-strong	Strong
Daily prices	No/partial with several reservations	–	–
Interest rates	–	Partial	–
Takeovers	–	Partial	No
New issues	–	Yes/partial	–
Stock recommendations	–	No	No(?)
Money stock	–	No(?)	–

Table 4.19 Seasonality effects of the Hong Kong stock market, 1975–87

Effect	Characteristic and evidence for Hong Kong
1 Weekend effect	Negative Monday returns No evidence
2 Calendar time hypothesis	Higher returns on Monday No evidence
3 Trading time hypothesis	No difference in the mean returns between trading days No evidence
4 January effect	Higher returns in January Positive evidence
5 Turn of the year effect	Higher returns during the first days of January and the last days in December No evidence
6 Turn of the lunar year effect	As for turn of year effect Positive evidence but with reverse direction for 1973–82

To the extent that the distribution of returns is not the same for all days of the week or months in the year then these can be deemed to be anomalies and signs of market inefficiency.[51] As such they are evidence against the Hong Kong market's being semi-strong efficient. However, the degree that these effects are exploitable also depends on transactions costs and the size of the potential excess return. All that can be said about the Hong Kong market is that it shares a fair amount of anomalies with other Asian and western markets although the direction of these effects is not necessarily the same.

The picture of the Hong Kong stock market which emerges is considerably more complex than the purely anecdotal 'back of an envelope' type of analysis which has sometimes been common in the financial press. In the aftermath of the October 1987 crash many unkind words were written about the Stock Exchange of Hong Kong ranging from 'casino' to 'Mickey Mouse'. The background to the crisis and the subsequent closure of the Exchange is described in Chapter 5, Section 5.2. There is now enough evidence to show that these were words of ignorance rather than of substance. The market is surprisingly sophisticated in some of its behaviour and in other aspects is no different from other developed markets in its degree (or lack) of efficiency.

Chapter five

Futures, gold, investment management and regulation

5.1 Introduction

This chapter, predictably, covers markets and institutions which are not directly related, although their activities, which include trading in derivatives, come under the heading of financial markets. Gold, which is a physical commodity, is an exception but its use as an investment vehicle allows it to cross the line, so to speak.

The two most important developments in these markets in Hong Kong have been the spectacular rise, and equally the spectacular fall, of the stock index futures market based on the Hang Seng Index (HSI) and the rapid development of Hong Kong as a regional investment management centre. Expertise, combined with Hong Kong's legal and regulatory system, brought together unit trusts, pension funds and private client advisory services. This generated secondary activities which impinged directly on the local financial markets. It is wise to be wary of the rapid rise of financial centres because of the speed with which developments can be overtaken by events. In the case of Hong Kong the development of more specialist markets for futures or commodities met with competition from nearby centres such as Singapore and Tokyo. However, there are certain characteristics which are likely to differentiate the markets in Hong Kong from those in neighbouring countries. These characteristics will be detailed and illustrated in the following sections. It is sufficient to indicate that the PRC has repeatedly stated its desire to develop its own domestic capital and financial markets using Hong Kong both as a model and, possibly on a linked basis, as the gateway to the West. Equally, the possibility for a commodities futures market for China operating in Hong Kong has been raised and discussed.[1]

Essential for the development of any financial market, and in particular those related to investment management, is the regulatory and legal framework. Hong Kong has gone through two major convulsions in this area during the 1980s. First, there were the imbroglios in the early 1980s relating to the failures of banks, practically all of of which related to some aspect of fraud. The basic details are outlined in Chapter 2, Section 2.2. The outcome of these crises was a thorough revision of the banking legislation culminating with the much stricter and carefully thought-out 1986 Banking Ordinance. Second, there was the October 1987 crash leading to the closure of the Stock Exchange. This created such a poor international impression, especially when leading members of the Exchange were prosecuted for illegal activities and bribery, that the Government had very little choice except to attempt a major reform. This took essentially three forms. First, the Securities Review Committee reviewed and made extensive recommendations regarding the operations and regulations of the Stock Exchange, the Futures Market and the Securities Commission.[2] Second, the Government replaced almost all the leading members of the Stock Exchange and encouraged, if not cajoled, it into a thorough review of its rule book and membership. Finally, a number of Ordinances were enacted including the Securities and Futures Commission Ordinance of 1989 which revamped and redefined the powers of the Securities Commission. Additional developments were linked to these, such as the adoption of a new constitution by the Futures Exchange, reviews of the Takeover and Mergers Code, legal measures against insider trading and so on. These developments are sketched out and analysed in Section 5.4 and then related to Hong Kong's position in the international capital markets.

5.2 Futures markets

Except for the gold market, which is considered separately in Section 5.3, Hong Kong did not have an organized futures markets until 1977 when the Government granted a licence to and permitted the establishment of the Hong Kong Commodities

Exchange Ltd (HKCE). The licence was due for review after 5 years. The Exchange initially traded in cotton and sugar, and then added soya beans in 1979 and gold in 1980. The cotton contract never developed adequately and was finally abandoned in 1981. The performance of the gold contract is dealt with in Section 5.3, but that did not develop successfully either. Soya beans futures are more actively traded with the primary participation of Japanese interests. Raw sugar is less actively traded. Indisputably the success story of the futures market was the HSI contract which started trading in May 1986.

When the licence of the HKCE was being reviewed, the Government made it a condition of the renewal that the management of the Exchange was reorganized, particularly after a spate of fraudulent practices perpetrated by members had been discovered in 1982. There were additional problems regarding the relationship of the holding company which effectively controlled the HKCE, the International Commodities Clearing House (ICCH) which undertook the clearing of the trades, and the Guarantee Corporation which backed the integrity of the contracts. The process of the reform of the HKCE was combined with the introduction of the HSI futures contract which led to the change in the name of the Exchange to the Hong Kong Futures Exchange (HKFE).[3]

The soya bean and raw sugar contracts are very straightforward. Soya beans are traded in 500 bags of 60 kg each with delivery for each consecutive month up to 6 months ahead. Sugar is traded in lots of 50 long tons in every second month starting from January. Delivery points for soya beans are Tokyo or Kanagawa and for sugar f.o.b. (free on board) in South-east Asian countries.[4] The HSI futures contract is simply the Index multiplied by HK$50. The delivery dates have been changed during the lifetime of the contract, but during its peak activities they covered the spot and the next 2 months. Delivery is in cash, but the closing price calculation has also been changed.[5] The relative importance of these contracts is shown in Table 5.1.

The HSI futures contract attracted most of the attention and criticism following the October 1987 crash. The meteoric rise and fall of the contract is worth detailing because it affords an analytical insight into the strengths and weaknesses of Hong Kong's financial markets. It is also a useful exercise of wider

Table 5.1 Turnover in the HKFE (in million HK dollars), 1986–8

	1986	1987	1988 (Jan–Apr)
HSI	89,784 (81.6)	585,078 (93.4)	7,208 (41.7)
Soya beans	17,756 (16.1)	38,936 (6.2)	9,389 (54.3)
Sugar	2,225 (2.0)	2,448 (0.4)	679 (4.0)
Gold	242 (0.2)	260 (0.0)	30 (0.0)

Source: *Report of the Securities Review Committee,* Hong Kong, 1988, p. 404
Note: Numbers in parentheses are percentages of the total.

implications as the experience of its trading allows a close observation of the 'birth and death' of a highly successful contract.

Table 5.2 chronicles the rapid rise in the trading activity of the contract which at one stage rivalled, in terms of numbers traded, that of the S&P500. Equally in the months following the October 1987 crash the contract languished at daily trading levels of a few hundred, rising above 1,000 contracts only in 1989.

The price behaviour of the HSI contract and the influence of its trading on the equity market have been the subject of a number of studies. The standard pricing model of a futures contract is that of the cost of carry.[6] The annual return of holding the portfolio of the shares included in the index can be expressed as follows:

$$(I_2 - I_1) + I_1\left(\text{Div}\frac{t}{365}\right) \qquad (5.1)$$

This is simply the change $I_2 - I_1$ in the value of the cash index over the opening and closing of a futures position plus the dividend returns Div on the index stocks multiplied by the number of days t to the date when the futures position is closed. Rather than hold the underlying shares in the index, investors may buy a futures contract instead. The return here will be

$$(F_2 - F_1) + I_1\left(r\frac{t}{365}\right) \qquad (5.2)$$

i.e. the change $F_2 - F_1$ in the value of the futures contract over its opening and closing prices, plus the interest r saved by not having

Table 5.2 HSI futures contract: trading volume in contracts, 1986-7

	Total monthly turnover	Average daily turnover
1986		
May	29,838	1,570
June	38,039	2,002
July	64,854	2,819
August	82,162	4,108
September	118,165	5,627
October	185,385	8,828
November	156,150	7,807
December	151,252	7,202
1987		
January	177,759	9,355
February	222,859	11,143
March	332,896	14,677
April	276,529	14,554
May	293,001	13,952
June	341,307	17,065
July	420,313	18,274
August	484,590	24,229
September	601,008	27,318
October	399,605	23,985
November	47,195	2,283
December	17,473	806

Source: Hang Seng Index Futures Market Review, various issues

to commit the whole sum of money I_1 to purchase the shares in the index. This is valued over the period t to the closing of the futures position.[7] At the expiry of the contract the futures price F_2 and the cash value of the index I_2 must be equal, i.e. $F_2 = I_2$. It now follows from expressions (5.1) and (5.2) that, on expiry when $I_2 = F_2$,

$$F_1 = I_1 + I_1 \left[(r - \text{Div}) \frac{t}{365} \right] \qquad (5.3)$$

In other words the price F_1 of the contract at the opening equals the cash value of the stock in the index adjusted by the cost of carry, which is simply the difference between the interest rate an investor may have to pay by borrowing either money to buy the underlying shares or the shares themselves (repo rate) minus the dividends receivable.[8] All these returns are expressed as annual yields over the appropriate time period. Expression (5.3) can be simplified to

$$\text{futures price} = \text{spot price}(1 + \text{cost of carry})$$

However, this expression does not allow for additional transaction costs such as levies, tax duties and Exchange commissions.

If this condition does not hold, then there will be opportunities for arbitraging between the spot and futures markets by buying in the 'cheap' market and selling in the 'dear' market. In the case of Hong Kong the arbitrage opportunities were (and still are) limited to the extent that the Stock Exchange has not yet permitted the official short selling of shares, i.e. selling shares that investors do not own in the expectation of buying them back at a profit. This has meant that the HSI futures market could have been arbitraged only if there was a premium on the futures contract, i.e. the price of the contract was higher than its theoretical price as expressed in equation (5.3). This would have involved selling the relatively expensive futures and buying the relatively cheaper stocks. The positions would then be unwound by reversing the transaction. If the futures prices showed a discount, short selling in the equity market in Hong Kong whilst buying the relatively cheaper futures could not have been executed without breaking the Exchange's rules.

There is some evidence that the HSI futures contract traded *ab initio* at a premium, which is unusual as most new contracts are underpriced whilst the market finds its way. A study in the *Asian Monetary Monitor* followed the pricing behaviour of the first three contracts traded (May–July 1986).[9] Significant arbitrage inefficiencies were found and were attributed to various transactions costs which stopped the convergence of futures and cash prices.

As the market developed and volumes increased a pattern became quite apparent. In the pre-October 1987 days most active contracts were those with 11–40 days to expiration. In the post-crash period trading was more concentrated in the spot month contract. Not surprisingly, the behaviour of the basis (the difference between the underlying cash value of the index and the futures price) appears to have been related to the volume of activity. Hopewell and Terpstra constructed a series of daily futures prices by extracting the prices of only the most actively traded HSI contract on any day.[10] Twenty-two contracts over 469 trading days were analysed from 6 May 1986 to 29 March 1988, thus covering the periods both before and after October 1987. The entire period exhibited an overall premium of about 0.74 per cent expressed as the (actual – theoretical)/theoretical price ratio of the contracts. The pre-crash premium stood at 0.95 per cent with the premium turning into a discount of 0.03 per cent in the post crash period. A number of additional tests were run exploring both the dynamics of the basis and the relationship between the pricing error (i.e. the difference between the actual and the theoretical values) and the changes in the spot index. In general, the pricing errors were not statistically significant in predicting subsequent movements in spot prices. This could be interpreted as a sign of a weakly efficient market. The overall conclusion of this study was that the persistence of premiums, and therefore of arbitrage profits, was to be found in the pre-crash periods and largely disappeared after October 1987. Perhaps the most interesting characteristic of the HSI contract was that it traded *ab initio* at a premium in contrast with the experience of other contracts such as the S&P500 and the Nikkei, both of which experienced discounts during their first trading months.

There are reasons to believe, however, that the measurement of the theoretical price of the HSI may not be as easily established as that of other contracts. For a start in Hong Kong there is no equivalent of the US repo rate to use as the cost of financing futures transactions. For Hong Kong this can be approximated by either the Hong Kong inter-bank offered rate (HIBOR) or the best lending rate (BLR). Second, there are as yet no studies for Hong Kong on the market impact effect, i.e. the effect on the prices of the actual buying or selling of futures. One way of approximating this, however, is by using the information on the bid–ask spread of the existing traded contracts. Third, the inclusion of interest rates in the pricing formula signifies not only the cost of financing a position in the cash market, but also the potential opportunity gain of having to pay only the appropriate margin for holding the market portfolio in the form of the futures contract. The rest of the capital necessary could be deposited and earn interest. In the case of Hong Kong, it was revealed in the investigations which followed the October 1987 crash that there was widespread disregard of the Exchange's margining rules applicable to clients. This must have distorted the pricing relations viewed from the point of view of the investors. Finally, it is worth repeating that the prohibition of short selling in Hong Kong meant that arbitrage could only (legally) take place in the cases of premiums appearing on the contracts but not on discounts. It is therefore not surprising that in another study by Yau *et al.* on the pricing of the HSI somewhat different results were obtained.[11] This study used daily data spanning May 1986 to December 1988. In determining the premiums or discounts the authors first calculated the differences between the actual and the theoretical prices and then subtracted the appropriate transaction costs. Before the October 1987 crash the spot month contracts exhibited an overall premium of 0.42 per cent on the spot index. After the crash this became an overall discount of 1.78 per cent.[12] When the 'mispricing' values were examined on a day-by-day basis against the transaction costs, the pre-crash period contained a large number of cases where opportunities for profitable arbitrage must have remained. Similarly, with transaction costs accounted for, most of the mispricing cases disappeared after the crash and those that persisted were well within the range of the transaction costs involved. Broadly similar results held for the prices of nearby as opposed to spot month contracts.

The existence of premiums too large to be explained by transaction costs could have been caused by institutional inertia and ignorance of the market. As will be shown later, the trading up to the crash was dominated by a very small number of very large institutional and private investors. This could have made arbitraging rather difficult as it would have involved large trades amongst a small number of traders. The retail investors, and there were many before October 1987, were too small to take positions and profit from them. Yau *et al.* offer another comprehensive and plausible explanation in terms of market sentiment and transaction costs:

> the persistent positive mispricing occurred before the Crash could be due to the over-optimism about the bullish stock market and to the fact that futures trading provides a greater leverage to play the market. Due to high transaction cost of

index arbitrage, opportunities arising from over-speculation were not taken away by arbitrageurs. After the Crash, the market volatility has declined drastically reducing the speculative bubbles. Mispricing has thus fallen into the arbitrage-free boundaries. This offers an alternative explanation of the disappearing mispricing in the post-Crash period other than the prohibitive size of transaction costs. The results from the post-Crash period seem to support that the futures market is getting more efficient as compared to the pre-Crash period[13]

As has already been indicated the October 1987 crash dealt an almost lethal blow to the HSI futures market. Trading volume remained quite low, and at the time when the Securities Review Committee was holding its hearings there was considerable pressure to close down the stock index futures market altogether. Thankfully less emotional considerations prevailed and the HSI contract received, if not a stay of execution, at least a reprieve. The events leading up to the closure of both the Stock Exchange and the Futures Exchange are worth recounting in order to put in perspective the role of the HSI futures contract during this period.[14]

On 16 October 1987 there was a total of 36,683 net open interest contracts on the long side, 94 per cent of which (34,490 contracts) were with clients; the other 6 per cent were house accounts. The long side was almost wholly speculative with a strong retail element of small investors. The short side was primarily institutional with 50 per cent or more of the sellers of contracts being market arbitrageurs. Their positions involved almost HK$4–6 billion worth of shares purchased in connection with arbitrage programmes. This was understandable in view of the large premiums on the price of the contracts which gave rise, in some cases, to annualized returns of 30 per cent. Business on both the client and the broking side was highly concentrated. Of the seventy-five net long brokers, three accounted for over 50 per cent of the net long positions; five brokers accounted for nearly 90 per cent of the net short positions, out of twenty-seven net short brokers at the time. More ominously, 50 per cent of the long positions were held by a single person and his associates. When the market crashed that single client owed nearly HK$1 billion, or about US$128 million, to his counterpart sellers! On Monday 19 October 1987 the HSI fell by 420.8 points. The Stock Exchange closed for the rest of the week, and when it reopened on Monday 26 October the HSI fell by another 1120.7 points, a total fall between opening of 19 October 1987 and closing on 26 October 1987 of 68.7 per cent. It has repeatedly been said that the Stock Exchange had decided to close precisely because the overhang of unwinding positions by the short holders would have depressed prices even further. More cynical observers have suggested that the closure was effectively an attempt to bail out the long positions of the few institutional and personal investors who faced potential losses of more than HK$55,000 for each contract they had bought. In essence the real cause of the difficulties rested with the inadequacy of the capital basis of the Futures Guarantee Corporation, which in theory was meant to back the integrity of the contracts, and the laxity with which margin rules were enforced.

The Futures Exchange was unfortunate enough to have a complex and interlinked system of clearing of trades and of the guaranteeing of contracts. The system worked well enough under normal circumstances but could not cope with the more extreme market situations. There is little doubt now that the Futures Exchange risk management was primarily, but not exclusively, at fault. As the Securities Review Committee concluded:

> we believe that the underlying cause of Hong Kong's unique experience of the October collapse was poor risk management and lax credit controls in both markets and at every level of the system, from individual brokers through to the futures market clearing house rather than the essential inherent features of the HSI futures contract.[15]

The root of the problem was that risk management was not integrated. Throughout this period the clearing of trades was undertaken by ICCH (HK) which in turn was owned by ICCH (UK). The latter was owned by six leading UK banks. The guarantee of the contracts was provided by the Futures Guarantee Corporation (FGC) which was owned by ICCH (HK) and ICCH (UK) plus a number of leading Hong Kong and international banks, including the Hongkong and the Standard Chartered banks. Its capital at the time of the collapse was a totally inadequate HK$15 million with an additional HK$7.5 million in reserves. When it became obvious after the crash that the long position holders would default, it became equally obvious that the FGC would not be able to meet its obligations. The situation turned out to be even more incestuously complicated as one of the main losers of FGC's inability to guarantee the defaulting longs would have been the Hongkong Bank itself, as its subsidiary Wardley had considerable short positions. But Hongkong Bank also owned 20 per cent of the FGC. The impasse was resolved by a rescue package put together by the Hong Kong Government whereby HK$1 billion from the Exchange Fund was matched by another HK$1 billion from the shareholders of the FGC and leading market participants. The sum was later topped up by another HK$2 billion.

The subsequent reforms of the regulatory system of the Futures Exchange (outlined in Section 5.4) explicitly took into consideration the issue of the capital adequacy and risk management of the futures trading position. However, the crash did taint the stock index market with a reputation it did not deserve.

In the aftermath of October 1987 futures markets were accused of contributing to the instability of the underlying equity markets and even actually causing its crash. Programme trading taken in conjunction with the 'triple witching hours' periods, when futures, options and options on futures expired, could cause large and rapid movements in prices. There is little evidence, other than purely anecdotal, of programme trading in the Hong Kong equity and futures markets. The Securities Review Committee rejected this proposition, and several others as well, as explanations for the crash:

> We do not think that the interplay of complex trading strategies on the futures markets triggered the fall in the SEHK. In this respect we note that futures did not trade at a discount to the crash market on either 16 or 19 October and we have seen no evidence to suggest that futures market strategies were the cause of significant cash market sales, although of course it is not clear what would have happened if the markets had remained open and there not been major defaults. However, there is equally little doubt that the

overhang of long arbitrage positions was a severely
complicating factor during the crash. If the guarantee
corporation had defaulted, the long arbitrageurs would have
had to unwind their positions on the cash market, estimated to
involve the sale of between HKD 4 and 6 billion worth of
shares, compared with average SEHK daily volumes of HKD
2.7 billion during September and HKD 3.9 billion in the final
run up to 19 October 1987. This would have doubled the
selling pressure of HKD 4.5 billion worth of trades which
eventually hit the market on 26 October, depressing stock
prices still further . . . . It has been suggested that the futures
market contributed indirectly to the crash by artificially
inflating prices, to a point where they were bound to fall
sharply. In principle this could happen through investors
extending their positions in the stock market because of the
availability of hedging facilities in the futures market; or
through the overall price level of the market being determined
on the Futures Exchange floor and transmitted to the stock
market via arbitrage. A variance of this . . . maintains that
Hong Kong was gripped in an upward spiral . . . seing stock
market prices rise, speculators invested heavily in lower-cost
futures. This created a premium between the futures and cash
market which prompted arbitrageurs to buy heavily in the
stock market, pushing prices up further, encouraging more
speculators into the futures market, and so on. However,
there is no clear evidence to support this interpretation of the
stock market rise . . . . But we note that trading directly
attributable to index arbitrage accounted for less than 5% of
the daily stock volumes.[16]

Hong Kong's futures market has not been alone in being
implicated in the destabilization of the underlying cash market.
Similar accusations were raised in the USA in the aftermath of
the crash. However, there is no systematic evidence that futures
either destabilize or increase the volatility of the cash markets.[17]
As has already been established for the HSI contract, the
persistence of pricing inefficiencies in a number of other future
contracts may be indicative of the limited extent to which
arbitrage activities are reflected back on the cash market. The
conclusions of studies such as those by Modest and Sundaresan,

Figlewski and Merrick are also partially reflected in the evidence available on the price behaviour of HSI contract.[18] An examination of the behaviour of the HSI on both the inter- and intra-day changes before and after the introduction of futures did not yield any evidence of greater instability.[19] Daily data on the HSI covering all the trading days from 3 January 1984 until 30 September 1987 were used. The tests did not extend to October 1987 onwards as the closure of the Exchanges and the sharp drop in the volume of futures trading would have distorted the results. For the daily data the percentage change was calculated using the appropriate daily closing price as follows:

$$\frac{\text{HSI}_t - \text{HSI}_{t-1}}{\text{HSI}_{t-1}} \times 100$$

The 'before' period covers 3 January 1984 to 2 May 1986 (577 daily observations) and the 'after' from 6 May 1986 until 30 September 1987 (350 daily observations), a total of 927 observations. The intra-day spreads were calculated from the difference between high and low daily figures of the HSI expressed as a percentage of the closing value, i.e.

$$\frac{\text{high} - \text{low}}{\text{closing}} \times 100$$

HSI Services Ltd has supplied the high − low figures as from 1 July 1985 only, and so the sample here covered 209 daily observations before and 350 after the introduction, a total of 559. The average daily percentage change of the HSI (and its standard deviation) and the average intra-day spread were the two key variables used to test for any changes in the volatility of the stock market following the introduction of futures trading. The 'last trading' and 'all other days' statistics cover the last trading day of the HSI futures contracts by calculating the volatility moments outlined above during those days and for all the rest of the trading days. Similar calculations were applied to the average intra-day percentage spreads based on the high − low figures during the last trading day for futures contracts and all other days. These calculations concentrated on the last trading days because investors may move aggressively in the cash market in order to influence the closing price of their own futures contract and hence may generate unusual volatility in the index.

The methodology of the testing primarily involved an examination of the time series of the daily percentage change of the HSI and the intra-day spread for evidence of stationarity through correlograms and the Box–Pierce Q test for white noise. Both series were tested for the whole period and for the 'before and after' periods. Chow stability tests against a time trend were also estimated for both time series. A number of subsidiary tests were also run, such as the correlation between the number of contracts traded on a daily basis and the percentage change of the HSI as well as that for intra-day spreads. Finally, the means and standard deviations of the two time series were estimated for the subperiods of 'before and after' as well as the means and standard deviations for last trading day and all other days. Statistical comparisons via the use of t and F tests were either inappropriate or redundant in most cases given the evidence for, or absence of, stationarity and normality in the distributions. However, these statistics provided additional information for the interpretation of the rest of the tests.

Table 5.3 summarizes the white noise and Chow stability tests. The white noise test employed here is the standard Box–Pierce Q test at the 5 per cent χ^2 significance level from six to forty-two lags at 6-lag intervals, i.e. seven tests altogether. The significant or non-significant test results in Table 5.3 refer to all seven tests for each category. In this case all were uniformly either significant or non-significant. Correlograms also confirmed these results for individual lag structures. The Chow tests proved less reliable. These were run by regressing the two variables, the daily percentage change of HSI and the intra-day spread, against a time trend and then performing the test using the regressions on the two subperiods i.e. 'before' and 'after'. In all tests coefficients were non-significant for the daily percentage change and the R^2 were very low and non-significant. All the time coefficients for the intra-day spread were significant, as were the R^2.

Table 5.4 shows the mean and standard deviation values calculated for 'before and after' situations and correlation tests on volume and index changes.[20] Two observations should be made here. First, the standard t and F tests are not applicable in the case of intra-day spread calculations as the series are clearly dependent and therefore not stationary. There is no evidence that the series are normal either.[21] This effectively eliminated the

Table 5.3 White noise and stability tests of inter-day and intra-day index changes

| Period | Lag | Box–Pierce Q, χ^2 | |
		Inter-day changes	Intra-day spread
Whole period	6	9.94	648.80*
	12	13.96	1105.49*
	18	17.63	1536.90*
	24	23.62	1880.91*
	30	26.34	2216.83*
	36	33.99	2533.69*
	42	34.69	2756.59*
Before	6	6.76	66.16*
	12	10.43	105.42*
	18	14.38	129.42*
	24	22.44	142.04*
	30	28.03	151.00*
	36	33.76	156.84*
	42	35.47	158.82*
After	6	9.03	168.75*
	12	12.47	237.12*
	18	16.49	303.14*
	24	21.11	327.78*
	30	30.47	345.14*
	36	33.53	375.45*
	42	36.34	378.86*
Chow test		$F = 0.78$	$F = 9.19*$

Note: * Significant at 5 per cent.

basis for the normal distribution based tests. Although there is strong evidence of independence, the daily percentage changes series is not normally distributed either.[22] Second, it is interesting to note that the studies by Santoni and Edwards of the S&P500 and other futures contracts are based on t and F 'before and after' tests.[23] The results of these studies are very similar to those of the present investigation. However, no evidence is offered as to the stationarity and normality, or otherwise, of the series involved. Indeed, once a series has passed a white noise test then statistical comparisons of moments of subperiods within the series should be redundant. Therefore, the results of these tests are given in Table 5.4 for purely indicative purposes.

Casual observation of the first and second moments of the daily percentage change of the HSI and of its intra-day spread as

Table 5.4 First and second moments of inter-day and intra-day HSI changes: correlations of volume and index changes

	Mean	Standard deviation
Daily percentage change in HSI		
Whole period	0.17	1.43
Before	0.14 ⎱ *	1.58 ⎱ **
After	0.22 ⎰	1.14 ⎰
Last trading days	−0.01 ⎱ *	0.97 ⎱ *
All other trading days	0.23 ⎰	1.15 ⎰
Intraday spread of HSI		
Whole period	1.19	0.68
Before	0.76 ⎱ **	0.52
After	1.45 ⎰	0.63
Last trading days	1.35 ⎱ *	0.46
All other trading days	1.46 ⎰	0.64

Correlation (volume is the total number of contracts traded daily)
(a) Inter-day changes and volume 0.09*
(b) Absolute value of interday changes and volume 0.18**
(c) Intra-day spread and volume 0.30**

Notes: 'All other trading days' covers the period after the introduction of futures trading.
* Differences not significant at 5 per cent or correlation not significant at 5 per cent.
** Differences significant at 5 per cent or correlation significant at 5 per cent.
For the appropriateness of these tests see main text.

shown in Table 5.4 would indicate that the inter-day volatility of the market rose in terms of averages although its dispersion declined. However, the intra-day volatility rose. In view of the white noise tests, the inter-day volatility in terms of the two moments is unlikely to have changed over this period, whilst intra-day volatility did not necessarily rise as a result of the introduction of futures trading. The moments of the last trading day versus all other days do not provide any clear signs that futures activity increased inter-day volatility. There is low but significant correlation between the volume of futures contracts traded and the absolute daily percentage change and intra-day spread. In other words the greater the volume of trading the greater the daily changes and spread. It would now follow that the introduction of stock futures trading in Hong Kong had no measurable effect on the stock price volatility. This is all the more remarkable given the evidence of persistent high premiums in the futures market and the potential for index manipulation. As outlined in Chapter 4, Section 4.3, the HSI contains a relatively small number of stocks some of which carry a very large weight in the index. This allows relatively small movements in their price to move the index by tens of points. One explanation for these results is that the introduction of futures trading in Hong Kong took place at the beginning of the bull market of 1986–7 and hence the overall upward trend of stock prices could not have been significantly influenced by futures activity.

The future of the HSI contract is less in doubt now than it was in the months following the October 1987 crash. The events of June 1989, when the Hong Kong stock market crashed again following the political unrest and massacres in Beijing, showed that a well-regulated market could cope with a single-day fall of more than 580 index points (22 per cent drop). Although price limits were put in effect, the market stayed open and margin calls were strictly and prudently enforced.

The next step for the development of the Futures Exchange will be the introduction of a HIBOR contract. The need for an interest rate hedging instrument in Hong Kong is undeniable as the discussion in Chapter 3, Section 3.3, has shown. The key question, however, will be whether there will be enough trading interest to maintain the market active and liquid.

5.3 The gold market

Financial markets in Hong Kong tend to appear in multiples, such as the four stock exchanges before 1986. The gold market is no exception as there are at present three organized markets, the Chinese Gold and Silver Exchange, the loco-London market and the futures gold market.[24]

The Chinese Gold and Silver Exchange is the oldest of the three, having been established in 1910. It is a purely local market in the sense that it deals in gold traded in a local Chinese weight, the tael which is equivalent to 37.429 grams, in 100 tael bars of 99 per cent purity. The local form of the market was even preserved through a special exemption in the Weights and Measures Ordinance which enforced a metric system in Hong Kong. The market is completely self-regulated and it is further characterized by its delivery system which, although it allows for spot delivery, does not specify a fixed date for settlement for most of the contracts. This is done by allowing all open positions to be carried forward for a day at a time without a specified time limit. If there is excess supply in the market, investors with long positions pay a premium to the shorts in order to have their positions carried forward for one more day. If there is excess demand with prices rising, the shorts would pay the longs for the carrying forward of open positions. The premium paid or received is fixed daily and is closely related to HIBOR. In a rather limited sense this is an undated futures market.[25] The bear market in gold in the late 1980s led to a large fall in the turnover of the local market, as much as 60 per cent, casting doubts on its continuing viability. However, in view of the restrictions in the trading of gold in neighbouring countries such as Taiwan, Thailand and the PRC, Hong Kong's physical market is likely to continue to thrive. In terms of gold imports Hong Kong still ranks among the top countries in the world and is an important regional centre after London and Zurich. In 1988 Hong Kong imported 460 tonnes of gold with 300 of these shared equally between Switzerland and the UK, and about 100 tonnes from Australia, the USA, Canada and South Africa. This compares with Japan's imports of 300 tonnes and Taiwan's imports of 330 tonnes.[26]

The second organized market is the so-called loco-London market which is simply an extension of the international gold market.[27] This market developed after the lifting of restrictions on gold imports into Hong Kong in 1974. It is primarily a spot market with delivery in London and payments effected in New York. This explains the 'loco' prefix signifying its local links with London. However, it is a purely professional market as opposed to the Chinese local market which attracts investors interested in the physical holding of gold as investment.[28]

The third market is the gold futures market, a part of the HKFE. The gold contract was introduced in 1980 but never really succeeded in trading in substantial volumes. For example, on average, the daily turnover during 1984–7 varied between twenty and twenty-eight lots, falling to a low of eight daily lots in the months after the October 1987 crash. The volume has partially recovered since then, but the contract is still not considered viable. The primary reason for this lack of interest is that the local investors use the Chinese market and the professionals are linked to the world market via the loco-London, leaving the futures somewhere in between.[29]

The gold futures contract carries a standard specification of trading 100 oz. of fine gold with delivery in Hong Kong. The spot month plus the following 2 months and all the even months are traded, giving eight different months of delivery.[30]

A number of other derivative gold instruments are available in Hong Kong. Two of them are worth mentioning. The Hongkong Bank trades the so-called Paper Wayfoong Gold. These are paper receipts of a certain number of tael of gold equivalent. The investors have no physical gold holdings although the bank guarantees the physical presence of gold. The paper receipt are purchased or redeemed at the current bid-offer price for a tael of gold. The other product is a gold-linked bull–bear bond in HK dollars issued by Banque IndoSuez in January 1988. Investors purchasing the bull part of the issue would receive on redemption an additional premium for every US dollar increase in the price of gold compared with its price at issue. Similarly they would suffer a loss for a price fall. Exactly the reverse arrangements hold for the bear part of the issue.

As the loco-London market reflects the overall international gold market situation, the efficiency of the gold market in Hong Kong can be examined in terms of the local Chinese market trading in taels. A study by Tai used the daily closing selling prices of the market from March 1981 to October 1983, a total of 606 observations.[31] A number of tests based on spectral analysis showed that the first differences between successive daily prices were not random. The conclusions of the paper were as follows:

First, the Hong Kong gold market was inefficient during the period of the analysis. Second, periodicity was present in the gold price series. If the Hong Kong gold market is inefficient, then there are opportunities for making abnormal profits by exploiting market inefficiency. On the other hand knowledge of the periodicities presented in the gold price series can assist investors with development of gold price forecasts and the development of successful trading rules.[32]

The study did not specify the possible causes of the market inefficiency present, nor were the periodicities mentioned explained in any detail. A similar study by Ho using data for 1981–2 from the Chinese local market also found it mostly inefficient.[33] It could be expected that a purely local market of an internationally traded commodity would not exhibit a great degree of inefficiency defined in terms of the correlation between successive daily price changes. Despite the different standard in the weight and purity of the gold traded it is not surprising that arbitrage between the loco-London market and the Chinese local market does exist. There is some evidence of arbitrage activity, particularly in times of selling pressure. The opportunities for arbitrage, however, do not necessarily increase the efficiency of any single individual market.

The future of the gold markets in Hong Kong will depend on the development of the regional markets. As already indicated the restrictions in gold trading in some neighbouring countries have created lucrative opportunities for Hong Kong. However, the opening of Tokyo's Commodity Exchange of Industry and the continuing low level of activity in the gold futures may put pressures on all the markets in Hong Kong in the near future.

5.4 Unit trusts and investment management

Unit Trusts are relatively new to Hong Kong both as an investment vehicle for local investors and as a management activity. The then unsophisticated markets of Hong Kong in the late 1960s and early 1970s were particularly badly hit by the frauds perpetrated by funds such as IOS and GRAMCO and unit trusts acquired an unjustifiedly poor reputation. In 1972 the Government introduced a bill to regulate the marketing or sales of funds to local investors. In 1978, instead of an ordinance, the Securities Commission and representatives of fund managers agreed to a Unit Trusts and Mutual Funds Code. The Securities Ordinance 1974 (as subsequently amended) and the Securities and Futures Commission Ordinance 1989 empowered the Commissioner of Securities to authorize unit trusts for operation and sale in Hong Kong. In 1983 the Hong Kong Unit Trust Association (HKUTA) was set up in order to both promote the interests of the industry and to promote unit trusts as a form of investment in Hong Kong.[34]

The rise of authorized unit trusts in Hong Kong was quite rapid. It is important, however, to stress that the promotion or sale of an authorized trust in Hong Kong does not imply that the trust, manager and trustees are domiciled in Hong Kong or are otherwise based in Hong Kong. It simply indicates that the trust, irrespective of its origins, has fulfilled certain requirements under the code and the relevant Ordinance. In 1983 there were about 100 authorized trusts. In 1986 they had increased to 211 and by 1987 their number had risen to over 260. In December 1987 there were thirty management groups with 268 broad funds under management which covered nearly 500 subfunds or umbrella groupings. Of these funds nearly 40 per cent were established locally, and the rest were domiciled overseas. At present, there are no comprehensive statistics for all unit trusts in Hong Kong as the HKUTA collects data only from its members. Of the 507 authorized trusts at the end of 1987 the HKUTA statistics covered 290. These trusts had HK$73.1 billion under management at the beginning of 1987 of which HK$3.9 billion was invested in Hong Kong securities.[35] By the middle of 1989 the total of unit trust funds and subfunds had risen to over 550.[36] Of these funds at least fourteen were specifically Hong Kong equity based, leaving aside the scores of others which included Hong Kong equity in Southeast Asia or newly industrializing country (NIC) funds.

The October 1987 crash affected unit trust funds quite substantially, particularly as some of them had to suspend redemptions or were unable to provide quotations. At the time this was blamed on the local investors who, apparently, treated trust funds as equity rather than adopting a buy-and-hold attitude. Surprisingly, however, following the June 1989 Beijing massacre with the single day drop in the HSI of more than 580 points, trust funds fared extremely well with no abnormal redemption demands. At the time this was viewed as a sign of the growing maturity of the investors and of the unit trust market in general.

The development of the unit trust industry in Hong Kong is tied closely to the development of Hong Kong as a regional investment management centre. There are a number of ways in which the importance of Hong Kong as a funds management centre can be appraised and quantified. Table 5.5 supplies some regional data and some data specific to Hong Kong indicating the significant presence of Hong Kong in this area.

Table 5.5 Hong Kong's comparative position in fund management, June 1987

Country or centre	No. of trusts	No. of managers	Total assets (US$ billion)	Average size of trust (US$ million)
Asia Pacific comprising	2,063	108	275	133
Japan	1,520	12	245	161
Hong Kong	238	35	10.6	45
Australia	135	23	7.4	66
Korea	112	9	5.3	47
UK	1,070	161	56	54
USA	2,200	208	810	368

Source: P. Pearson, 'Hong Kong's attraction for fund managers' paper presented to the Conference on Investment in Hong Kong, Stock Exchange of Hong Kong, 1987

Given the presence of other competing centres in the Pacific rim, Hong Kong's position is attributed to at least three key factors. First, the role of both the institutions and of Government policy in establishing Hong Kong as a truly liberal and well-organized offshore centre cannot be overemphasized. There are no foreign exchange or capital movement controls, but there is a coherent but flexible regulatory framework on unit trusts and there are all the legal and financial ancillary facilities necessary to run the organization and management of funds. Second, the taxation system favours income and capital gains from the ownership of securities as it imposes no taxes on dividends or capital gains on the disposal of securities. This is an important consideration for Hong Kong trusts deriving income or gains arising within Hong Kong. There are also further exemptions such that no revenue-related charges are imposed on the running of unit trusts in Hong Kong. Finally, Hong Kong's position is reinforced by either the relative underdevelopment of other centres or the less favourable taxation treatment there. However, the penetration of the 'unit trust habit' is still relatively low in Hong Kong. One way of measuring it is to calculate the ratio of domestic unit trust assets to the total equity market capitalization.

In Hong Kong in 1987 this stood at 6.2 per cent, in the UK at 8.4 per cent, in Japan at 8.3 per cent and in the USA at 31.2 per cent. Another method is to calculate the ratio of unit trusts to personal financial assets. In Hong Kong in 1987 this stood at about 0.25 per cent, in the USA at 11 per cent and in the UK at 3 per cent. The total number of unit trust holders in Hong Kong in 1988 was estimated as about 25,000.[37]

In addition to unit trusts specific mention must be made of pension funds and insurance-related funds business.

There are a large number of provident, superannuation and retirement schemes in Hong Kong. At the end of September 1986 more than 4,429 schemes covering at least 200,000 employees in the private sector had been approved by the Inland Revenue. An equal number of civil servants or of government-related or government-supported organizations were also covered by pension and retirement schemes.[38] The Wyatt Actuaries Company of Hong Kong produces a regular survey of pension funds in Hong Kong.[39] The 1988 survey covered thirty-three managers with 193 pension schemes etc. under management. The distribution of funds amongst managers was highly skewed with three of the main merchant banking (deposit-taking company DTC) houses, Jardine Fleming, Schroders Asia and Wardley, having the lion's share of forty-six, thirty-nine and thirty-two schemes respectively. The combined assets of the surveyed funds at the end of 1988 stood at HK$21.2 billion with the average scheme or fund size at HK$110 million. Over a 6 year period (1983–8) the funds dedicated 64 per cent of their assets to equity, 24 per cent bonds and 12 per cent to cash. The assets were roughly equally distributed between Hong Kong (31 per cent) and the USA (25 per cent) with the rest of the world taking the other 44 per cent. The currency exposure not in HK dollars was nearly 70 per cent.

The role of pension and retirement funds is bound to grow, especially as the Hong Kong Government briefly considered but then dropped a proposition to introduced a centralized provident fund. The October 1987 crash took its toll on the assets of these funds, but the growing sophistication of the investing public and the substantial component of equity in these funds are bound to increase their attractiveness. This is also reflected in the growth of the insurance business in Hong Kong and particularly the part associated with life.[40] Table 5.6 outlines some of the relevant data concerning the life aspect of the insurance business in Hong Kong as it is more closely related to investment management. The figures in table 5.5 are highly selective. For example, they exclude data from the other 277 insurers operating in Hong Kong in 1988 of whom 150 were incorporated outside Hong Kong and the other 127 were local. It is clear, however, that life business is of growing importance. Total life insurance premiums grew by 21 per cent during 1981–5, rising to a growth of over 80 per cent during 1986–7. It is estimated that although term or whole-life insurance still constitutes the bulk of the business underwritten, about 20 per cent of the individual life premiums in 1987 were derived from endowment or investment-linked insurance compared with 4 per cent in 1985. There are reasons for believing that the growth in life-related insurance services will continue. Demographic and social trends in Hong Kong will encourage this. Smaller families and less reliance on family support in contingencies and a wealthier population but also a rising average age will encourage greater participation and sales.[41]

Table 5.6 Data on selected locally incorporated life insurance companies, 1984–5

	1984	1985	1986
Life companies (no.)	4	4	3
Life funds (HK$ million)	3,140	4,325	5,278
Gross premium of life companies (HK$ million)	480	925	648
All other companies (no.)	42	41	41
All other insurance funds (HK$ million)	7,234	9,379	10,071
	(4,247)	(5,011)	(5,673)
All other gross premiums (HK$ million)	6,140	6,956	7,040
	(1,760)	(2,009)	(2,335)
Total life funds (HK$ million)	7,387	9,336	10,952

Source: Hongkong Bank, *Economic Reports*, several issues
Note: The numbers in parentheses are life funds (or, where applicable, premiums on life insurance) by composite insurance companies in million HK dollars; all other gross premiums include reinsurance premiums.

The evidence outlined so far concerning the growth of investment-related sectors can be elaborated further by reviewing the performance of the managers and the institutions against commonly accepted financial benchmarks. The multinational character of most fund managers operating in Hong Kong makes comparisons or conclusions which are specific to Hong Kong rather difficult.

One standard approach to the measurement of performance of portfolios (funds) is to use expected returns and the covariance of returns to construct an efficiency frontier against which individual performances can be measured. This can be done by either taking combinations of funds and treating them as single assets or simply taking the underlying mixture of assets and calculating the two moments.

Given weights x_i attached to individual assets, the expected rate of return $E(R_i)$ and its variance of $\sigma^2_{p_1}$ for a portfolio consisting of n assets are respectively

$$E(R_p) = \sum_{i=1}^{n} x_i E(R_i)$$

$$\sigma^2_p = \sum_{i=1}^{n} \sum_{j=1}^{n} x_i x_j (\text{cov } R_i R_j)$$

where the subscript p refers to the portfolio and cov $R_i R_j$ is the covariance of the returns on the ith and jth securities. By using standard portfolio techniques, combinations of these assets can yield a frontier which shows optimum combinations of returns and risk. An example is shown in Figure 5.1. The curve AB is, in effect, an envelope curve of a large number of individual combinations of assets. Combinations lying inside the curve are not preferred to those on the curve as they will involve the same risk but smaller returns and vice versa. One way of judging the performance of unit trusts and fund managers is to construct a frontier from all the returns underlying the assets invested in. Given the international character and investment policy of most funds the frontier will contain the risk–return information of assets from many different countries. Specific funds or management companies may not be investing in all or even some of the assets or countries included in the risk–return efficiency frontier. Indeed, they may be specializing in only some of them. The object of this exercise, however, is to observe the performance of funds against a 'universe' of assets. A specific illustration of the efficiency frontier can be found in a study comparing the performance of retirement schemes managers in Hong Kong.[42] Here the efficiency frontier was calculated by using the envelope curve of portfolios of wide asset combinations and, in particular, Hong Kong, Japanese, US, Australian, and German equities, and US, UK and German bonds over 1983–8. The median measurement of investment performance (MIP) over the same period in terms of risk and return was also plotted as a single point. Figure 5.2 is a broad summary of these findings. The median returns for retirement funds surveyed over 1983–8 were 36.2 per cent, 4.4 per cent, 34.7 per cent, 41.2 per cent, 5.2 per cent and 11.4 per cent respectively, with the number of schemes in the survey growing from eighty-one to 179 over this period.

The efficiency frontier of Figure 5.2 tells half the story, however, when it comes to appraising the performance of individual fund managers when the returns must be evaluated against the risk taken. The Sharpe index (reward to variability), defined as:

$$\frac{r_i - RF}{\sigma} = \frac{\text{risk premium}}{\text{variability}}$$

where r_i and σ are the return and the standard deviation of the ith portfolio or fund and RF is a risk-free interest rate, can be used here.

For the sixty-two pension funds surveyed in Hong Kong over 1983–8 the highest Sharpe index stood at 1.86 and the lowest at 0.56, a difference of over three times. However, there are problems in interpreting this index in the context of Hong Kong since retirement fund management is heavily concentrated in the hands of a few companies. Therefore, the results could reflect the overall performance of these few managers rather than of the whole spectrum. This can be corrected by examining the average results per manager, but here again the changing investment environment makes these comparisons valid only when examining similar funds in similar markets during the same time periods.[43]

International diversification could undoubtedly help to improve performance of any portfolio which included Hong Kong equities. There is considerable evidence that stock markets in different countries do not tend to move together during either normal or crisis periods. For example, one study spanning 1 July 1987 to 29 January 1988, thereby covering both before and after the October 1987 crash, found that the stock indexes of the USA, the UK, Japan and the FRG, recalculated in US dollar terms so as to employ a common unit of measurement, were highly correlated but the relationship was very unstable:

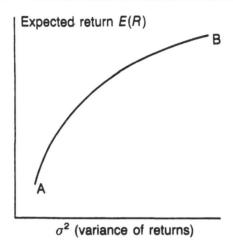

Expected return $E(R)$

B

A

σ^2 (variance of returns)

Figure 5.1 Efficiency frontier of combinations asset

If one examines the correlations of the levels of stock prices before and after the crash, however, the correlations change dramatically. For example, the correlation of the UK index with the US index is about 0.90 for the whole period. Before the crash, however, (3 months before October 1987, AFF) the correlation is −0.56, while after the crash (3 months after October 1987, AFF) it is 0.56. Conversely, the correlations for the US and German Stock indexes are 0.93 for the whole period, 0.75 before the crash and −0.01 afterwards. This instability is precisely what one would expect if the relative stock price indexes are random walks with no long-run relationships between their levels.[44]

However, there were positive and statistically significant correlations between the changes in the indexes for the period 1 July 1987 to 29 January 1988. This is not surprising since financial transactions and trade in goods and services could be expected to affect the indexes in the same direction. Taking a longer time period sample (January 1957 to December 1987) yielded roughly similar results as to both the level and changes in the level of these indexes.[45]

The relative performance of Hong Kong's stock market and its international links are explored in Table 5.7. Two observations

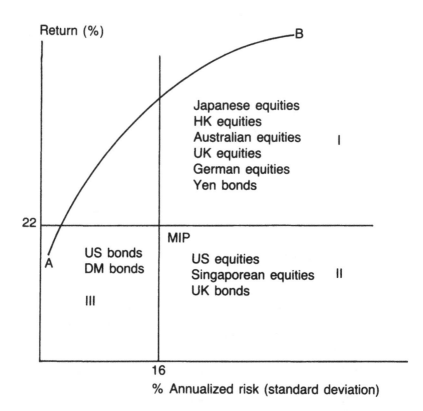

Figure 5.2 Retirement fund performance in Hong Kong 1983–8

Note: The efficiency frontier AB shows the optimum combinations of all the assets
indicated. Quadrants I, II and III indicate the general return–risk situation of investing
all the portfolio in any single asset, and MIP is the actual achieved median return of
all the funds surveyed. The assets are not listed in any particular order other than the
quadrant they fall in relation to the MIP. Figures and orderings are approximate.

should be made here. First, although there is correlation between
the levels of Hong Kong's stock market activity and other
centres, the correlation varies considerably. This explains why
international diversification of Hong Kong-based funds and
portfolios yield risk–return benefits. Second, Hong Kong's
notorious volatility and high yield are not based on fiction.
Indeed, the source from which Table 5.5 is taken lists sixteen

Table 5.7 Correlation, risk and return: Hong Kong and other major stock markets, 1971–85/6

(1)	(2)	(3)	(4)
Stock market	Correlation with Hong Kong (R²)	Annual return (%)	Standard deviation of return
Hong Kong	1.00 (1.00)	25.01	40.86 (43.07)
USA	0.26 (0.06)	9.95	15.41
Japan	0.28 (0.07)	24.58	20.75 (16.35)
UK	0.29 (0.08)	13.73	28.28 (24.95)
FRG	0.18 (0.03)	16.69	20.09 (15.78)
Australia	0.29 (0.08)	9.28	26.81 (23.36)
Singapore	0.41 (0.16)	11.30	32.46 (32.39)
World (US$) (Morgan Stanley)	0.32 (0.10)	13.00	13.85 (13.18)
EAFE (US$) (Morgan Stanley)	0.28 (0.07)	17.09	17.21 (14.40)

Source: B. Solnik, *International Investments*, Reading, MA: Addison Wesley, 1988, pp. 40–1, 45

Note: The number in parentheses in column 2 is R^2, i.e. the square of the correlation coefficient. Data for correlation calculations are for 1971–85. For returns and risk the period spans 1971–86. EAFE stands for the Europe, Australia and Far East Index (i.e. non-US) of Morgan Stanley Capital International. All the calculations were US dollar based which meant that returns included an exchange risk. The numbers in parentheses in column 4 are risk measured in domestic currency.

exchanges, as well as Hong Kong, in the risk–return calculations over 1971–85. Hong Kong tops the list in terms of the highest volatility and returns which also explains, in reverse, why Hong Kong equities may find favour in portfolios of overseas-located funds. Similar results were obtained in a study which examined the interrelationships between Asia Pacific markets and the USA over 1977–88. The correlation coefficients were as follows: Australia, 0.29; Japan, 0.36; Korea, 0.03; Malaysia, 0.29; the Philippines, 0.07; Singapore, 0.15; Taiwan, 0.15; Thailand, 0.04; Hong Kong, 0.16. On an annual basis, for all the countries covered there was at least one negative correlation coefficient, with Korea heading the group with six. Hong Kong had two negative signs, one in 1977 and one in 1983.[46]

Further studies using causality tests based on weekly index data (1977 to mid-1988) have established a unidirectional influence from the US equity markets to those of Hong Kong.[47] A study of the returns performance of Asian Pacific markets (including

Hong Kong) adjusted for the exchange rates yielded some predictable results. Over the period examined (1979–88) Japanese investors would not have benefited greatly by diversifying away from yen denominated assets, whereas Hong Kong investors using HK dollars as the investment currency would have fared no better or worse than if the US dollar had been used instead.[48] Overall, investment in Asia Pacific region securities in general and Hong Kong in particular appears to offer possibilities for diversification and resultant return–risk increases–decreases. However, there are still differences between specific countries and some doubts as to the overall stability of the observed covariation of returns. These considerations, as well as the transaction costs involved, may limit the potential diversification gains.

The performance of unit trusts registered in Hong Kong measured in terms of returns and risk produced rather mixed results.

A study in Hong Kong used the 1987 weekly bid prices of 129 unit trust funds trading in Hong Kong to calculate the risk–return relationship and the effects of diversification on fund performance.[49] The unit trusts covered a wide spectrum of equities from Japan, Hong Kong, Australia, Singapore and the Philippines, and portfolios of Southeast Asian, Far East, US, UK, European and international assets. Most of the funds experienced a higher standard deviation of returns than the markets in which they were invested. Equally, all funds had an unsystematic risk, measured by the residual standard deviation of the linear regression estimation of the characteristic line of each fund, which was greater than zero. The Hong Kong equities funds had the highest average beta coefficients indicating a greater sensitivity to the underlying market. In general, the higher portion of unsystematic risk to local risk for all funds indicated that most funds could benefit by diversification. The average ratios of price change to standard deviation of funds showed that Hong Kong and US equities funds were doing better than the rest since about half of them had a higher ratio than the general market, thus outperforming the market in that respect. A study by Ip and Ho using a longer time period (1983–7) and covering only the performance of Asia Pacific mutual funds (unit trusts) arrived at broadly similar conclusions.[50] Funds appeared to have wide margins in terms of further diversification to reduce unsystematic risk. Hong Kong equity funds tended to have the lowest ratios of systematic to unsystematic risk with 23 per cent of their total risk still avoidable through further diversification. In terms of market efficiency few Hong Kong equity funds outperformed the market. Many of the funds surveyed performed worse than a random portfolio on a risk-adjusted basis.

The results of these studies confirm the possibility of further gains through diversification in these markets. For example, a study using three portfolios consisting of Hong Kong and US, Japanese or European shares with ratios varying from 100 per cent to 100 per cent either way produced interesting results. The data covered 3 year periods ending in June 1984, June 1985 and June 1986. Because the returns were converted into US dollars, they included currency as well as movements of the underlying equity. The return and risk were calculated using the Hong Kong index versus the S&P500 and Japanese and European indexes. Unhedged diversification into the US market over 1981–4 and 1982–5 would have resulted in increased returns and reduced risk, but for 1983–6 diversification would have led to risk–return reduction. In all cases diversification into the Japanese market produced risk reduction and returns increase, but only up to a point where further diversification reversed the trend. The behaviour of the European portfolio was not dissimilar to that of the Japanese.[51]

Finally mention must be made of the costs of investing in unit trusts in Hong Kong. In one study trusts traded in Hong Kong were classified according to their objectives. Two hundred and two funds were classified under seventeen broad categories such as money market, regional, equity regional, fund of funds etc. Three types of costs were calculated: the spread, initial and redemption charges, and the cost incurred of buying a fund holding it for 1 year, making one switch within the year and then selling it. The cheapest funds according to all three classes of costs were regional money market funds and the most expensive were secondary equities and global funds. The reasons for these differences were explained by the fact that money market funds are expected to produce a relatively low yield and the management of the underlying assets is simple. Equity funds cost more to run and also present more difficult challenges to the managers.[52]

The evidence outlined so far indicates a growing degree of sophistication of both the investing public in Hong Kong and the market for funds management. Given the expertise and the presence of a large number of financial intermediaries, coupled with Hong Kong's liberal legal and regulatory regime, the future of fund management appears to be bright. Of particular importance will be the growth of pension and retirement funds. The approach of 1997 may not in fact aggravate these prospects as long as pension rights are encashable and portable and the foreign exchange risk is minimized through the pegged HK dollar. It is true that Hong Kong investors have had unimpressive experience with unit trusts, particularly during the October 1987 crash. However, an investing public of growing sophistication will not fail to notice the benefits of diversification and the growing availability of both regional and international instruments of investment coupled with expert advice in a competitive environment.

5.5 The regulatory framework

Hong Kong's regulatory system for the banking and financial markets underwent a massive and fundamental change between 1986 and 1989. The changes were in response to major, and costly, banking scandals which exposed the weaknesses of the banking supervision and to the October 1987 crash. In the latter case the SRC Report put forward a host of recommendations pertaining to the equities and stock markets. Independently of this official activity, the Stock Exchange itself, aided and abetted by the Government, thoroughly revised its own rule book. At the same time the Government was also reviewing all the related ordinances of the investment and financial markets and put into motion a number of changes.

Regulation of financial markets transcends the pure legal framework in which it is presented because of the inherent assumption that financial markets produce quasi-public services and hence should come under the ambit of regulation. Like any other regulatory issue of any market activity there are costs and benefits involved. This is not a new question in economic and financial analysis. The costs of regulation are the resources dedicated by either the state or private organizations in supervising, enforcing and complying with the rules. This can be quite considerable and can be justified only by the expected gains to investors. Presumably, an efficient market would provide enough information that participants would only need to use prices as a guide to their actions. Purely fraudulent activities would be taken care of by the criminal law. But because financial markets are perceived to produce or trade in services that are quasi-public, market forces alone will not necessarily lead to market practices which distribute the benefits and risks amongst participants fairly. Hence the need for the state to step in. Again intervention does not always succeed, if success is measured in terms of the benefits to the customers. Regulation can frequently end up in restrictive practices benefiting the existing market participants rather than the investors. This is simply an extension of the argument that competitive process, and its attendant benefits, should take precedence over any arguments based on the potential imperfections of markets which may necessitate regulation.

Hong Kong has always taken great pride in the minimum interference by government or regulatory authorities in any of its financial institutions. Other than the Commissioners and the Secretary for Monetary Affairs, the key official in all decisions concerning regulations of the financial markets is the Financial Secretary. Not surprisingly, therefore, there was a long and sometimes acrimonious debate over the regulation issues, particularly those of the securities and futures markets, as they involved quasi-political as well as purely economic or financial questions.

Other than various licensing requirements under an assortment of ordinances, the first concrete steps to set up a regulatory body for banks, and later for DTCs, came with the 1964 Banking Ordinance, following, predictably, a banking crisis in 1961. This Ordinance set up the Office of the Commissioner of Banking whose powers were extended and repeatedly modified until the most comprehensive reviews of all took place culminating with the 1986 Banking Ordinance. The creation of DTCs in 1976 brought them under the powers of the Commissioner as well. The functions of the Commissioner as defined by the Ordinance are quite wide, but they fall into three broad areas. First, the Commissioner licenses or revokes the licenses of banks and

DTCs. In other words, the Commissioner can act as a barrier to entry or force a bank or DTC to discontinue its presence and activities in Hong Kong. There are checks and balances in these very drastic powers including decisions ultimately made by the Governor in Council. Second, the Commissioner receives regular monthly reports from all the licensed institutions on their operations and balance sheets. This is the most obvious way in which the capital adequacy, liquidity and specified loan ratios of the Ordinance can be inspected and, if necessary, enforced. Finally, the Commissioner, through a number of supervisory and advisory powers, can promote sound banking activities in Hong Kong. The Ordinance imposed a number of restrictions on the structure of the assets and liabilities of banks and DTCs. The most important of these is the capital adequacy ratio defined in terms of the amount of capital as a percentage of risk-weighted classes of assets in the books of the banks or DTCs. The initial ratio was set at 5 per cent, with risk weights varying from zero to 100 per cent. The requirement is imposed on all locally incorporated banks and DTCs. In September 1988 the Commissioner announced that Hong Kong would move progressively towards the weights and ratios of the Basle Banking Agreement. This ratio is higher although in some cases the risk weights were different from those in the Ordinance. The bank and DTCs have an additional liquidity ratio of 25 per cent to observe and cannot lend more than specified proportions of their balance sheets to any single customer. All these are primarily prudential rather than credit-restricting requirements.

The discussion in Chapter 2, Section 2.2, outlined the main causes of bank failures in Hong Kong in the 1980s. Almost all these had their roots in some form of fraudulent or irregular practice. At the time the Office of the Commissioner was criticized for a lack of diligence in not spotting what turned out to be extensive loans to directors, cheque-kitting practices and so on. Part of the blame turned out to be the lax accounting standards adopted by these banks and their advisors. It is also important to stress that fraud and dubious lending practices are by no means exclusive to Hong Kong as the recent UK experience with Johnson Matthey and the extremely expensive debacle with the US Savings and Loans Associations showed. The quick adoption of the Basle Banking Agreement signalled

Hong Kong's wish to demonstrate to the international banking community its desire to maintain the highest and strictest possible standards.

The regulatory situation of the financial markets until 1988-9 was also representative of Hong Kong's reactive rather than lead response to market developments.[53] The key sets of rules were to be found in the various versions of the Securities Ordinance which was passed initially in 1974. The Ordinance set up the Securities Commission and the Office of the Commissioner for Securities whose main function was to supervise the Stock Exchange and apply and enforce the relevant ordinances concerning the protection of investors, takeovers and mergers, unit trusts and the licensing of members of the investment and related industries. In 1976 a separate Commission on Commodities Trading was set up whose Commissioner was also the Securities Commissioner. This body oversaw the trading activities of the commodities futures contracts.

The four stock exchanges (later unified into one in 1986) and the Futures Exchange had, of course, their own internal rule books, subject always to the approval of the Securities Commission or the Futures Commission.

Although structurally these bodies appeared to have well-defined powers and responsibilities, the October 1987 crash was to prove otherwise. It must be stressed that it was not just a major event which simply buckled the resistance or strength of these regulatory institutions but a series of developments all of which generated a 'domino' type of effect at a time of stress. The weakness of the regulatory system of the financial markets in Hong Kong has been exhaustively detailed in the *SRC Report*. As many of the criticisms and recommendations concern technical and quasi-legal matters the following summary touches on the broad issues only.

First, the legal and institutional framework that existed in 1987 emphasized self-regulation in the sense that the official authorities were supposed to provide the support and guidance. However, these authorities lacked both the resources and the initiative during a period of very rapid changes. Two examples illustrate this predicament. The manpower shortage at the Securities Commission was such that in the mid-1980s the vetting of unit trust authorization applications stretched over a period of

2 years. Furthermore the development of a successful unified stock exchange in 1986 produced a powerful and motivated group of executives who pushed for the business development side of the Exchange whilst disregarding both the rule book or the need to set an appropriate administration for the surveillance of members, listing regulations and the settlement system. The Securities Commission was unable to control this group of executives with the result that decisions such as that to close the Exchange for 4 days during the October 1987 crash were apparently taken with little or no regard to consultation or proper procedures.

Second, the settlement system of the unified exchange still maintained the archaic paper (physical delivery of shares) settlement over 24 hours. Although this may appear as a purely administrative or bookkeeping matter it proved crucial to the events leading to the crash.[54] As the volume of trade mounted, the 24 hour system broke down completely with brokers failing to settle ever mounting deals. Indeed, the chairman of the Exchange gave this backlog problem as one of the reasons for the closure. Small brokers, who represented the majority of the total membership of the Exchange, were particularly aggrieved as they did not have either the credit facilities or capital backing of large international houses who could carry the potential default risk of unsettled trades. Coming to an agreement as to the settlement period and the eventual move towards a 'paperless' systems proved difficult and was possible only after lengthy negotiations.[55] The settlement system and its reform raised further issues of a central clearing agency which would also guarantee trades, promote greater transparency of share ownership and, to the extent that it is still not permitted, prevent short selling of stock

Third, the Futures Exchange had developed a clearing and risk management system which was confused and ineffectual. As the discussion in Section 5.3 has shown, the interlocking ownership of the clearing house (ICCH) with the FGC and the Exchange itself led to conflicts of interest and poorly defined lines of responsibility. The explosion in the volume and value of the HSI futures contract was not matched by increases in the capital of the FGC or effective monitoring of the margin rules on clients.

The implementation of the *SRC Report* took various forms. In the case of the Stock Exchange internal reforms were well on stream before the Committee reported. Following the arrest of the chairman in January 1988 on charges of corruption, the Government proceeded to handpick a completely new council and promoted the appointment of new and professional executives to run the Exchange. At this point it must be stressed that accusations at the time about the degree of corruption of Hong Kong's financial markets in general and the Stock Exchange in particular now sound misplaced and somewhat hypocritical. At roughly the same time the American stock markets were being shaken by the Ivan Boesky insider deal scandal, UK markets faced major questions over the Guinness bid for the Distillers Company and later the Japanese Government resigned over the Recruit shares scandal and the Greek Government was forced by major banking frauds into elections which it lost. This is not to justify the irregularities in Hong Kong, but to point out that Hong Kong does not have a monopoly over bribes and illegal practices.

The newly revamped council, executive and rule book of the Exchange could then face with greater equanimity and authority the second major reform based on the SRC recommendations.[56] The Securities and Futures Commission Ordinance of 1989 unified the rules concerning the functions and powers of the Securities and Futures Commission, abolished the old commissions and replaced them with a much larger and more powerful body. Therein lay the considerable controversy regarding this Ordinance, as the finance community in Hong Kong was in general fearful and sceptical about the expanded body and questioned both its usefulness and its cost effectiveness.[57]

The third major group of reforms centred around the Futures Exchange. This involved several stages. The Futures Exchange set up a wholly owned subsidiary Clearing House which also assumed the responsibility for all risk management functions related to clearing backed by capital contributed by members, insurance and bank guarantees. This ended the complex and ineffective tripartite arrangement as the Clearing House now guarantees the integrity of trades as well as having a close relationship and interface with the risk exposure of the traders. After considerable resistance from some members the Exchange also adopted a new constitution which clarified membership requirements, duties and rights.[58]

The final set of reforms concerned a revision of the Takeovers and Mergers Code, provisions for the disclosure of interest of major shareholders in companies and finally the drafting of much firmer provisions regarding insider dealing, an area still poorly defined in Hong Kong.[59]

The October 1987 crash may turn out to be a blessing in disguise for Hong Kong as it gave the necessary impetus for the appropriate regulatory reforms to be instituted. The new institutions, and in particular the Futures Exchange, were put to a severe test following the Beijing massacre in June 1989. The HSI fell on two separate occasions by 339 points, a 10.8 per cent drop, on 22 May 1989 and by 581 points, a 22 per cent drop, on 5 June 1989. The HSI fugures market was also subjected to the highest volatility it had ever experienced with the June 1989 contract trading between 3,390 and 1,910 points breaching the 300 points a day limit on five occasions. Margining rules were strictly adhered to and the decline in the volume of open interest contracts was containable and less than expected indicating a professional and mature market. Similarly the Stock Exchange dealt with the massive price falls in an orderly manner and with continuous trading.[60]

The major question still outstanding is the speed with which the new Securities and Futures Commission will both encourage and foster self-regulation. The continuing attraction of Hong Kong as a financial centre must tread the tightrope between too much regulation taking the spirit and speed out of the markets and too little regulation encouraging the (unjustified) reputation of markets which cannot be trusted or which cannot provide minimum guarantees of integrity. The present set of regulatory institutions and ordinances represents Hong Kong's attempt to strike that particular delicate balance.

Chapter six

The foreign exchange rate, monetary and fiscal policy

6.1 Introduction

The absence of a central bank or of a similar type of institution in Hong Kong has meant that issues of monetary policy have always been connected to the exchange rate regime. As has already been mentioned in Chapter 2, the role of the two note-issuing banks (NIBs), Hongkong Bank and Standard Chartered has been akin to that of a central monetary authority, at least in terms of control over the quantity of cash. However, even this statement is not quite accurate in view of the frequent changes in the note issuing arrangements. The role and function of the Exchange Fund, also briefly mentioned in Chapter 2, has undergone a number of subtle changes, especially after July 1988, but, as an institution, it is still not near an embryonic central bank.

From the end of the Second World War until November 1967, the HK dollar note issue was fully backed by sterling assets. The devaluation of sterling during that year caused considerable upheaval as it required adjustments and compensation to banks which lost out on their sterling holdings. However, more importantly, although the HK dollar was devalued in line with sterling against the US dollar, it was only partially adjusted. This was the first step to a move away from the strict colonial system whereby both the reserves and the backing of the currency were tied to sterling. The floating exchange rate regime for sterling which was introduced in June 1972 allowed the Hong Kong authorities to take further steps away from this link and towards a connection to the US dollar. The note-issuing arrangements had required the two NIBs to buy a certain type of asset from the

Government – certificates of indebtedness (CIs) – and to use these to back the notes printed. The NIBs were now required to submit HK dollars instead of sterling in order to acquire the CIs so as to print more notes. Between 1972 and 1974 the HK dollar exchange rate was pegged to the US dollar. However, continuous pressure on the HK dollar and the inability or unwillingness of the monetary authorities to resist them finally led to the flotation of the HK dollar in November 1974. This exchange regime and the arrangement whereby increments in the note issue were not being backed by foreign currency remained unchanged until October 1983. Then, as will be detailed below, the HK dollar was pegged once again to the US dollar and the note-issuing arrangements were changed once again.[1]

6.2 The foreign exchange market

The development of the foreign exchange market in Hong Kong can be traced back to the abolition of all foreign exchange controls in 1973 after the HK dollar was unpegged from sterling in 1972. A further impetus to the market was given by the rapid increase in the number of foreign banks starting business in Hong Kong after 1978. It was also helped by the rise of the deposit-taking companies (DTCs) as a distinct financial entity. During the period of the moratorium on new licences for banks (1975–8), acquisition of an existing DTC was an indirect way of setting up a presence in Hong Kong. The relative underdevelopment of the local money market also meant that banks and DTCs had to rely on overseas sources for funds. All these developments contributed to the establishment of a lively and active foreign exchange market.[2]

The foreign exchange market in Hong Kong deals almost exclusively in US dollars rather than HK dollars against all other major currencies. This is not surprising especially in view of the pegging of the local currency to the US dollar. The currencies dealt with in order of importance are the Deutschmark, the yen, sterling and the Swiss franc. The major participants in the market are banks and, to a lesser extent, DTCs. The majority of the deals and transactions are inter-bank, and account for more than 85 per cent of all the business done. All the major international banks are represented, with their positions reflecting their specializations in the international market. Therefore, for example, the Deutsche Bank is active in Deutschmarks, the Bank of Tokyo in yen, and Citibank, Chase, Bankers Trust and others are active across the board of the rest of the currencies.[3] Banks with strong local links such as the Hongkong Bank and Standard Chartered dominate the more limited trades of the HK dollar against other currencies.[4] A comparative league for Hong Kong compiled by *Euromoney* in August 1982 shows the banks offering the best deals (IB, inter-bank; C, corporations).

DM–US$	£–US$	Yen–US$	SFr–US$
Citibank	Chase	Citibank	Chase
(IB)	(C)	(C)	(C)
Deutsche Bank	NatWest	Chase	HKB
(IB)	(IB)	(C)	(C)
	Citibank	Bank of Tokyo	Citibank
	(IB)	(IB)	(IB)

Twelve foreign exchange brokers are members of the Hong Kong Foreign Exchange and Deposit Brokers association which grants them official recognition by the Hong Kong Association of Banks (HKAB). About 30 per cent of all transactions are undertaken through brokers who do not take positions themselves but simply bring buyers and sellers together. Two of the largest broking firms, Marshalls and Tokyo Forex and Tullet International, make between 500 and 600 deals per day. Commissions are competitively determined with discounts for large quantities offered by most brokers.[5] The majority of the transactions are spot with about 20 per cent of the trades in forward or swap deals.

The value of the transactions in the market averages a daily US$30 billion. At these levels the Hong Kong foreign exchange market currently accounts for no more than 10 per cent of the total world turnover. In this respect the market is still in a very minor league compared with London or New York.

A relatively recent innovation in the products and service offered in the market are bearer exchange rate option certificates (BEROs). As Hong Kong has not yet established a currency futures and/or options markets other than forward or swap deals arranged on an individual basis, there are no traded instruments to hedge exchange risks with. BEROs were initially issued by

Barclays in either call or put form for relatively small sums, £–US$ for £5,000 and US$–DM for US$10,000. The bank also made a market in the certificates in order to ensure a cash value for these options.[6] Further developments included banks offering loans for deferred spot currency transactions. This involved banks lending customers a sum of money, usually Deutschmarks, yen, sterling or Swiss francs. A margin deposit was required and this was varied as the currencies fluctuated against the US dollar. An interest differential was charged or paid depending on whether the bank charge on the loan was greater than the interest earned on the deposit. The customer could close the position by converting back to US dollars, collecting the profit or paying back the loss. These accounts were purely speculative and, in a sense, offered the next best alternative to trading currency futures in Singapore's International Monetary Exchange.[7]

The efficiency of Hong Kong's foreign exchange market has been tested in a number of studies. The weak form of market efficiency stipulates that past changes of a variable are not predictors of future changes. Hong Kong provides an interesting case for the testing of this proposition because of the changeover from a floating to a US dollar pegged system since October 1983. This allows for 'before and after' type of tests as well as for examining the effect on the market's efficiency of a change in the exchange regime.

One of the earlier studies by Ho employed monthly data of exchange rates for HK and US dollars, sterling and Deutschmarks spanning November 1974 to December 1979.[8] The Ljung–Box test for the autocorrelation coefficients of the changes in these three exchange rates was estimated. The results for the markets for US dollars and sterling did not reject the null hypothesis, thus indicating some evidence for weak efficiency but not for the Deutschmark market.

A study by Chan employed a considerably more sophisticated set of tests using daily rather than monthly data for the HK dollar to US dollar rate from April 1980 to September 1983.[9] Specifically, in addition to the standard white noise autocorrelation tests the series were also tested for normality as well as for periodic non-randomness. The data were split into four subperiods covering roughly the 4 years between 1980 and 1983. A number of white noise and normality tests were then applied to explore both the distribution of the daily changes of the exchange rate and the degree of autocorrelation. The Smirnov–Kolmogorov D normality test rejected the hypothesis that the changes were normally distributed, although the zero mean test was accepted. Individual autocorrelations from the 1982 and 1983 subperiods were found to be significant. Similarly, the Box–Pierce Q test showed some evidence of dependence for the same two subperiods. These significant results were reversed at the 1 per cent confidence level. Overall the behaviour of the foreign exchange market was shown to be consistent with the weak form of market efficiency but with a question mark over the 1982 and 1983 periods. But even for these periods the evidence was far from conclusive.

Another study by Lui undertook an interesting 'before and after' survey by utilizing data on the HK dollar to US dollar exchange rate spanning January 1982 to December 1984.[10] Given that in October 1983 the HK dollar rate was fixed to the US dollar, the study yielded 434 observations before the link and 259 after. This study is of particular importance as the pegged rate regime since 1983 has relied on an arbitrage mechanism between a controlled and a free market. The details of this arrangement are examined in the next section. Since all the data in this study are the free-market prices, the behaviour of the exchange rates after the peg was introduced can be tested against the benchmark (official) fixed rate. Lui's study examines the statistical distributions of both the absolute values of the HK dollar to US dollar rates and the day-to-day changes. In both cases the means and standard deviations differ significantly, with the 'after' period exhibiting a decrease in both moments. Neither distribution is normal. It is important to remember, however, that as was pointed out in Chapter 5, Section 5.3, tests relying on comparisons of first and second moments drawn from statistical distributions which are neither stationary nor normal must be interpreted with care. The series of daily changes in the exchange rate were then tested for autocorrelation using both individual and group Box–Pierce tests. These tests showed that there was evidence of dependence but the results were very sensitive to small variations in the number of lags. Furthermore for the 'after' period, the average change in the exchange rate over the sample taken was -0.00007 or 1.75 per cent in annual terms. Even if there was some dependence in the daily changes, the overall effect was likely to be very small. It would now follow that despite the statistical evidence there was very little reason to believe that the market was weak inefficient in the 'after' period, although it may have been less so in the 'before'.

It is important to observe that the studies by Chan and Liu overlap in the 'before' period, as Chan's data span April 1980 to September 1983 and Lui's span January 1982 to December 1984, an overlap of 21 months. In both cases the evidence for the 'before' period points to a weak efficient market. The two studies partially confirm each other's findings. Based on these results, there is no evidence that the introduction of the pegged system reduced the efficiency of the market in so far as the dependence tests are, in general, more reliable for the 'after' period than for the 'before' period.

The significance of these tests lies not so much in their academic interest but in the insight that they offer on the workings of the market. A controlled foreign exchange system did not appear to decrease the market's efficiency although, not surprisingly, it reduced its volatility in terms of the first two moments of the distribution of the changes in the exchange rates.

In general, the competitive pressures on Hong Kong's foreign exchange market reflect a number of considerations, not least the question of maintaining the peg against the US dollar. The official policy towards the internationalization of the HK dollar has been cautious and negative. However, this attitude was reversed in 1988 with the authorities being more confident in their ability to control the market. The rapid development of the domestic equity and medium-term capital market plus the growing internationalization of the Hong Kong stock market may well boost the role of the HK dollar as a trading and investment currency. Furthermore the relatively lower labour and office costs compared with Tokyo and the excellent telecommunications of Hong Kong plus its time zone position will continue to offer its foreign exchange market a competitive edge in the region.

6.3 Foreign exchange rate policy

Undoubtedly the most important policy decision taken by the Hong Kong Government in the post-war period has been the pegging of the HK dollar to the US dollar in October 1983.

As already described above, Hong Kong was a member of the sterling area and its currency was linked to sterling. The sterling devaluation of 1967 and finally the floating regime introduced in 1972 acted as the main impetus to decouple the HK dollar and link it instead to the US dollar. Between November 1974 and October 1983 the HK dollar was allowed to float. Its performance in terms of a trade-weighted index is shown in Table 6.1. The new series data in the table are based on a basket of fifteen currencies weighted by their bilateral trade importance for Hong Kong. The major difference between the old and the new series reflects the rising role of China as Hong Kong's trading partner. Furthermore, for different time periods, starting with 1975, separate trade weights are used rather than a uniform set in order to capture the changing patterns of trade. From 1983 onwards the index reflects the average trade pattern of 1984–6.[11]

Table 6.1 HK dollar, effective exchange rate index (trade weighted), 1975–88

Year	Old series (base December 1971)	New series (base October 1983)
1975	104.8	150.6
1976	108.6	157.4
1977	110.8	161.4
1978	99.4	146.1
1979	91.1	134.4
1980	90.8	133.7
1981	86.3	126.5
1982	85.5	125.3
1983	72.6	107.4
Sept	66.8 ⎫	98.7 ⎫
Oct	64.9 ⎬	96.1 ⎬
Nov	68.2 ⎭	100.9 ⎭
1984	71.1	106.6
1985	75.0	115.7
1986	66.3	110.1
1987	–	105.8
1988 (Jan)	–	101.6

Source: *Hong Kong Monthly Digest of Statistics*, Special Review, November 1987

As the figures indicate, the HK dollar reached its lowest point in September–October 1983. This was the outcome of a number of processes that had been in action before 1983, but the uncertainty surrounding the Sino-British negotiations concerning the fate of the colony after 1997 created a heavy speculative run. The confidence crisis spread to the property sector which had an immediate impact on the stock market. During 1982 the Hang Seng Index (HSI) fell from a high of 1,445.3 to a low of 676.3, a drop of more than 50 per cent. There were also panic runs on liquidity-strapped banks, a number of where were heavily overexposed to the property sector. As investors shifted currencies the pressure on the HK dollar mounted. The Government felt it essential to intervene in order to restore confidence in the currency, and hopefully, through a reverse domino effect, on the rest of the market. The intervention took the form of pegging the currency to the US dollar through the medium of the note issue and the Exchange Fund.

The Exchange Fund was first established in 1935 following the abolition of the silver standard in Hong Kong in order to provide the sterling equivalent backing for the currency of the territory. Up to that time the note issue of originally three banks but ultimately two, the Hongkong Bank and Standard Chartered, was backed by either silver or sterling securities. After 1937 there was no obligation to redeem notes into silver coins. The NIBs exchanged the proceeds of the sales of silver with CIs issued by the Fund. In a sense the fund became the equivalent of a colonial currency board providing the mechanism of 100 per cent convertibility of the note issue into sterling. However, the Fund did not guarantee a fixed parity.[12] Over the years the functions of the Fund diversified and extended. Following the floating of the HK dollar in November 1974 and the change of the rules whereby CIs were now purchased not with sterling but with HK dollars, the operational rules of the Fund changed as well. Whereas previously the Fund maintained only a small working balance in HK dollars with banks, it now opened up proper accounts with the two NIBs and it was also allowed to borrow HK dollars in the inter-bank market. The purpose of this changeover was to allow the Fund access to HK dollar funds in order to provide the reserves necessary to carry out its functions.[13] Its borrowing powers were extended in December 1981 in order to allow the Fund to operate more freely in the inter-bank market so as to influence interest rates.[14] In 1976 the Coin Security Fund which provided the backing for the coin issue and the 1 cent notes in terms of HK dollars and other assets was merged with the Exchange Fund.

An even more significant change took place during 1976–8 regarding the fiscal reserves of the Treasury held in either HK dollars or foreign currencies.

> The fiscal role of the Exchange Fund dates from a decision in 1977 to transfer to the Fund the Treasury's HKD balance (apart from working balances) against the issue of interest bearing Debt Certificates, the bulk of the Treasury's foreign currency balances having been transferred in 1976. Between 1972 and December 1981 the Exchange Fund's HKD assets (and some of the foreign currency assets) therefore comprised (a) the counterpart of accumulated budgetary surpluses i.e. the Government's fiscal reserves – and (b) HKD balances against the issue of CIs. When the Exchange Fund's borrowing scheme was introduced in December 1981 the HKD assets would have begun to reflect these transactions.[15]

Further variations in the role of the deposits of the Fund with the banks were introduced by 1979. The Fund could now arrange to have its HK dollar deposits treated either as inter-bank deposits, which under the liquidity regulations of the time required a 100 per cent cover, or as any other deposit, in which case the cover was reduced to 25 per cent.[16] It must be noted that under the 1986 Banking Ordinance no mention is made of this provision. Incidentally, even if the Fund did actively 'reclassify' its deposits in order to affect the liquidity of the banks, the effect of that would have been minimal given the totally free availability of bank-created liquid assets in Hong Kong. In July 1988 as part of yet another change in the functions of the Exchange Fund, the Treasury could be requested to open an account with the Fund and to transfer to it its working balances with the rest of the banking system. As already indicated the Fund had been the ultimate holder of budgetary surpluses but did not have a direct control or role over the Treasury's accounts with the banking system.[17] In July 1988, further changes were introduced in the relations of the Fund with the Hongkong Bank and the inter-bank markets. These will be examined in Section 6.5. The Fund is managed by the Secretary for Monetary Affairs and the staff of the Monetary Affairs Branch. There is also an advisory committee concerning the uses and composition of the Fund.

The total size of the Exchange Fund is perhaps the best guarded but best guessed at secret in Hong Kong. The Fund never publishes accounts nor gives figures, although the increases in its size can be calculated from the fiscal surpluses in any year. Ghose has presented a comprehensive series of estimates covering 1955–62 with the Fund's assets rising from HK$718 million in 1955 to HK$1,359 million in 1962: in 1967 its value was put at HK$350 million, in 1972 at HK$768 million and in 1977 at HK$15.5 billion.[18] In 1981 the estimated assets stood at HK$35 billion, of which HK$20 billion were fiscal reserves and the rest monetary. During the 1980s, a third of the assets of the Fund were kept in HK dollar deposits and the rest mostly in foreign government bonds or those of international financial institutions and foreign currency deposits including US dollars, sterling, yen, Deutschmarks and Swiss francs.[19]

The US dollar peg mechanism since 1983 is based on the arrangement of the note issue via the two NIBs, Hongkong Bank and Standard Chartered. The notes issued must be backed by CIs which can be purchased from the Exchange Fund for US dollars. The Fund will also buy back CIs for US dollars. The peg was effected by the Fund guaranteeing a fixed price of HK$7.8 worth of CIs for every US dollar surrendered, and vice versa, when the two banks purchased or exchanged their CIs for US dollars. Since now every additional HK dollar issued was backed by US dollars, any inflow or outflow of US dollar funds was likely to have a direct effect on the note issue and, by extension, on the liquidity of the banking system and on interest rates. However, the exchange rate in the open market was left free to fluctuate. The mechanism relied on arbitrage between the free market and the fixed rate of exchanging CIs for US dollars to bring the two rates in line. The two NIBs extended the pegged rate privilege to interbank transactions in US dollars but not to their transactions with the non-bank public.

Table 6.2 illustrates the cash arbitrage system in action and the expected effect on the money supply. The cash holdings of the banks and the public will expand or contract depending on the pressures in the free foreign exchange market and on the subsequent changes in interest rates. These variations will have an impact on the stock of money which in the case of Hong Kong

Table 6.2 The cash arbitrage system and the pegged exchange rate

Parity rate
US$1 = HK$7.80

Free-market rate appreciates to HK$7.60	Free-market rate depreciates to HK$8.00
Action	*Action*
1 Banks sell US$1 to an NIB and receive HK$7.80 cash; banks then buy back US$1 in the free market for HK$7.60, making a profit of HK$0.20	1 Banks use US$1 to buy HK$8.00 in the free market; they then sell HK$7.80 cash to an NIB for US$1, keeping HK$0.20 as profit
2 *Alternatively*, banks sell HK$7.60 in the open market receiving US$1, which is then sold to an NIB for HK$7.80 cash, again generating a profit of HK$0.20	2 *Alternatively*, banks sell HK$7.80 cash to an NIB for US$1 which they then sell in the free market for HK$8.00, again generating a profit of HK$0.20
Results	*Results*
1 To the extent that the NIBs use the US dollars acquired to print more HK dollar notes and the public end up holding more cash, the money stock may rise; the liquidity of the banking system will increase	1 To the extent that the NIBs obtain US dollars by surrendering cash (CIs) to the Exchange Fund and the public end up with smaller cash holdings, the money stock may decrease; the liquidity of the banking system will decrease
2 Demand for the US dollar will increase, leading to a rise in its free-market price	2 The free-market price of the US dollar will fall as more are supplied
3 The overall increase in liquidity may ease interest rates thus weakening further the free-market price of the HK dollar	3 Interest rates may rise as the result of reduced liquidity of the banking sector

is defined broadly as follows: M1 which consists of notes plus demand deposits with banks, M2 which consists of M1 plus bank savings, time deposits and non-negotiable certificates of deposit (NCDs) held by non-bank customers, and M3 which is M2 plus DTC deposits and NCDs held by non-bank customers. Table 6.4 in Section 6.6 shows the components of the money stock in greater detail.

6.4 The pegged system in operation

The system of foreign exchange rate support outlined above seemingly relied on the cash arbitrage between the free foreign exchange market with the two NIBs as intermediaries. The arbitrage under the rules of the system is open only to the banks, including the NIBs, but not to the general non-banking public.

The core of the mechanism, including the authorities' perception of the cash arbitrage, can be found in the statement of the Secretary for Monetary Affairs made at the time of the introduction of the peg:

> Following the agreement between the Government and the two note issuing banks, certificates of indebtedness which are issued by the Hong Kong Government Exchange Fund to the note issuing banks to be held as cover for their issues, will henceforth be issued and redeemed only against payment in US dollars, at the fixed exchange rate of US\$ 1 = HK\$ 7.80 . . . . To assist the smooth and equitable functioning of the arrangement, the note issuing banks have agreed with the Government that they should provide *notes* to, and accept them from, other banks on the same basis as they themselves deal with the exchange fund i.e. against payments in US dollars at the rate of US\$ = HK\$ 7.80 . . . . It should be stressed that the market rate will hold close to the announced rate without any need for increased transactions in bank *notes*. The mere fact that deposits are convertible (at maturity, where relevant) into notes and that HK\$ notes are ultimately convertible (via certificates of indebtedness) into foreign currency will, assisted by the forces of competition and arbitrage, ensure convertibility between HK\$ deposits and foreign currency deposits at a rate determined principally by the fixed rate for certificates of indebtedness, without any intermediate transactions in notes having taken place.[20]
> (author's emphasis)

Similarly the Hongkong Bank, the main note-issuing bank, informed other banks that

> The note issuing banks have agreed that they in their turn will require payment in US dollars where Hong Kong dollar *notes* are drawn from their Treasuries and will make payment in US dollars where Hong Kong dollar *notes* are deposited. For all

such transactions the prevailing parity will be used.[21] (author's emphasis)

It is important to note that the Government was at pains to point out that the arbitrage operation which would have kept the open market rate at US$7.80 would not come via cash (i.e. note) transactions, because of (a) the convertibility of the HK dollar deposits into HK dollar notes and (b) the convertibility of HK dollar notes into US dollars although not necessarily into US dollar notes. The latter qualification was also obvious from the specific instructions issued by the Hongkong Bank. US dollar payments for HK dollar notes and vice versa would be affected either through offsetting transactions with inter-bank accounts in the USA for US dollars or by an equivalent transaction in Hong Kong for HK dollars. No US dollar notes were to change hands.[22]

It is also important to stress that both the Secretary for Monetary Affairs and the Financial Secretary, in announcing the details of the link, laid great emphasis on the role of changes in interest rate. The implication was clearly that the outcome of the cash arbitrage would be changes in interest rates and it was the developing interest rate differentials which would affect the US dollar flows.

Unfortunately most of the premises on which the Government had based the system were not true, and indeed as events were to show the system did not work as expected. At the time of extreme pressure for revaluation during December 1987 to February 1988, the Government had to threaten to introduce the artificial and distorting measure of negative interest rates to relieve the pressure on the HK dollar. This is not to say that the pegged system was unsuccessful, because it was, and it has kept the HK dollar at the chosen parity. However, the mechanism established to do this did not work as expected.

The arbitrage operation has been outlined schematically in Table 6.2. In the case of an appreciation of the HK dollar in the free market, non-NIBs would be faced with two arbitrage options:

(i) arbitrage with the US dollar by obtaining HK dollars at HK$7.80 from an NIB, reselling in the open market to buy back US dollars and keeping the HK$0.20 difference per US dollar transacted.

(ii) arbitrage with the HK dollar by using them to buy US dollars in the open market at HK$7.60 and then selling US dollars back to an NIB at 7.80, again keeping the HK$0.20 arbitrage profit.

Banks using option (i) must have US dollar funds for arbitrage operations. These can be obtained as follows:

(a) switching existing US dollar deposits into arbitrage operations;
(b) borrowing US dollars in the inter-bank market;
(c) borrowing HK dollars in the inter-bank market and then switching the funds into US dollars;
(d) using their US dollar cash holdings.

In the first case the bank will exchange the US dollars for HK dollars with an NIB receiving HK dollars *cash* at the rate of HK$7.80. The bank can then purchase the US dollars back in the open market at HK$7.60, thus making a profit. To the extent that these transactions were for cash, the stock of money will increase as the non-bank public will swap US dollars for HK dollars cash. Alternatively, the public will end up with more HK dollar deposits and fewer US dollars. The results of case (b) are identical, except that the profit made will depend on the interest rate charged on the US dollar loan. Indeed, this is also the case with (a) because the bank will forgo the interest earned on lending the US dollar funds used for arbitrage. In case (c) the banks will use the borrowed HK dollars to purchase US dollars in the free market for HK$7.60. The US dollars will then be sold to an NIB for HK$7.80 cash, the loan will be repaid and HK$0.20 kept as profit. As with the previous cases, the interest charged will be crucial in determining whether the arbitrage is profitable. The bank will end up with more HK dollars cash and the stock of money will be affected to the extent that the NIBs printed more notes. Finally, in case (d) the bank will surrender the US dollars cash to an NIB in return for HK dollars cash at the rate of HK$7.80 and then use the HK dollars to buy back the US dollars in the open market at HK$7.60. The public may end up with more HK dollars cash if the bank bought the US dollars for cash. Otherwise, the bank will have more cash and the public will have more HK dollar deposits. The total amount of notes will rise by the amount of notes that the NIBs printed as they received dollars in exchange for HK dollars cash. The effects on the HK dollar interest rates would be to lower them as banks became more liquid or there was a net increase in the amount of HK dollar funds available to the inter-bank market.

In option (ii) banks can obtain the necessary HK dollars as follows:

(a) switching their existing HK dollar inter-bank deposits into arbitrage operations;
(b) borrowing in the HK dollar inter-bank market;
(c) borrowing US dollars and exchanging them for HK dollars;
(d) using their HK dollar cash holdings.

In cases (a) and (b) the banks will obtain US dollars at the free-market rate of HK$7.60. The US dollars obtained will then be surrendered to an NIB for HK dollars *cash* at HK$7.80 thus yielding a return of HK$0.20. Banks will now have fewer HK dollar inter-bank deposits and more HK dollars cash. In case (c) the banks will swap US dollars at an NIB for HK dollars at HK$7.80 and then buy back US dollars in the free market at HK$7.60. In cases (a) and (b) the public will end up with fewer US dollars and more HK dollar deposits or HK dollars cash, and the banks with more HK dollars cash. In case (c) the banks will sell the US dollars to an NIB for HK$7.80 cash, then buy back the US dollars in the open market at HK$7.60, repay the loan and make HK$0.20 profit. To the extent that this transaction is carried out for cash, the public will have more cash holdings and less US dollar deposits and the banks' cash position will be unchanged except for their cash profit. Otherwise the banks will end up with more cash and the public with more HK dollar deposits and less US dollars. In case (d) the banks will use their HK dollar cash to buy US dollars in the free market and then surrender them to an NIB for HK dollars cash. The banks' HK dollar cash holdings will remain unchanged except for the cash profit. The public will end up with more HK dollars cash rather than HK dollar deposits (and less US dollar deposits) if the banks choose to transact in cash. The effect of all these cases on the note issue, and by extension on the M1, M2 and M3, will depend on how many HK dollar notes the NIBs choose to print by purchasing CIs for US dollars from the Exchange Fund with the US dollars they received from banks, and the net change in the holdings of cash of the non-banking sector.

Exactly symmetrical arguments would hold if the HK dollar had depreciated against the US dollar in the open market. Option (i) would have banks using the US dollar to arbitrage by buying HK dollars in the free market and then exchanging them back for US dollars with an NIB at a profit. The exchange would have taken the form of surrending HK dollars *cash* with the NIB and receiving in return a US dollar deposit. Option (ii) would have involved arbitraging with HK dollars cash surrendered to an NIB in exchange for US dollars which would then be used to buy back HK dollars in the open market. The results of the arbitrage operation under these options would have led to a shortage of inter-bank HK dollar funds as banks ran down their liquid assets in an effort to obtain HK dollar notes. Also, the public would have ended up holding less HK dollars cash. This would have driven interest rates up which combined with the increased supply of US dollars, would have raised the price of HK dollars versus US dollars. The effect on the note issue would be contractionary to the extent that the NIBs cancelled out notes printed by exchanging CIs for US dollars with the Exchange Fund. Figure 6.1 outlines these sequences of events. It is important to note the complication introduced by the non-cash transactions between the banks and the public and the fact that the rules, if followed, must involve HK dollar *cash* transactions between the banks and the NIBs.

Taking both options (i) and (ii) together it is obvious that a number of conditions must hold for the arbitrage operations to work or take place at all. First, the expected return from arbitrage must be greater than either the alternative use of funds or the cost of borrowing. It would then follow that if interest rates were such as to make arbitrage operations profitable then the inter-bank market rates would be the first to be affected.[23] Second, to the extent that the arbitrage operations involve arbitraging with the HK dollar (i.e. option (ii)), inter-bank interest rates will move directly with the arbitrage transactions. Therefore, increases (decreases) in the demand for HK dollar inter-bank deposits will drive interest rates up (down) and thus make arbitrage less (more) profitable. Third, the outcome of some of the arbitrage operations will mean that banks end up with more cash. As this is a conscious policy decision it must be profitable at the margin. Reducing cash holdings may involve

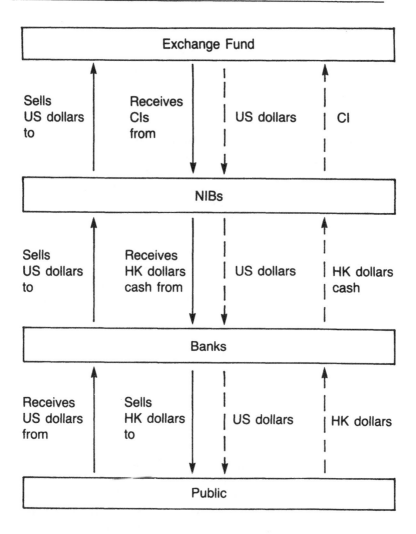

Figure 6.1 Summary of the cash arbitrage mechanism

Note: The solid arrows indicate appreciation of the HK dollar versus the US dollar. Exactly the reverse reasoning applies for depreciation, which is indicated here by the broken arrows. All transactions are based on US dollars.

increasing loans, but this may not be achieved quickly and may involve further interest rate adjustments.

In summary there are three key factors in this process of arbitrage:

(a) HK dollar *cash* transactions are an integral part of the chain, and under the official specifications cannot be bypassed or substituted by deposit transactions.
(b) The arbitrage process will affect the inter-bank market and hence inter-bank interest rates at some stage.
(c) The variations in the cash holdings of banks may or may not be reflected in those of the public, depending on whether the transactions of the banks with the non-bank public in the free foreign exchange market are undertaken for cash or through deposit transfers. The effects on the HK dollar stock of money will depend on whether the public has shifted in or out of US dollars to HK dollar deposits or HK dollars cash. The cost in terms of forgone interest rates will also be a factor in these switches. The effects on the note issue in general will depend on the reactions of the NIBs to the arbitrage operations.

The crucial question now hinges on whether the cash transactions just described did take place and how much they actually influence the interest and exchange rates.

6.5 An appraisal of the arbitraging process

To begin with the cash arbitrage operations are open only to banks and not to the general public. The arguments concerning the convertibility of HK dollar deposits into cash are therefore completely irrelevant except to the extent that banks (but not the DTCs, which were excluded from the scheme) could withdraw HK dollar inter-bank deposits in *cash* and then convert these into US dollars through the two NIBs. The existing clearing agreements preclude this possibility as all transactions are ultimately channelled through the ten settlement banks of the clearing system including the Hongkong Bank. The general public could not arbitrage the market through their own banks as the fixed conversion rate was available only to the banks, via the NIBs, and not to them. In other words, the convertibility of the

HK dollar bank deposits into HK dollars cash and cash into US dollars was appropriate only to inter-bank transactions. Indeed, even if the convertibility of the bank deposits could somehow have been shown to be relevant to this issue, the total of demand, savings and time deposits in HK dollars in 1983 stood at HK$124 billion. With time deposits excluded the total still stood at HK$74 billion, several times greater than the estimates of the Exchange Fund at the time. The Government could not have shown that it had the resources to back its promises, unless of course the resultant changes in interest rate would have been large enough to stem any flows away from the HK dollar.

Second, the cash arbitrage operation undertaken by banks would be limited to the extent that banks wished to maintain a minimum cash to deposit ratio. In other words, if banks switched out of HK dollar notes to US dollars, they would obtain more US dollar deposits rather than cash. The extent of this switch would be limited by the demand for HK dollar notes by their customers. Furthermore the banks may have found it unprofitable to maintain large cash holdings in periods of appreciation of the HK dollar in the free market. In any case the profitability of the arbitrage would always be restricted by the ruling levels of inter-bank interest rates.

Third, a technical hitch in the system was detected soon after its inception and caused a great deal of criticism and discussion at the time. It was claimed that the support system would create a two tier system whereby HK dollar notes would be at premium over deposits, at least as far as the banks themselves were concerned. It was then claimed that the existence of DTC subsidiaries of licensed banks would ensure that banks could always obtain HK dollar notes without having to surrender US dollars. Their DTC subsidiaries could open an account with one of the NIBs and then withdraw notes and transfer them over to the parent bank. Leaving aside the practicality of the scheme whereby banks would attempt to exploit the hour-by-hour fluctuations of the exchange rate via indirect cash transactions, this criticism, if anything, strengthened the argument for the irrelevance of the convertibility of deposits into cash. Again, the non-bank public could not arbitrage the market, only banks could do this, and even then only by cash transactions.

Finally, and more realistically, in setting up this mechanism the case had to be considered whereby banks could draw down their inter-bank balances in the form of cash, or even borrow in the inter-bank market, in order to use the arbitrage opportunities. Equally, banks could switch out of US dollars, obtain HK dollar balances and either lend them to banks which would switch them again into HK dollars cash for arbitrage in the free foreign exchange market or do the switching themselves. It would now follow that any such significant movements would alter the inter-bank interest rates sufficiently to cancel out the arbitrage benefits. This is a purely factual question. Did the banks use *cash* transaction in the free market when the rate of exchange diverged from HK$7.80? Unfortunately there can be no conclusive answer to this question. There are no figures for daily cash movements in or out of the two NIBs or of the daily cash positions of all the other banks. Even if there were, it would have been difficult to differentiate the normal cash transactions of banks, reflecting the actions of their depositors from those of purely arbitrage operations.

The motivation for banks to arbitrage depends crucially on the expected return. In the example given in Table 6.2 the appreciation against the fixed rate was of the order of 20 cents or equivalently 2.56 per cent on the parity. If a bank could make this profit on a daily transaction basis it would translate to an annual compounded return in excess of 10,000 per cent! Equivalently of course if the overnight rate at the inter-bank market was less than 10,000 per cent per annum, then the arbitrage would be profitable! These are, of course, extreme examples which simply set hypothetical limits to the arbitrage operations.

For the period November 1984 to January 1988, covering 51 months, the average free market rate stood at HK$7.8025 with a standard deviation of 0.0170 or equivalently a potential discount or premium on the parity price of 0.21 per cent. Since these are monthly data this translates back to an annual return of approximately 2.5 per cent. The figures are very broad and, as they are monthly averages of daily data, hide potentially greater variations and in particular intra-day fluctuations. During this period inter-bank interest rates ranged as indicated in Table 6.3. It would now follow that, on average, the expected returns on arbitrage since 1984 were likely to be below these rates making

198

arbitrage a potentially unprofitable activity except on a few occasions. These admittedly crude comparisons are further complicated by the possibility that the arbitrage may have also been part of a swap deal involving the HK dollar–US dollar forward market. There are no systematic data or studies on the efficiency of the HK dollar–US dollar forward market.

Table 6.3 Spread (minimum and maximum) of inter-bank interest rates in Hong Kong, 1983–8

| | Interest rate (% p.a.) | | |
	Overnight	7 days	1 month
1983	$\frac{1}{2}$–32	4$\frac{1}{2}$–30	6$\frac{1}{2}$–26
1984	$\frac{1}{2}$–48	1–39	3$\frac{1}{2}$–28
1985	$\frac{1}{2}$–12	2$\frac{1}{2}$–9	4–8$\frac{1}{2}$
1986	$\frac{1}{2}$–15	2–12	3$\frac{1}{2}$–9
1987	$\frac{1}{2}$–9	$\frac{1}{4}$–8.1	$\frac{1}{4}$–7$\frac{1}{2}$
1988	$\frac{1}{2}$–9.8	$\frac{1}{4}$–9.7	$\frac{1}{4}$–9.7

Sources: Hong Kong Monthly Digest of Statistics, various issues

Despite any potential imperfections of the forward market, covered interest rate arbitrage operations between the HK dollar and the US dollar would have been an additional factor bringing the spot rate nearer to the official level. In view of the repeated assertions by the Hong Kong Government that it would defend the parity level, it would be reasonable to assume that the forward rate would not deviate significantly from HK$7.80 level. Therefore, for example, if forward rates in terms of the HK dollar decreased (an appreciation of the HK dollar), then, given the level of inter-bank interest rates, the spot rate would be expected to appreciate. In practice, however, forward rates deviated quite frequently from the HK$7.80 level and this would have necessitated quite large adjustments in interest rates in order to bring the two exchange rates back in line. It would therefore appear that covered arbitrage operations were far from perfect, probably because interest rates did not change enough or because investors did not believe in the viability of the pegged system. However, the latter is an assertion that would only hold during periods of sustained upward or downward pressure on the rate, rather than reflecting day-to-day transactions.

A study by Chan produced evidence of the overall weakness of the arbitrage process.[24] The study postulates that there are two basic ways that the arbitrage effects will work through to the spot HK dollar to US dollar rate. First, the cash arbitrage process will cause changes in the note issue which will be reflected in the stock of money and therefore in the exchange rate. However, changes in the spot rates can cause the stock of money to change via the arbitrage operations already described. The model is formulated as follows:

$$\Delta M_t = a_1 + \Sigma b_i \Delta S_{t-i} + \Sigma c_j \Delta M_{t-j} \qquad (6.1)$$

$$\Delta S_t = a_2 + \Sigma d_i \Delta S_{t-i} + \Sigma e_j \Delta M_{t-j} \qquad (6.2)$$

where ΔM_t and ΔS_t are changes in the stock of money and spot rate and their appropriate lagged values over $t-i$ or $t-j$.

Second, a similar model could be formulated for the covered arbitrage operations, IRF_t, defined as:

$$IRF_t = \frac{1 + n(r_{US} - r_{HK})}{1 + n \; r_{HK}}$$

where r_{US} and r_{HK} are the appropriate US and HK interest rates and n is the maturity period of the forward contract. Here the covered interest arbitrage relation could be influenced by changes in the spot rate, but equally the spot rate could change because of the changes in the IRF. This model was specified as

$$IRF_t = A_1 + \Sigma B_i \Delta S_{t-i} + \Sigma C_j \; IRF_{t-j} \qquad (6.3)$$

$$\Delta S_{t-1} = A_2 + \Sigma D_i \Delta S_{t-i} + \Sigma E_j \; IRF_{t-j} \qquad (6.4)$$

The modelling of these relationships is simple in the sense that what is tested here is the potential flow of causality. The data used were the average monthly exchange rates from January 1985 to June 1988, the monthly figure for the money stock definition M1, M2 and M3, and the average monthly overnight and 1 month inter-bank rates for Eurodollars and HK dollars. In addition to estimating the statistical significance of each equation for differing lag variables, the Granger causality test was also applied to determine the direction of the influence. In general, the statistical tests indicated no significant causality between changes in the money stock and exchange rates and vice versa. Poor results were obtained in terms of the significance of the coefficients of equations (6.1) and (6.2). The causality tests were inconclusive for equations (6.3) and (6.4). However, there was some evidence that the US–HK 1 month interest rate differential was statistically significant in the context of equation (6.4).

Tests like the one described above using average monthly data of foreign exchange rates are likely to miss out the inter- and intra-day effects of interest rate differentials or the expectation effects of changes in the stock of money. However, this study indicates that there is no clear evidence that the cash and interest rate arbitrage worked in Hong Kong in the way they were expected.

There is some further interesting evidence on the weakness of the interest rate effect on the arbitrage operations and the spot HK dollar exchange rate. Hsu argued that, in view of the fact that the note issue in Hong Kong was controlled by private banks, there was no guarantee that the arbitrage profits would provide sufficient incentives for the banks to close the gap between the official and free market exchange rates.[25] Taking the period between November 1983 to December 1984, Hsu found that:

Of the fourteen months in this period there are only two months, December 1983 and January 1984, during which the exchange rate stayed closely to the official parity. From February to December 1984, the exchange rate tended to depart significantly from the official parity, and the departures were far greater than what could be explained by the transactions costs, i.e. the costs for individual banks to hold cash during their transactions with the Exchange Fund. Assuming that the annual yield on the assets held by the banks is as high as 20 percent and that each of the banks' transactions with the Exchange Fund takes one day to complete, the exchange rate would not have exceeded HK$ 7.804 or fallen below HK$ 7.796 per US dollar had the banks always arbitraged to take advantage of the gap between the market exchange rate and the official parity. The fact that the exchange rate more often than not fell in the range outside the limits suggests that arbitrage did not always take place and that the exchange system differs from a straightforward US dollar peg.[26]

Hsu went on to compare the movements in the spot rate with those of the note issue. Normally the arbitrage mechanism would have resulted in net increases in the note issue when the spot rate appreciated in comparison with the official rate and vice versa. However, there was no systematic evidence that this was the case over the sample period. This type of comparison is always suspect and inconclusive in view of the fact that the net amount of notes issued by banks will reflect their overall portfolio decisions, including the cash demands of their depositors and seasonal factors, and not just arbitrage operations.

As has already been explained, for the arbitrage mechanism to work cash transactions had to be effected so that banks could end up, in general, with greater HK dollar cash balances during periods of appreciation of the HK dollar exchange rate against parity and smaller balances during periods of depreciation. Therefore, one way of observing the arbitrage process at work would be to track the behaviour of cash balances in the portfolios of banks during the period of the linked exchange rate rather than variations in notes issued. The model's predictions are straightforward in so far as higher rates than HK$7.80 (i.e. the HK dollar depreciating against the US dollar) would be associated with lower cash ratios and vice versa. However, testing of this proposition would meet with considerable obstacles. First, the cash arbitrage would have to take place on a day-to-day basis, or even an hour-to-hour basis, in order to capture the profitable discrepancies. Leaving aside the physical impossibility of these transactions which would slow down the process and therefore make it more amenable to observation, there are no published figures for the daily cash positions of banks. At best there are end of month figures which, as has been indicated are susceptible to seasonal variations and factors unrelated to exchange rate movements. The sum total of cash held by banks, or the proportion of cash relative to either total assets or HK dollar denominated assets, may change because of unrelated portfolio decisions of banks, changes in customers' demands and so on. Furthermore, as was shown in the discussion of the options available to the banks according to Table 6.2, there was no way of predicting what would happen to the public's or the banks' cash holding in some of the cases outlined. Second, the published figures for cash holdings include those for the Hongkong and Standard Chartered Banks. During the arbitrage activities associated with an appreciation of the rate against parity the Exchange Fund will end up with more US dollar deposits and a greater amount of issued CIs. When non-NIBs surrender US dollars in the form of inter-bank deposits to the two NIBs, they will receive HK dollar cash in return. The NIBs will provide the cash by turning over US dollars to the Exchange Fund in return for CIs and then use these to print more notes. The NIBs now have equally matched positions in so far as the rise in their note issue (a liability) will be matched by a rise in CIs (an asset). As the NIBs themselves hold cash as part of their assets, the note issue could figure in both sides of their balance sheets. Hence the cash to asset ratios, which include the cash held by the NIBs, are likely to introduce an element of distortion in the overall aggregates. There is, of course, the separate issue of cross cash holdings, i.e. the Hongkong Bank holding notes issued by Standard Chartered and vice versa. As there are no separate figures for these, the question remains unresolved. These two banks may hold higher (lower) cash ratios during appreciation (depreciation) of the exchange rate as a consequence of their note-issuing activities rather than as a matter of choice.

Table 6.4 shows the results of a simple correlation analysis between the average monthly foreign exchange rate against the US dollar and the cash-to-asset ratio either in terms of the HK dollar denominated assets only or in terms of all the assets of all banks in Hong Kong. The total period examined here, which includes incidents of upward and downward pressure, yields a small, but non-significant, correlation coefficient with the right sign for HK dollar assets only. Only the subperiods of pressure are both significant and have the right sign. These are far from conclusive tests but they are broadly consistent with the predictions of the theory. For the total period, given an average exchange rate of HK$7.80, any movement of the cash-to-asset ratio would cancel out, resulting in a non-significant correlation coefficient. The signs of the coefficients for the appreciation and depreciation periods are correct and broadly significant. Therefore, if the cash-to-asset ratio behaviour of banks is any guide, its behaviour is consistent with, but not a proof of, an arbitraging posture during successive periods of upward or downward pressure on the parity rate. On the basis of both the broad evidence presented and the logical implications of the cash arbitrage mechanism it is difficult to believe that the pegged rate was maintained other than through interest rate movements.

Therefore, the question as to what could cause interest rates to change must remain.

Table 6.4 Correlations between the exchange rate (monthly average) and the cash-to-asset ratio of banks (end of month)

Period	Cash-to-asset ratio (HK$ assets only)	Cash-to-asset ratio (total assets)
Nov 1983–Jan 1988	−0.074 *	0.11 *
Apr 1984–Dec 1984 (depreciation)	−0.64	−0.59 **
Apr 1985–Oct 1985 (appreciation)	−0.90	−0.94

Source: Hong Kong Monthly Digest of Statistics, various issues
Notes: Periods of appreciation or depreciation were defined as at least 3 successive months or more during which the exchange rate was mostly or continuously either below or above HK$7.80.
* Not significant at 5 per cent.
** Marginally fails the 5 per cent significance test.

In the normal course of events an inflow of US dollars should drive local interest rates down as banks exchange US dollars for HK dollars from the two NIBs. Similarly, banks faced with a net switch from US dollars to HK dollars should be able to offer lower deposit rates. As Hong Kong does not have a central bank and the Exchange Fund does not deal with the general public, the interest rate movements must be caused by a different mechanism. The only possible and logical answer is that the Exchange Fund itself, either through the two NIBs or by guaranteeing their operations, buys or sells dollars in the inter-bank market. An inflow of US dollars would lead to a switch of HK dollars from the Exchange Fund to the accounts of other banks or their customers. This would increase liquidity and hence decrease local interest rates. Banks would acquire additional inter-bank HK dollar deposits equal to the US dollar deposits just generated through the switch. There is also the further possibility that existing US dollar deposits in Hong Kong would be switched to HK dollars. In this case the total amount of deposits (HK dollars plus US dollars) would not change. The reason for this is that the Exchange Fund holds its deposits with the banking system in Hong Kong just like any other private client. As will be shown below, this absence of a special treatment or classification of

Government deposits generated a host of problems. However, the Hong Kong Government has never admitted publicly that it operated in the foreign exchange market, but since the measures announced in July 1988 this has changed. A more probable version of the operations is that the two NIBs operated the system on behalf of the Government. There is anecdotal but no concrete evidence that the Hongkong Bank supported the peg by forward deals that maintained appropriate covered parity interest differentials, albeit in an imperfect forward market. Furthermore, the thin and shallow inter-bank market could easily be manipulated by relatively small movements of funds, thus allowing easier control of interest differentials. The complete dominance of this market by the Hongkong Bank made the task all the easier. However, the situation has been changing. In December 1987 the authorities in Hong Kong were forced to introduce a unique set of measures to stem the speculation on the upward revaluation of the HK dollar. The measures involved imposing an interest rate charge on banks' holdings of HK dollar inter-bank credit balances via the clearing mechanism operated by the Hongkong Bank. The aim was to discourage investors from holding HK dollars. There were two schemes which could be put into action: either a tariff of progressively higher penalty rates depending on the size of the inter-bank clearing balance or a flat rate charge. The penalty interest rate(s) would be calculated against an announced 'specified rate' and the sums so collected would then be passed on to the Government. The banks would be at liberty to pass the interest rate charge on to their customers. The purpose of the scheme was to introduce a uniform mechanism whereby banks could impose negative interest rates on the HK dollar balances of their depositors in order to discourage any further inflows into HK dollars. The HKAB introduced a separate scheme detailing the manner in which the banks themselves would pass the charge on to their depositors. The essence of the scheme was that current and savings accounts in excess of HK$1 million would be liable to charges. During periods when the negative interest rate scheme was to be enforced the banks would not accept HK dollar time deposits including swap deposits of less than 3 months' duration. Call deposits would not be accepted either.[27]

It must be stressed that to date the negative interest rate

scheme has not been activated. In other words the 'specified rate' was kept permanently at zero. However, the scheme remains in force and the authorities have indicated that they would activate it if circumstances warranted it.

The effects of a negative interest rate scheme on the Hong Kong economy in general and the money market in particular would be very damaging, irrespective of any effect it might have on the exchange rate. For a start, as the banks advised their clients, holders of balances in excess of HK$1 million would either have to place them on accounts in excess of 3 months or dispose of them altogether, presumably in other currencies. This would have led to a rapid switch to assets such as equities, CDs, commercial paper or cash which were not liable to the negative interest rate charges. Given the relative state of underdevelopment of Hong Kong's short term capital market, any large and sudden movement of funds was guaranteed to generate equally abrupt interest rate movements. Furthermore the HK$1 million rule was arbitrary and liable to widespread abuse by the simple expedient of opening up multiple accounts of less than HK1$ million under different names. Furthermore, the authorities were subject to a flood of requests for exemptions from charities, non-profit institutions, pension funds etc. There were also doubts over the legality of the negative charges imposed on customers, opening up the prospects of extensive litigation if the scheme was ever enforced. Finally, there were the unpredictable macro-economic effects of the imposition of charges. For example, banks wishing to avoid the administrative inconvenience and poor public relations involved in negative interest rates could attempt to reduce their clearing balances by extending their lending. Ultimately, this would have been a zero-sum game since, presumably, all banks would have attempted the same. The net effect would have been a surge in the HK dollar money stock leading to possible inflationary pressures, augmented by the falling interest rates. The property market might also have been adversely affected by rapid changes in mortgage interest rates or surge of speculative buying. The domestic economy would have adjusted by rising prices rather than by changes in the exchange rate.

The negative interest rate scheme was a hasty reaction to a serious pressure to revalue the HK dollar. Movements of short-term capital were dealt with by the introduction of a scheme which had potentially very serious long-term consequences on the real economy. Furthermore, the imposition of negative interest rates would have had to be short in duration given the nature of the speculative capital movements involved. The authorities could not have been serious in contemplating a repeated 'on-off' series of actions as the disruption in the money market would have been enormous. The absence of long-term capital market instruments and paper would have meant that the embryonic yield curve in Hong Kong would have been given several abrupt twists. Overall the scheme was one of display of determination rather than a seriously thought-through policy measure. There are signs, however, that even the authorities themselves believed as well and that they treated the negative interest rates incident as a period of breathing space which allowed them to bring forward a much more sensible set of policy measures and reforms.

In July 1988 the Monetary Affairs Office issued a new set of directives concerning the operations of the Exchange Fund through the Hongkong Bank. At the time the measures were widely believed to herald the first steps towards the establishment of a central bank in Hong Kong and therefore merit close scrutiny.[28]

The essence of these measures was an attempt to create a mechanism whereby the authorities could operate in the inter-bank market in order to influence the liquidity of the banking system, interest rates and therefore the exchange rate. The way this was done was rather convoluted and initially led to some misunderstandings as to the nature and purpose of the mechanism.

The Hongkong Bank is at the heart of the clearing system which was established and run by the HKAB. For the purposes of clearing the Hongkong Bank is called the Management Bank. There are nine additional banks, called Settlement Banks, which have to maintain a clearing account with the Bank. All the licensed banks in Hong Kong also have to maintain a clearing account with either the Management Bank or one of the Settlement Banks. Ultimately the Hongkong Bank enjoys a monopoly in the clearing system since it does not need to maintain a clearing account. It now follows that the net clearing balances (NCBs) of all the institutions, including also the DTCs who have to use the system indirectly, is reflected in the balance sheet of the Hongkong Bank. Until July 1988 the Bank had the additional privilege of interest-free loans in using the surplus clearing balances of banks but could charge penalty interest rates on those banks with a clearing overdraft.

The overall net clearing balance of the banking system has an important influence on interest rates. Surplus banks can lend funds in the inter-bank market and deficit banks can borrow them. Variations in the net supply of liquidity in the market will cause short-term interest rates to vary and will therefore affect the exchange rate of the HK dollar. In view of the monopoly position of the Hongkong Bank in the clearing system, and by extension in the inter-bank market, any variation in the composition of its balance sheet would also affect interest rates. It is on precisely this particular relationship that the measures hinged.

The Bank is now required to maintain an HK dollar account with the Exchange Fund, and the size of this account must be no less than the NCB of the rest of the banking system. If the account is less than the NCB, then the Bank would be charged an interest on the shortfall payable to the Fund. If the NCB is in debit (i.e. overall the banking system is effectively borrowing from the Bank) then again an interest charge will be levied. The interest rate to be charged will be based on either the BLR or the Hong Kong inter-bank offered rate (HIBOR), whichever is higher. Additional premiums can be charged over and above these rates.

The Fund can use the account which the Bank will maintain with it to settle its transactions with the Bank itself or with other banks. This means that the size of the account can be varied without any specific reference to the NCB and thus the Bank can be forced to undertake offsetting transactions if it does not wish to pay the interest charges on the shortfall.

Finally, under these new arrangements the Treasury will be required to hold balances with the Fund as well as with the rest of the banking system. This means that the source of HK dollars for the Fund's account, in addition to the Treasury deposits, will be the NCB of the banking system in the sense that the Bank will keep a sum not less than the NCB total in the account.

The accounting arrangements of the new scheme were simple.

The opening of the Bank's account with the Fund created a liability for the Fund which must be matched with an asset, and the asset here will be the HK dollar deposit of the Bank not less than the NCB. Variations in the NCB will be reflected in the account held with the Fund, but these variations will reflect changes in the inter-bank market. Except for the variation in the NCB, there are two other ways in which the assets of the Fund can change: first, by the issue or redemption of CIs as the note issue varies, and second by variations in the Government's budgetary surplus or the emergence of a deficit which is financed by the balances held by the Exchange Fund.

The situation for the Bank is equally simple in so far as the opening of the account with the Fund created an asset equally matched by the HK dollars deposited.

The crucial element in all these arrangements is the amount that the Bank must maintain in the account with the Fund. Under the previous arrangements, if the Fund intervened in the money market by buying or selling HK dollars, its actions were likely to have little or no effect. Supposing that the open market rate for HK dollars weakened from HK$7.80 to HK$7.82. The arbitrage process would have led to a decrease in the overall supply of HK dollar denominated funds, thus pushing inter-bank interest rates up. The Fund could have assisted directly in this process by selling US dollars or borrowing HK dollars. However, the problem with this form of action would have been that the Fund would have acted just like any other customer of the Bank. If it had bought HK dollars for US dollars, this would have led to a simple swap of deposits held within the Bank. Furthermore, as interest rates in the inter-bank HK dollar market tightened, customers of the Bank could have lent their HK dollar balances to other banks, thus increasing the NCB and relieving the pressure. The authorities summarized this situation following this type of open market operation by the Exchange Fund as follows:

> If, however, other customers of the Hongkong Bank are at the same time switching out of HK dollars into US dollars and to the extent that Hongkong Bank covers the short US dollar position by recouping the corresponding amount from the foreign exchange market, the tightness in the inter-bank market will inadvertently be relieved. Other customers of the

HKB may also be taking advantage of the high HK dollar inter-bank interest rates available by running down Hong Kong Association of Banks-type deposits with, or drawing down BLR facilities made available by HKB and placing those funds with other banks in the form of deposits which attract inter-bank interest rates. This again will unhelpfully relieve tightness in the inter-bank market.[29]

Under the new arrangements, however, open market operations of this type will have a more direct and unequivocal effect. In all its transactions with the money market the Fund may choose to instruct the Hongkong Bank to either credit or debit the account that it holds with it. For example, suppose that the Fund was buying HK dollars (selling US dollars) as part of a support operation; then there would be two cases to consider. If the HK dollar bought by the Fund came from the Hongkong Bank itself then its account with the Fund would be debited. This would cause its balance to fall short of the NCB. The Bank would then undertake an offsetting transaction such as borrowing HK dollars in the inter-bank market in order to reduce the NCB and avoid paying the penalty interest rate. Its action would be complementary to that of the Fund in so far as interest rates would rise. If non-bank customers attempted to shift their HK dollar balances to the inter-bank market in order to benefit from the higher interest rates, then the Bank would be obliged to neutralize the inflow by borrowing additional sums in the inter-bank market.

If the Fund had sold US dollars to bank X, then the Hongkong Bank's account with the Fund would be debited, but simultaneously the Bank would debit the clearing account held with it by bank X. The outcome here would be that the NCB would decrease matching the fall in the account held by the Bank with the Fund. The reduction in the NCB would force interest rates up. Again, any inflows of funds into the market, given the size of the Bank's account with the Fund, would lead to a rise in the NCB, thus forcing the Bank to undertake additional offsetting transactions. In essence the new arrangements have created a clearing balance for the Bank itself with the added financial penalty of interest rate charges if this balance is less than the NCB.

There is a further instrument which the authorities can use to influence interest rates, namely the deposits that the Treasury holds with the banking system:

> Under the new system, in addition to the bulk of the fiscal surplus, the Treasury is also required to maintain an account with the Exchange Fund and may be asked to transfer its balances in the banking system to the EF accounts in exchange for interest-bearing debt certificates. If funds are transferred from the Treasury's bank accounts to the Exchange Fund, the Hongkong Bank's account will be debited first and the Hongkong Bank will then debit the clearing balance of the banks from which the Treasury funds are transferred. This will lower the NCB and raise interest rate. A redemption of debt certificates by the Treasury will raise the net clearing balances and lower the interest rate.[30]

The total effect of these measures has been the creation of a basic framework to undertake open market operations. The Hongkong Bank, which is the key agent in these transactions, has now been deprived of the interest-rate-free loans from its clearing functions. Simultaneously the Bank has been made to carry the brunt of any adjustments relative to the NCB on the assumption that it will do so rather than pay the interest rate penalty of any shortfalls of its account with the Fund. The Bank also lost the interest-rate-free source of funds via its previous use of the NCB. In fact there is some evidence that the stock market's reaction to these measures was to mark down the price of shares of the Bank by an amount significantly higher than that of the rest of the market or than the prices of shares of other banks.[31] One estimate of the potential loss to the Bank of the interest-free use of the NCB put it at about HK$50 million per annum, which is relatively small compared with the bank's average profits.[32] The Bank still remains at the hub of the clearing activities. Even when the Fund deals with other banks, ultimately the clearing and adjustment process will come through the Bank. Therefore, to avoid any 'informational' advantage still accruing to the Bank, the Fund will disseminate to the money and foreign exchange market the size of the Bank's balance with the Fund at the close of the previous day and the net effect of operations on it carried by the Fund during the previous day. Therefore, for example, in the first disclosed operation in the market on 7 September 1988 the Fund undertook some unspecified transactions which resulted in a reduction of the Hongkong Bank's balance with the Fund by HK$150 million. This would have caused the Bank to undertake offsetting transactions leading to a reduction of an equivalent sum in the NCB and thus raising interest rates.[33]

The relative effectiveness of these measures will depend to some extent on the willingness of the authorities to pursue actively open market operations and allow for greater fluctuations in interest rates. In view of the failure of the cash arbitrage scheme to maintain the linked exchange rate during periods of pressure, this is a welcome change in the approach to monetary policy. That the authorities are now willing to follow through these measures was evidenced by announcements made during the budget speech of 1989. The Government intends to expand the open market operations by issuing short-term Exchange Fund bills:

> These bills will constitute direct, unsecured, unconditional and general obligations of the Government for the account of the Exchange Fund. Given that these bills would be used for monetary purposes, they would be for the account of the Exchange Fund and not for general revenue as in the case of Treasury bills elsewhere.[34]

The Government considered this an essential move in view of the fact that the assets presently available for trading in the Hong Kong money market are limited. In other words, the buying and selling by the Fund of these new government bills will be used to affect the liquidity of the inter-bank market and hence of interest rates. There were also further announcements that the operations of the Exchange Fund would be augmented by the possibility of opening a foreign exchange dealing desk and transactions would be carried out with other banks as well rather than with the Hongkong Bank only.

Inevitably, the July 1988 measures raised the question as to whether the authorities had taken the first steps towards introducing a central bank in Hong Kong. The necessity, or otherwise, of a central bank in Hong Kong has long been a hardy annual in discussions concerning the monetary policy of the territory.[35]

Given the reversion of the territory to the PRC's sovereignty in

1997, the deliberate establishment of a central bank before then seems unlikely as it may lead to the necessity for a delicate political decision. Setting up an institution independent of the Bank of China (BOC) group may appear provocative and, equally, letting a mainland bank assume the powers exercised at present by the Hongkong Bank on behalf of the administration may seem compromising from the point of view of the Hong Kong Government. Ultimately the question boils down to issues of practicalities. One approach has been to list the functions, duties and responsibilities of a central bank and then check off those which are or are not applicable to Hong Kong (monopoly of note issuing, lender of last resort, availability of discount window etc.) Equally, others have pointed out that the 'functions approach' may be irrelevant as far as Hong Kong is concerned, given the realities of the existing system. According to this view the key question is whether the Government can control the monetary base and hence high powered money stock.[36]

In the case of Hong Kong the list of functions and controls exercised by a central bank is partially fulfilled by the Hongkong Bank. As to the question of whether or not the monetary base is controlled, the answer must be a qualified negative for a number of reasons, the most obvious being the establishment of a pegged exchange rate regime. Once the authorities have decided on the level of the exchange rate, the stock of money must adjust to whatever level is necessary to ensure that the interest rates are such as to support that rate. Longer-term considerations will also include the inflation differential between Hong Kong and its major trading partners, and in particular the USA. First, there are no general reserve requirements imposed on banks and the liquidity ratio is purely precautionary rather than credit limiting. Second, the convertibility of HK dollar notes into US dollars at a fixed rate is available only to banks. To the extent that banks are obliged to convert bank deposits into HK dollar notes as demanded by their customers, the overall size of the note issue can be construed as being the bottom line as far as the simple definition of high powered money applies for Hong Kong. In this sense the total size of the note issue ultimately limits the lending activities of the banks subject to the precautionary cash-to-deposits ratio that the banks themselves determine, and subject to the amount of US dollars that the banks expect to be able to obtain in order to switch them into HK dollars cash. The latter qualification is crucial. Banks can always obtain as much cash as they want by offering US dollars to the Fund via the two NIBs. The Fund will simply issue CIs to the NIBs in return for US dollars and the CIs will back the additional note issue. Therefore, to repeat, the convertibility of HK dollar deposits into cash is limited only by the overall availability of US dollar funds to the market in general and to individual banks in particular. The Fund is assumed to have enough US dollar funds to back the HK dollar issue fully, but this consideration is relevant only in the case when banks offer HK dollar notes in exchange for US dollars. In other words, the Fund guarantees convertibility of HK dollars cash to US dollars at a fixed rate only to banks. Therefore, this aspect of convertibility is irrelevant to the general non-bank public. If the public wished to switch HK dollar assets (deposits or cash) into US dollars they could do so in the open market. The arbitrage mechanism would then ensure that this conversion would take place at the pegged exchange rate. Therefore, there are three 'convertibility' issues to be considered: the convertibility of HK dollars cash into US dollars at a fixed rate open only to banks, the convertibility of HK dollar assets to US dollar assets open to everyone and finally, the obligation of the banks to repay their deposits in HK dollars cash. It is in this last case that the note issue operates as high powered money, that is, switching HK dollar deposits into cash, and is subject to the availability of US dollar funds which the banks can convert into HK dollar notes. The Fund does not have the US dollar reserves to guarantee the convertibility of all HK dollar assets into US dollar at the fixed rate, but in any case this is irrelevant for the credit creation of banks. The next question which arises is whether the account that the Hongkong Bank holds with the Exchange Fund counts as part of the monetary base.

At one extreme would be the possibility that the Hongkong Bank could choose to pay the interest rate penalty and let its account with the Fund diverge from the NCB. More realistically, however, the NCB can vary independently of the wishes of the authorities and it is only through their actions and the Bank's reactions that the liquidity of the inter-bank market can be regulated. To the extent that the Fund can become the ultimate supplier of liquidity in the market, then the authorities have introduced an arrangement whereby they can affect interest rates and hence the lending activities of the banks, albeit through an indirect mechanism.

The issue of central banking can best be summarized in terms of the willingness of the authorities to control interest rates far more directly and to take the first tentative steps towards progressively involving the whole of the banking system in the exercise of monetary control, as opposed to the Hongkong Bank only. Perhaps the most important long-term effect of the July 1988 measures would be the creation of a more active short-term paper market in Hong Kong to complement the equity and the underdeveloped long-term bond market. In this sense the discussion over the creation of a central bank in the form of a 'revamped' Exchange Fund was not necessarily irrelevant, but the context in which it was being conducted perhaps was.

6.6 Determination of the stock of money and external flows

The links between the domestic money supply, the movements of foreign capital (i.e. US dollar inflows and outflows) and the operations of the Exchange Fund are straightforward once it is appreciated that before July 1988 the Fund operated as another private customer of the Hongkong Bank.

In a banking system with a central bank, inflows of US dollars will affect the domestic stock of money if the central bank stands willing and able to exchange US dollars for the domestic currency at a fixed rate. Of course, it is understood that commercial banks keep a part of their assets as deposits with the central bank. A bank which receives a US dollar deposit can exchange it in the market for an asset or deposit ultimately through a transaction with the central bank. The domestic stock of money will rise by an equivalent amount and, if deposits with a central bank are deemed reserve assets, then the capacity of the commercial bank to create additional deposits via lending will also rise.

However, in the case of Hong Kong in the pre-July 1988 period, the impact on the stock of money, could come via the note issue. Figure 6.2 illustrates the case of one of the banks with which the Exchange Fund holds deposits, here assumed to be the Hongkong Bank. An inflow of US dollars will increase the US dollar deposits and assets of the Bank. If the deposits are switched into HK dollars with a private customer then the total HK dollar deposits do not change as only the ownership of the HK dollar deposit is changed (transaction 1). If the switch takes place via the Exchange Fund, say through the Fund buying HK dollars from the public in the open market, again the sum total of HK dollar deposits remains unchanged (transaction 2). In the case of an inter-bank deposit in US dollars which is then switched into HK dollars via a cash transaction the stock of money will rise by the additional amount of cash that the Hongkong Bank had to print (transaction 3). Note, however, that the Fund's US dollar holdings will increase by the equivalent amount of US dollars credited to it by the Hongkong Bank in exchange for CIs. The additional cash will increase the liquidity base of the systems and may lead to additional lending by banks.

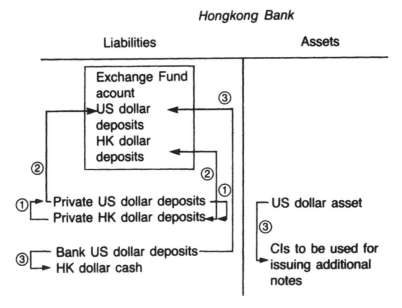

Figure 6.2 The Exchange Fund and the stock of money in Hong Kong

These considerations raise further technical issues on the determinants of the money stock in Hong Kong, some of which were discussed in the previous section. Given the linked foreign exchange system since 1983 a component of the domestic money supply is now related to the US dollar, and therefore, by extension, to the stock of money in the USA. Indeed Hong Kong has been called the fifty-first state, at least in monetary terms! This is not a particularly helpful approach for a number of reasons. First, the complications regarding the convertibility of HK dollar deposits into HK dollars cash has already been discussed. Second, since 1983 it is only the size of the note issue which is directly linked to the US dollar. As Table 6.5 shows, the cash component of the money stock in Hong Kong represents a fluctuating percentage of three definitions of money stock. As will be shown below, money stock multipliers in Hong Kong were not particularly stable over time.

Table 6.5 The money stock and its components, 1982-9

Year	M1			M2			M3		
	A	B	C	A	B	C	A	B	C
1982	27,485	94.9	43.8	206,688	58.5	9.4	250,240	59.6	7.6
1983	30,896	91.5	44.9	257,685	53.8	9.1	306,939	54.7	7.5
1984	36,791	90.6	39.7	314,081	54.9	7.6	374,879	55.5	6.3
1985	45,266	92.3	40.3	390,239	49.8	8.6	457,803	50.9	7.2
1986	56,094	91.9	37.3	518,131	45.8	8.1	582,208	46.4	7.1
1987	81,902	90.1	33.5	677,042	45.9	7.9	743,353	46.1	7.2
1988	88,834	89.2	37.6	824,648	43.0	8.4	893,342	43.5	7.6
1989	94,183	89.8	40.1	988,836	40.8	8.4	1,060,207	40.9	7.8

Source: *Hong Kong Monthly Digest of Statistics*, various issues
Notes: M1, notes and coin with the public plus customers' demand deposits with licensed banks.
M2, M1 plus customers' savings and time deposits with licensed banks plus NCDs issued by licensed banks and held outside the monetary sector.
M3, M2 plus customers' deposits with licensed and registered DTCs plus NCDs issued by DTCs and held outside the monetary sector.
A, the sum total of each money stock definition including foreign currency, where appropriate (HK$ million).
B, HK dollar component of A (per cent).
C, the amount of cash and coin in the hands of the public as a percentage of the HK dollar component of each definition.

Third, there are no reserve requirements for banks in Hong Kong except for a specified minimum liquidity ratio. Under the 1986 Banking Ordinance, as well as under its previous versions, cash was only one of the various assets in the imposed liquidity ratio. It would therefore follow that fluctuations in the cash available would not necessarily affect the banks' capacity to create deposits by lending. As indicated in Chapter 2, Section

2.4, the liquidity ratio contains assets which the banks themselves can create. Given the absence of both government bills or bonds and assets of a central bank in Hong Kong, the only constraint on deposit expansion was, and is, the demand for loans and the level of interest rates charged. In all fairness, however, it must be stressed that the authorities never claimed that the liquidity ratio was meant to operate as a reserve ratio. However, as the liquidity ratio has been the key obligation on the asset structure side of the banks, then it could have acted as a proxy for the reserve ratio. The capital adequacy (risk-weighted) ratio mentioned in Chapter 2, Section 2.1, is a further restraint on the asset distribution of banks, but its significance lies in its effects on the profitability of different types of lending rather than on the money stock multiplier.

There are a number of studies for Hong Kong which attempt to explore the size and determinants of the money stock multiplier. The standard multiplier model takes the following form.[37] Banks hold a proportion a of their deposits D in the form of reserve assets CB. In the case of Hong Kong the only truly exogenous 'reserve' asset is cash:

$$CB = aD$$

The public also holds a proportion γ of their deposits D in the form of cash CP:

$$CP = \gamma D$$

It now also follows that the total cash C (reserve asset) available is

$$C = CB + CP$$

The stock of money is now defined as

$$M = D + CP$$

Since

$$C = aD + \gamma D = (a + \gamma)D$$

and given that

$$M = D + \gamma D = (1 + \gamma)D$$

it follows that

218

$$M = \frac{1+\gamma}{\alpha+\gamma}C \qquad\qquad [6.1]$$

or

$$M = mC$$

where m is the deposits multiplier. It now also follows that

$$\frac{dM}{M} = \frac{mdC}{M} + \frac{Cdm}{M}$$

thus decomposing the percentage growth of the money stock into the cash or reserve component and its multiplier m.

This simplified version of the money stock determination has come under a considerable amount of criticism from the exponents of the so-called 'New View'. Most of the arguments in the debate are of some relevance to the case of Hong Kong.[38] The key element of the debate centred on the uniqueness of banks as credit-creating institutions, and by extension on the definition of money and on the fact that monetary authorities attempt, in general, not to control the monetary base but to influence interest rates. Monetary authorities set the level of interest rates and then provide the amount of C necessary to sustain it. Subsidiary issues in the debate included the stability of the multiplier m which of course depends directly on α and γ. Banks do not maintain the legally required ratio α exactly, i.e. they maintain excess reserves, and of course γ is influenced by interest rates, growth of income and wealth and all other factors which influence portfolio allocation.

In the case of Hong Kong some simple approximations of the size of the multiplier m can be given by calculating the values of α and γ. Table 6.6 gives a range of possible values with those for column 3 being the ones more likely to reflect Hong Kong's reality for a number of reasons. For a start, the interchangeability of current and savings accounts via simple electronic transfers means that the savings accounts, which yield interest and are used for transactions purposes, are perhaps the most relevant in terms of money definition. Second, accounts with DTCs, given the restrictions on both their minimum size and their time duration, are less likely to perform the transactions functions of the savings accounts with banks.

Table 6.6 The public's (cash-to-HK dollar deposits) × 100 ratio, 1982–8

	(1) HK dollar deposits (all institutions)	(2) HK dollar deposits (banks only)	(3) HK dollar savings accounts (banks only)
1982	8.45	10.60	18.48
1983	8.28	10.10	21.65
1984	6.87	8.40	20.03
1985	7.94	9.68	20.75
1986	7.87	9.04	19.69
1987	8.00	8.89	17.86
1988	8.61	9.51	25.11

Source: *Hong Kong Monthly Digest of Statistics*, various issues

Table 6.7 Banks' (cash-to-HK dollar savings deposits) × 100 ratio, 1982–8

1982	3.9	1986	3.1
1983	4.4	1987	2.8
1984	3.5	1988	3.5
1985	3.1		

Source: *Hong Kong Monthly Digest of Statistics*, various issues

$$\alpha = 0.034 \qquad \gamma = 0.205$$

$$M = \frac{1+\gamma}{\alpha+\gamma} = \frac{1.205}{0.239} = 5.04$$

Table 6.7 shows the banks' cash-to-HK dollar savings deposit ratios. Taking the average of the ratios from the figures in both tables yields

It must be stressed that in terms of equation (6.1) this is a complete hybrid as it does not reflect any of the M definitions used in Hong Kong. This multiplier figure broadly implies that over a 7 year period an increase of HK$1 in the cash issue would allow banks to increase savings deposits by about HK$5.0.

Peebles presented an extensive set of money multiplier calculations for Hong Kong classified in terms of M1, M2 and M3 and spanning a much wider period from 1965 to 1985, nearly 21 years.[39] Depending on the definitions and the time period chosen, the values range from 1.87 to 2.54 for M1, 5.04 to 11.05 for M2, and 9.89 to 11.99 for M3.

A study undertaken by Lee and Yao measured the impact on the changes in M1 and M2 of changes in the monetary base and in the equivalent coefficients α and γ.[40] Interestingly, the study covered periods of both fixed and floating exchange rates, thus allowing for the effect of a balance-of-payments constraint on the growth of money. Table 6.8 summarizes some of the results. In this study the monetary base, high powered money, was defined as being determined by external flows – the 'balance-of-payments' effect. Obviously the external constraint on the growth of money stock decreased during periods of floating exchange rate.[41]

Table 6.8 The monetary base and its impact on money stock 1961–78 (per cent of the change attributable)

	1961–72 (fixed exchange rate)	1977–9 (floating)	1971–8 (1971–4 fixed, 1974–8 floating)
M1	78.2	57.3	71.9
M2	75.6	50.2	70.2

Source: S.Y. Lee and Y.C. Yao, *Financial Structures and Monetary Policies in Southeast Asia*, London: Macmillan, 1982, p. 238
Note: Although the study does not specify this explicitly, the monetary base is assumed to be the amount of cash in circulation with the public.

The July 1988 measures introduced a new variable in the form of the NCB account of the Hongkong Bank with the Exchange Fund. Although this could be construed as a reserve asset which enters the multiplier formula, its use is dictated by foreign exchange consideration. To repeat the obvious, the authorities can either fix the exchange rate or the stock of money, but not both. However, the exact mechanics of the relationship are more complex in the case of Hong Kong, and the variables entering the money stock multiplier do not appear to be stable over time.

6.7 The pegged exchange rate and the monetary–fiscal policy mix

The system outlined in Section 6.5 backing the pegged exchange rate is supposed to work automatically on interest rates via changes in liquidity and the stock of money. Since 1983 the key element in Hong Kong's monetary policy has been the maintenance of exchange parity. Fiscal policy was expected to play a purely neutral role in so far as the Government attempted to balance the budget or use the resultant surpluses to add to the reserves which then helped to sustain the pegged exchange rate. However, the existence of persistent surpluses in the Government's budget does have implications for the level aggregate demand and therefore for the exchange rate. The institutional arrangements in Hong Kong concerning the Government balances, the accumulated fiscal surpluses held with banks and the use of these balances have important monetary and policy implications. In this section we outline the impact of fiscal policy in Hong Kong focusing on the monetary implications and its influence on the exchange rate.

Fiscal policy can be expected to have an impact on an economy in two ways: on a microeconomic basis by changing relative prices of goods or factors or shifting sectoral or regional balances and on a macroeconomic basis by affecting the level of aggregate demand. Hong Kong's experience with fiscal policy has been primarily in terms of the Government's efforts to maintain a balanced or a surplus budget in the context of minimum intervention and low taxes.

Elementary macroeconomic analysis shows that balanced budgets do have an impact; they are not neutral. Although the standard 'textbook' balanced budget multiplier with a value of 1 is too simple and rests on too many unrealistic assumptions, at least it draws attention to the possibility that even modestly balanced budgets will not leave the level of economic activity unchanged. In the case of Hong Kong, the absence of large government debt and the fact that the Government hardly ever needed to borrow also meant that the monetary impact of fiscal policies was likely to be small. If a budget deficit is met by borrowing from the banking sector, then fiscal policy is not only expansionary in itself, but by causing the stock of money to rise generates a secondary monetary impact as well. The exchange rate policy of the authorities would also determine the extent of this monetary impact. The effects on the stock of money of fiscal measures could be either sterilized or allowed to have an impact depending on the exchange rate regime. The existence of a large amount of government debt, as opposed simply to the government borrowing occasionally, can generate wealth effects via changes in interest rates or expectations about inflation. Again, in the case of Hong Kong where only about HK$1 billion of government bonds were in existence and were hardly ever traded, the wealth effects must have been very small. As has already been shown in Section 6.6, institutional arrangements in Hong Kong have meant that the monetary impact of fiscal policies was likely to be defused since the absence of a central bank made the public sector just one more customer for the banking system in general and the Hongkong Bank in particular.

The arrangements behind Hong Kong's pegged exchange rate were supposed to influence interest rates through a quasi-automatic system of cash arbitrage. Use of the Mundell–Fleming open economy model allows a systematic evaluation of the options open to Hong Kong's policy makers. In Figure 6.3 an increase in aggregate demand caused by, say, a decrease in the Government budget surplus would shift the IS curve to IS'. Given the pegged foreign exchange against the US dollar and the reasonable assumption of perfect capital mobility from the point of view of Hong Kong, domestic interest rates would rise to r' and the level of income to Y_1. The BB curve is drawn at the level of international interest rates r' and, specifically, the Eurodollar rate. The higher interest rate differential $r' - r$ would now cause a capital inflow which, unless sterilized, would increase the domestic supply of money. This would cause the LM curve to shift to LM', lowering interest rates back to r and causing income to rise to Y_2. Exactly the reverse reasoning would apply if the Government increased its budget surplus, with interest rates falling and then rising as a consequence of the capital outflow. The inflows or outflows of funds would generate pressures on the IIK dollar to US dollar fixed rate, opening up cash arbitrage possibilities. The effect of these arbitrage operations would then be reflected in inter-bank interest rates and possibly in the overall liquidity of the banking system. Given enough time and sufficiently persistent arbitrage activities, the amount of bank loans, and hence deposits, could be affected. The arbitrage system, as shown in Section 6.4, never really worked in this way for a number of reasons including imperfections in the cash arbitrage between the official and the open foreign exchange market and the relatively large interest rate differentials necessary to have made arbitraging profitable.

Second, and more pertinently to fiscal policies, the existence of

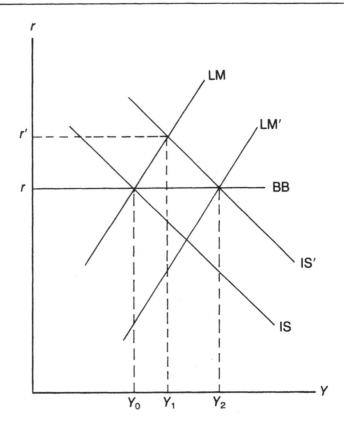

Figure 6.3 Fiscal–monetary policy mix

surpluses in the Government budget did not translate back to movements in the stock of money. In the context of Figure 6.3 an increase in the budget surplus would have shifted the IS curve downwards and, if the surplus was not allowed back into the money stock, the LM curve upwards. In Hong Kong the budgetary surplus accumulates as claims against either the domestic private sector or overseas entities. As the Hong Kong Government has virtually no debt to repay, the surplus simply increases its assets rather than decreases its liabilities.

Under the present institutional arrangements variations in the size of the budgetary surplus held with the Exchange Fund would have very little or no impact on the stock of money. The financial and money statistics in Hong Kong do not differentiate between private and public sector deposits, and to some extent, neither do the liquidity ratio regulations.[42] However, there are some distinctions that need to be clarified. For example, one source states:

> There is one important and outstanding problem with the deposit figures as collected. They still include money balances of the authorities which are not strictly deposits of the non-bank public. Nor is it clear whether the deposits which the authorities hold at short term and which are subject to 100% liquid asset cover, are reported in the statistics as part of the ordinary deposits total or whether they are recorded in the interbank liability items.[43]

Another source makes a different claim but offers no source for verification:

> Unfortunately the Hong Kong Government has chosen not to publish the level of its deposits in banks. Analysts are told only that the Government deposits with seven days or less to maturity are subtracted from demand deposits in calculating M1, so that the M1 figure is accurate in this respect. That is, M1 will fall when government deposit levels rise, and vice versa. But the other money measures are faulty at present because the government deposits are not excluded from the totals.[44]

Although the present 1986 Banking Ordinance does not mention the 100 per cent liquidity ratio rule in the specified liquid assets, it is understood that the short-term deposits of the Exchange Fund with any bank still require 100 per cent liquid reserves, although the deposits of other government departments do not. Shifting government funds from short- to longer-term deposits would change the liquidity requirements. Whether the Government did alter the time maturity of its deposits deliberately or not is not known, but if it did it would be unlikely to have been effective in view of the excess liquid reserves carried by the banks as a whole in Hong Kong. In any case, the liquidity ratio was never imposed as a form of credit control but as a safeguard for depositors.

Subject to this caveat, it would now follow that increases in the budget surplus would not cause the money stock to change as deposits from the private sector would shift to the Government with no other change in the liquidity position of the banks. Even if the Government was to hand back the surplus in the form of a tax rebate, the stock of money would remain unchanged. However, the Government may shift out of HK dollars to other currencies. This change in the composition of its portfolio would affect Hong Kong interest rates and hence aggregate demand. It would not, however, affect the HK dollar definition of money stock as the Government would have had to purchase US dollars or other currencies by exchanging its own holdings of HK dollars. The question of the note issue is a separate one, but in any case notes account for a small percentage of the total money stock and, for all intents and purposes, they are irrelevant in the cash arbitrage mechanism. The July 1988 measures did not change these conclusions significantly. As described above, the account which the Hongkong Bank is to maintain with the Exchange Fund varies with the size of the NCB of the banking system. Its variations are meant to influence inter-bank liquidity and hence interest rates. The size of the budgetary surplus is, of course, completely incidental to any day-to-day variations in the level of interest rates and therefore of the exchange rates. Under the new arrangements the Treasury will also maintain a balance with the Exchange Fund. To the extent that this arrangement may provide the Exchange Fund with additional funds to influence the inter-bank market, this will help the exchange rate policy of the authorities but there will be no direct impact on the money stock.

It is important to reiterate, however, that, unlike systems with a central bank whose liabilities are reserve assets, Hong Kong's supply of money is not linked directly to the borrowing (or loan repaying) activities of the Government. Hence the monetary impact of the surplus in terms of affecting the stock of money, the interest rates and therefore the exchange rate is indirect through the operations (if any) of the Exchange Fund.

6.8 Measuring the budget surplus or deficit

A considerable amount of creative accounting needs to be undertaken in order to arrive at a figure of the deficit or surplus in overall government spending in Hong Kong. The standard

figures given in the *Hong Kong Annual Digest of Statistics* cover
the General Revenue Account, but they are deficient for a
number of reasons.[45] First, the figures on both revenue and
expenditure exclude those of the Urban and Regional Councils
and the Housing Authority. Although these bodies have financial
autonomy they are none the less an integral part of the public
sector. Second, certain items in the General Revenue Account
are rather arbitrarily classified as revenues or expenditures. For
example, proceeds from the occasional government loans are
included in the revenues. Loans can be seen as the residual of the
difference between expenditures and taxes and other forms of
non-tax inflows, rather than revenues. The acquisition by the
Government of an equity stake in the Mass Transit Railway
Corporation (MTR) is classified as expenditure. Some authors
prefer not to treat these equity contributions as part of
government expenditure, although it can be argued that they are
a form of investment indistinguishable from expenditure on
building hospitals or roads. Finally, and most importantly, in
order to arrive at the surplus or deficit position of the whole of
the public sector rather than just 'central' Government, so to
speak, a number of further adjustments need to be made.
Specifically, the General Revenue Account includes transfers to
the Capital Works Reserve Fund (CWRF), the Development
Loan Fund (DLF), the Home Ownership Fund (HOF) and, as
already indicated, the MTR. The CWRF was set up in 1982 for
the express purpose of financing public works and acquisitions of
land. The CWRF tended to accumulate surpluses over a period
of time which did not appear in the General Revenue Account,
although the source of these surpluses was the general revenue of
the Government. In order to arrive at a more accurate estimate
of the overall surplus or deficit, these surpluses must be added
back to the General Revenue Account. The sums involved can be
quite significant, thus changing the size of the surplus and
therefore the overall fiscal stance of the Government. Therefore,
for example, for the 1988–9 estimates the General Revenue
Account showed a surplus of HK$5.5 billion which increased to
HK$7.3 billion when the surpluses of the CWRF, the HDF etc.
were added. Indeed, by the end of fiscal year 1987–8 these funds
had an accumulated total surplus of HK$14 billion.[46]

The revised and more accurate Consolidated Account Balance

therefore contains the General Revenue Account expenditures less any receipts from loans classified as revenues, less any payments for equity for MTR plus all the relevant expenditures of the Urban and Regional Councils, the Housing Authority, the CWRF, the DLF and the HOF, subventions to the private and quasi-private sector and expenditures on public works financed by the Asian Development Bank. Similarly, to arrive at the overall surplus or deficit, the revenues on a consolidated basis must be subtracted from the consolidated expenditures adding back the surpluses (or deficits) of these separate funds. Table 6.9 shows the overall consolidated surplus or deficit over a 10 year period. On average the surplus represented about 2.6 per cent of GDP.

Table 6.9 Surplus (+) or deficit (−) in the Government's budget (consolidated accounts in HK$ billion), 1977–87

1977–8	+2.1 (3.0)	1982–3	−0.5 (0.3)
1978–9	+1.7 (2.2)	1983–4	−2.2 (1.0)
1979–80	+2.7 (2.5)	1984–5	+1.8 (0.7)
1980–1	+11.0 (8.0)	1985–6	+4.3 (1.6)
1981–2	+8.3 (5.0)	1986–7	+7.7 (2.5)

Sources: *Hong Kong Annual Digest of Statistics*; H.C.Y. Yo, in H.C.Y. Ho and L.C. Chan (eds) *The Economic System of Hong Kong*, Hong Kong: Asian Research Service, 1988, pp. 18, 36

Notes: Numbers in parentheses denote the surplus or deficit as a percentage of GDP. All numbers and measurements at current market prices (1977–87).
As fiscal years start in April the comparison with annual GDP figures is an approximation. Since 9 months of any fiscal year are in the first calendar year of these figures, calculations are undertaken on that basis. Therefore, for example, the ratio of surplus to GDP for 1977–8 uses the 1977 GDP figures.
Overall average contribution to GDP is 2.69 per cent.

Purely for comparison, Table 6.10 shows the surplus or deficit of the current account of visible and invisible trade as a percentage of GDP. Although the trade figures generally contribute a larger percentage, the overall average of both surpluses/deficits is not widely different.

Table 6.10 Surplus (+) or deficit (−) in the current account balance (visible and invisible) as a percentage of GDP (current prices), 1977–87

1977	2.32	1982	−3.63
1978	−3.56	1983	−2.01
1979	−2.90	1984	4.20
1980	−4.59	1985	5.68
1981	−5.60	1986	4.57[a]
		1987	5.40[a]

Sources: *Hong Kong Annual Digest of Statistics*, 1987; *Economic Background 1987*, Economic Services Branch, Hong Kong Government, 1988
Notes: Overall average contribution to GDP irrespective of sign: 4.0 per cent. [a] Preliminary or provisional estimates.

6.9 Measuring the fiscal impact: a simple approximation

A simple model of national income determination, disregarding the monetary sector as the interest rate effect will simply reduce the overall size rather than change the sign of the multiplier, yields

$$Y = \beta(Y - T) + G + (X - \mu Y) + Z$$

where $T = tY$, T is taxes, t is the marginal propensity to tax, β is the marginal propensity to consume, μ is the marginal propensity to import so that imports $M = \mu Y$, G is government expenditures, X is exports and Z represents all other expenditures. If it is assumed that $dT = Y dt + t dY$ and that $dT > dG$ by a factor X^*, where $X^* > 1$ (i.e. the Government plans for a budget surplus) so that $dT = X^* dG$, then

$$\frac{dY}{dG} + \frac{dY}{dt} = \frac{1 - \beta X^*}{1 - \beta + \mu}$$

If now $\beta X^* < 1$ then the overall effect of the surplus will still be expansionary. The explanation for this is straightforward. If an additional dollar of tax revenue reduces demand by β (the marginal propensity to consume) but the Government proceeds to spend more than (HK$ $\times \beta$) but less than one dollar, then it will still generate a surplus but the overall expenditure in the economy will have risen. Table 6.11 shows the average and the marginal propensity to surplus for Hong Kong in the last 17 years. The table contains two sets of figures. R/G and $\Delta R/\Delta G$

refer to the average and marginal propensities to surplus out of total revenues whereas T/G and $\Delta T/\Delta G$ are the average and marginal propensities to surplus out of tax revenues only. In the context of this very simple model the relevant figure should be $\Delta T/\Delta G$ since in the case of Hong Kong a substantial proportion of government revenues come from the sale of land which is a purely commercial transaction. The figures in Table 6.11 yield a value of X^* based on taxes equal to 0.36 and a value of X^* based on revenues in general equal to 0.79. Existing estimates for the marginal propensity to consume in Hong Kong put the long-term value at about 0.7. This yields an estimate of βX^* based on taxes of about 0.25 (or based on all revenues of 0.55).[47] Therefore, the possibility exists that the surplus in the budget can contribute positively to aggregate demand. This may be particularly important in Hong Kong when larger surpluses materialize following years of rapid growth. The surplus may therefore act counter-cyclically.

Table 6.11 The average and marginal propensity to surplus in the consolidated budget, 1970–87

	R/G	T/G	$\Delta R/\Delta G$	$\Delta T/\Delta G$
1970–1	1.26	0.73		
1971–2	1.23	0.72	1.08	0.70
1972–3	1.29	0.76	1.50	0.88
1973–4	1.09	0.68	0.41	0.42
1974–5	0.93	0.56	0.44	0.20
1975–6	1.06	0.66	−6.48	−5.16
1976–7	1.13	0.71	1.73	1.09
1977–8	1.22	0.71	1.61	0.70
1978–9	1.14	0.67	0.89	0.56
1979–80	1.17	0.66	1.26	0.63
1980–1	1.50	0.64	2.29	0.58
1981–2	1.28	0.59	0.63	0.42
1982–3	0.98	0.53	−0.42	0.25
1983–4	0.94	0.53	0.42	0.60
1984–5	1.04	0.59	4.16	2.37
1985–6	1.10	0.67	1.71	1.51
1986–7	1.15	0.69	1.53	0.11
Average (st. dev.)	1.14 (0.13)	0.65 (0.06)	0.79 (2.12)	0.36 (1.52)

Source: H.C.Y. Ho, in H.C.Y. Ho and L.C. Chan (eds), *The Economic System of Hong Kong*, Hong Kong: Asian Research Service, p. 18
Note: G is total Government spending, R is all revenues and T is tax revenues only; the Δ calculations are the changes over the previous period. Figures adjusted as indicated in the text.

It must be stressed that this numerical estimate is no more than an approximation. A number of simplifying assumptions underlie these results. First, the model estimates impact rather than dynamic multipliers. There is no time pattern or any measurement of the length of periods involved. Second, the tax system is assumed to be proportional to income. This is true to some extent in Hong Kong where the average and marginal tax rates merge, but it is not true for all levels of personal income and family circumstances. Indirect taxes can also be expected to vary with GDP, but this is not necessarily the case for flat fees and levies. The feedback from the external transactions is allowed only via a very simple import demand function dependent on income. Last but not least, different types of government expenditures will have different macroeconomic impact.

These modifications, if allowed for, would change the results but would be unlikely to yield very different conclusions from the ones arrived at, namely that there is reason to believe that the budget surplus in Hong Kong may have an expansionary effect on aggregate demand. The actual size of this impact, however, may well be small and its limited monetary effects are unlikely to have short-term or even medium-term effects on exchange rates.

6.10 Conclusions

If an attempt was made to summarize Hong Kong's monetary and fiscal policies in the 1980s, then six words would suffice: exchange rate stability and fiscal surpluses. The success or failure of these policies can be analysed under two separate headings: first, the degree by which the policies were beneficial for the economy of Hong Kong, and second, the success of the instruments chosen to execute these policies.

Taking the simpler and more straightforward of the policies first, that of fiscal surpluses, its influence on the economy of Hong Kong is likely to have been stabilizing. As indicated, under certain circumstances surpluses may have had an expansionary effect on the economy but, as shown in Section 6.9, their impact was likely to have been small. A study of the macroeconomic impact of fiscal policies in Hong Kong concluded that:

A comparison of the budget balances with changes in per

capita real GDP shows that for most years the budget provided some offsets to changes in private sector demand. Budget surpluses were realised mostly in periods of rapid economic growth while deficits were incurred in the depressed years of 1974/75 and 1982/83. However the actual budget balance is not an accurate indicator of the macroeconomic impact of government revenue and expenditure since each item in the budget may differ in its ability to generate or destroy income. A weighted budget balance, obtained by giving weight to each budget item to reflect its macroeconomic impact may give a different picture.[48]

It is important also to stress that the policy-makers in the Hong Kong Government viewed fiscal policy primarily in terms of prudence and neutrality rather than as an active instrument of intervention. The ability to accumulate surpluses allowed (or excused) reducing both profit and income tax and maintaining them at low levels. The accumulated surpluses deposited in the Exchange Fund were meant to be used in periods of deficient growth in revenue or to undertake large-scale infrastructure works.[49] The overall size of the public sector in Hong Kong has remained fairly constant in relation to real GDP and in any case never exceeded 20 per cent.[50] Therefore, even if the authorities had wished to use public sector expenditures or taxes as macroeconomic instruments, it would have required significant variations for the impact to be of any importance.

The question of the success of the monetary policies pursued in Hong Kong raises much wider issues. The pegging of the exchange rate has been a controversial policy decision for a number of reasons. First, it meant that the authorities had little or no control over the stock of money and of interest rates. Second, the defence of the peg forced the Government to take extreme policy measures, although mercifully, it did not have to implement them (negative interest rates). Third, the existence of the peg may very well have caused some of the speculative runs that the peg was supposed to have avoided. Speculators may always decide to test the resolution of the authorities and this can become a game of bluff and counter-bluff. So far the Hong Kong government has indisputably won the battles. It would now follow that an appraisal of the pegged exchange regime must take into account the costs and benefits of the policy decision including all the intangible ones. Perhaps the toughest test of the policy came in the aftermath of the events of May–June 1989 in China when the exchange rate of the HK dollar did not come under any noticeable pressure. The authorities were quick to point out the very tangible benefit that this must have had on confidence at a time when any good news was badly needed. As indicated, however, one of the reasons why the pegged exchange rate survived this test was that massive deposit withdrawals from the Bank of China group had forced it to sell a large amount of US dollars in the market in order to raise the HK dollars necessary to honour the deposits being withdrawn. Therefore, in a sense one form of panic action (plus protest gesture) helped to offset another potential panic reaction (a real run on the HK dollar). However, there is a fair amount of empirical evidence that allows some approximation as to the costs and benefits of the pegged exchange system. The evidence is neither exhaustive nor conclusive, but it casts an interesting light on this controversial issue. Two particular areas are examined here: the effect of the peg on Hong Kong's exports and on the rate of inflation.

Given Hong Kong's export-driven economy it could be argued that a stable exchange rate, at least against a major trading partner, would benefit export performance. There are several arguments for this proposition, the major one being that it reduces uncertainty over expected export revenues and establishes orderly prices in the buying country. However, the empirical evidence on this issue is far from conclusive. A study of Hong Kong's export performance over 1977–84, covering a period of both floating and US dollar pegged exchange rate regimes, showed that indexes of exchange rate variability had no effect on export demand.[51]

A variation of this argument for the peg has been that the depreciation of the US dollar against all major currencies over 1986–8 had benefited Hong Kong's exports by maintaining US dollar prices in the USA stable and by making them relatively cheaper than competing exports from other newly industrialized countries. However, this argument is reversible, in that any appreciation of the US dollar will have the opposite effects. But even here the evidence is less than encouraging. Estimates of the elasticities of demand of Hong Kong's export volume were greater than 1 for the USA but less than 1 for the UK and the FRG. In general, the level of gross national product (GNP) of the importing countries was a more important export-determining variable.[52]

However, intriguing results were obtained in a number of studies examining the impact of exchange rates on textile and apparel imports to the USA over a number of periods between 1977–86.[53] These findings are quite important for Hong Kong as textiles and apparel are major export commodities to the USA. The study casts doubts on previous findings whereby changes in nominal exchange rates had little or no impact on imports of textiles etc. to the USA. These findings are reversed when real exchange rates (i.e. nominal rates adjusted for the differences in price levels amongst trading countries) are used instead. This conflicting evidence can be looked at in two different ways. It can be claimed that, if exchange rate movements did not influence textile and apparel imports to the USA, then the linked exchange rate system did not make any difference to Hong Kong's export performance to the USA. This conclusion is based on the evidence that exports to the USA from countries whose exchange rates did change against the US dollar did not appear either to benefit or to suffer as a result. If exchange rate movement did influence imports to the USA, then Hong Kong's exports had a relative advantage over imports from countries whose exchange rate rose against the US dollar but not against those whose rate fell. If the US dollar appreciates after its long decline over 1986–8 then exports from Hong Kong to the USA are likely to suffer as they will lose this relative price advantage.

It must be stressed that these are far from conclusive results as both the time periods examined and the definitions of variables used are crucial to the reliability of the estimates. But at least studies like these indicate that blind and unquestioning adherence to the belief that exchange rate stability and price elastic export demand functions are both important and real should not be articles of faith but testable propositions.

The linked exchange rate was expected to yield an additional benefit to Hong Kong in terms of aligning its rate of inflation with that of the USA. Once again the benefit could be measured in terms of improved export performance and the possibility that Hong Kong would experience a lower inflation rate than it would otherwise have had. At the same time, however, and as a consequence of the pegged system, the authorities in Hong Kong would lose control over an important aspect of domestic monetary policy and would face greater fluctuations in domestic interest rates and the danger of higher rather than lower domestic prices given the potential threat of imported inflation.

There is considerable evidence that by early 1985 the rate of increases in consumer prices in Hong Kong had adjusted to that of the USA.[54] But the rate of inflation in Hong Kong over the period 1983–7 was determined by a number of far more complex factors than just the rate of inflation in the USA. For example, the prices of food imports from China, an important component of the price index, had been kept down by the gradual depreciation of the renminbi against the HK dollar. Similarly the rapid rise of the yen against the US dollar–HK dollar was not reflected in the import prices from Japan, because of the attempt by Japanese exporters to maintain their market shares and sales volumes. Also, since 1986 domestically generated inflationary pressures started to widen the Hong Kong–USA inflation differential. One key contributory factor was the developing labour shortage in Hong Kong with the consequent wage increases and the rapid rise in consumer disposable income.[55]

The scant econometric evidence on the determinants of the rate of inflation in Hong Kong does not yield any clear conclusions except to cast doubts on the consistency by which changes in money stock affect the price level and to re-emphasize the importance of import prices.[56]

The evidence of the possible effects of the pegged exchange rates on the variability of interest rates is no clearer. As the data in Table 2.23 have shown, the number of changes in the best lending rate and their amplitude in terms of the standard deviation of the percentage point change do not appear to have increased after 1983. There is some evidence, however, that the HIBOR variability increased after the introduction of the peg.

On balance, the introduction of the pegged exchange rate system in Hong Kong yielded mixed benefits in terms of control over inflation and interest rates. Over the period 1983–7 the fact that imported inflation played a minor role in determining domestic price rises can be considered purely a matter of luck. There is no guarantee that prices of food imports will remain under control or that the rate of inflation in the USA will not accelerate. Furthermore, the increased variability in interest rates, at least in one segment of the market, must have imposed costs and increased uncertainty.

Ultimately, however, any test of the effectiveness or otherwise of the monetary and fiscal policies pursued in Hong Kong must rely on the criteria of whether the aims of the authorities were achieved. It can therefore be argued that Hong Kong's rapid economic growth, the relative price stability and the ability of the monetary system to cope with very hard confidence shocks is the proof of success. This may well be admitted with the proviso, that in Hong Kong, as elsewhere, policy decisions are taken without any attempt to quantify their costs and benefits. The best example in this case is the pegging of the exchange rate which is now effectively an article of faith for the authorities, a dangerous position to be trapped in. Even here, however, the claim for its success has been in terms of maintaining confidence rather than helping exports, controlling inflation etc. Confidence factors are difficult, if not impossible, to quantify or measure. Hence the claim for success must rest with subjective criteria. The authorities' attitude to economic policy in Hong Kong has been non-interventionist and liberal. That principle has been adhered to closely and consistently. Thus, to the extent that good economic policies are predictable (i.e. consistent) policies, Hong Kong's experience has been quite successful.

Chapter seven

Summary and conclusions

The picture which emerges from this survey of Hong Kong's financial markets is one of continuous flux, development and adjustment. The future movements and directions of change are conditioned to a great extent by the imminence of the 1997 changeover. Surprisingly, however, the rapid internationalization of financial activities may well have defused some of the negative effects. Given that the relations between Hong Kong and the PRC are those of growing mutual dependence and as long as the liberal and regulation-free environment of Hong Kong can be maintained, there is no reason to believe that Hong Kong's position as a financial centre will not be sustained after 1997. To a considerable degree banking and capital market activities are not directly related to the Hong Kong–PRC 'import–export–re-export–processing' nexus but rely on Hong Kong's position as an offshore centre. It would be unrealistic, however, to expect that if that nexus was damaged or broken then this would have no repercussions on financial activities. As was pointed out in Chapter 1 the importance of the direct links between Hong Kong and the PRC can easily be exaggerated in terms not of their quantitative importance but of the degree to which they run in both directions.

The banking market in Hong Kong has seen a major incursion by the Bank of China group which presented the Hongkong Bank group with possibly the only potential threat in its pre-eminence in the purely local banking scene. The large numbers of foreign banks in Hong Kong, and particularly the Japanese, testify to Hong Kong's importance as an offshore financial centre. The degree of competition in the banking market can easily be

separated into the purely domestic (i.e. local) and the international aspects. The Interest Rate Agreement dominates the
relationship amongst all the banks on the retail side. The
wholesale side of the domestic market is dominated by the
deposit-taking companies (DTCs), most of which are bank
owned. Here the process of elimination of the smaller licensed
DTCs has been aided and abetted by the authorities who
ultimately would like to see a two tier system emerging. Despite
the heavy concentration of the local banking market in the hands
of a very small number of banks, there appears to be no
systematic relationship between profitability and size. The
restrictions imposed on competition via interest rate have
frequently been bypassed both by financial engineering (money
market funds) or at an earlier stage via the use of DTCs. In this
sense it is interesting to observe how official regulation came to
shape the form of the market. Equally interesting has been the
division of labour which developed between banks and DTCs in
the non-equity capital market. The rise (and almost fall) of the
fixed-rate certificates of deposit (FRCDs), the development of
some types of commercial paper and the first reluctant steps to
make the HK dollar an international investment currency were
all part of the growth of the DTC market.

The structure of the assets and liabilities of banks and DTCs as
well as the rapid growth of both deposits and loans in foreign
currencies rather than HK dollars reflected these developments.
To the extent that banks and DTCs could control the composition
of their balance sheets it was shown that they responded to
profitable opportunities (FRCDs) and reflected the offshore
character of Hong Kong's markets (inter-bank borrowing and
lending). Similarly the demand for loans in HK dollars was
shown to be stable and well defined in terms of a small number of
variables, except that interest rate elasticities appeared to be low.
Overall the changes in the banking market reflected the evolving
structure of the market in terms of greater competition from
abroad but limited competition on the domestic side.

Because of its volatility and high returns the equity market is at
greatest risk of being either overglamorized or dismissed out of
hand. The market was shown to be dominated by a small number
of shares, some of which moved together as a group. The degree
of efficiency of the market, in the way defined by economists,

appears to be low. An inefficient market is, broadly, a market where consistent above-average returns can be made without these returns eventually being competed away. The various tests which have been applied to the Hong Kong equity market give an overall impression of inefficiency. This impression is qualified in a number of ways not only because of the shortcomings of some of the investigations but also because of the essentially dynamic and therefore changing nature of the market itself. Two aspects need to be noted here, the unification of the four stock exchanges in 1986 and the introduction of an extensive scheme of regulation in 1988–9 which is expected to increase the overall transparency of the market.

The developments of the equity market are closely interlinked with two important financial activities, the trading of financial futures and investment management. The latter is not limited to Hong Kong equities, but Hong Kong's position as an important offshore centre has made this a booming activity. The liberal laws and controls on unit trusts and fund management in general have made Hong Kong an extremely attractive centre. The performance of unit trusts and of fund managers based in Hong Kong can be appraised in a number of ways including the effect on portfolio performances of Hong Kong equities. The Hong Kong equity market ranks amongst the world's top in terms of volatility and therefore of returns. The reputation for volatility generated extensive negative publicity for the Exchange when it was combined with the closure of the market during the October 1987 crash. The closure of the market was blamed on the Hang Seng Index futures market which had expanded virtually uncontrolled until, according to the views at the time, the tail wagged the dog. This was an unfounded allegation as research and investigation were to prove later. There is no evidence that the introduction of futures trading increased the volatility of the underlying cash market. If the futures created any problems for the equities market this was because of the lax enforcement of basic risk management rules rather than because of any inherent imperfections of the markets themselves. This was an important incident in the financial development of Hong Kong because it showed that the introduction of new instruments or new variations in existing markets could be handled successfully only if standard and accepted regulatory procedures were also followed. The Securities Review Commission of 1988 produced extensive and detailed recommendations concerning the regulatory framework of Hong Kong and the necessary reforms. These recommendations were put into action by the Stock Exchange and Futures Exchange and by the complete reorganization of the Securities Commission. These reforms combined with the 1986 Banking Ordinance have now equipped Hong Kong with a wide-ranging and modern armoury of regulatory tools. Indeed, at the time when these rules were being implemented the question was frequently asked whether Hong Kong was 'regulating away' its reputation as a liberal and flexible financial centre. Ultimately the answer must lie in the extent by which market participants perceive that the costs of the regulation in terms of inflexibilities, bureaucratic delays, financial outlays for compliance, etc, are outweighed by the benefits of more transparent and orderly markets.

Perhaps the single most important policy action which helped to shape Hong Kong's financial market was the decision to peg the HK dollar to the US dollar in 1983. This decision effectively deprived the authorities of any control over interest rates and the stock of money. The benefits of this action were seen more in terms of a confidence factor than in terms of pure financial returns. With the run-up to 1997 it was seen to be essential to maintain the stability and the fixed rate convertibility of the local currency against the US dollar. The mechanism for establishing and maintaining the peg had an essentially Hong Kong flavour about it in being unique in some of its details. The peg was achieved through the note issue, still in the hands of two private banks, and through arbitrage activities between a fixed and a freely floating exchange market. This simple mechanism failed to work as expected, and it has been modified both by the blunt expedient of introducing negative interest rates and by the more subtle technique of direct open market operations by the authorities. The pegged exchange rate system has been proved successful because it suited the 'hands-off' approach of the authorities to economic policy in terms of relinquishing control over the stock of money, and because it maintained confidence in the financial system during periods of political strain. However, this policy cannot be divorced from the fiscal stance of the Government which encourages growing budgetary surpluses. This is considered prudent housekeeping in an almost naive Thacherite way, but it also helped to provide the resources to ensure that the pegged exchange rate remained so.

The development of Hong Kong's financial markets had certain unique elements, not least because of the territory's unique history and political future. At the same time, however, the internationalization of these markets became the best guarantee for their continuing existence and development in the post-1997 period. If Hong Kong's liberal and open policy towards banking, finance and trade is maintained, then there is no reason why the institutions that have chosen Hong Kong as their base of operations will not continue to do so in the future.

Notes

Chapter one: Introduction

1 Perhaps the best examples in English are the numerous articles on Hong Kong's banking and foreign exchange system which have appeared over the years in the *Asian Monetary Monitor*. These are referred to individually in the following chapters.

2 The three indexes are the consumer price index (CPI) (A), which covers 50 per cent of mostly low income households, (CPI) (B) covering 30 per cent of households and the Hang Seng CPI which covers 10 per cent of upper income households.

3 The following section draws from the empirical estimates of E.K.Y. Chen, *Hyper-growth in Asian Economies*, London: Macmillan, 1979, *passim*, and G. Peebles *Hong Kong's Economy*, Oxford: Oxford University Press, 1988, Chapter 2, *passim*. Other much more general surveys of Hong Kong's growth experience can be found in A.J. Youngson, *Hong Kong: Economic Growth and Policy*, Oxford: Oxford University Press, 1982, and D. Lethbridge (ed.), *The Business Environment in Hong Kong*, Oxford: Oxford University Press, 1984 (2nd edn). For an unusual interpretation involving a sociocultural approach see also E.K.Y. Chen, 'The economics and non-economics of Asia's Four Little Dragons', *Gazette, University of Hong Kong* 35 (1) (Supplement): 23–30, 1988.

4 See also Chapter 6, Section 6.9, where the contribution of the surplus to the overall level of aggregate demand is discussed.

5 T. Lee 'The symptoms and causes of structural change', *Asian Monetary Monitor* 13 (1): 10–23, 1989.

6 See 'A survey of the yen block', *The Economist*, 18 July 1989, and T. Lee, 'Intraregional trade and investment in East Asia', *Asian Monetary Monitor* 13 (3) 1–11, 1989.

7 *Hang Seng Bank Economic Montly*, October 1987.

8 See, for example, Joint Association Working Group, *Report on Hong Kong's Labour Shortages*, Hong Kong: Griffiths Management Ltd, 1989.

9 Some attempts have been made in that direction, significantly, at the initiative of the private sector. See, for example, *Building Prosperity: A Five Part Economic Strategy for Hong Kong's Future*, prepared by SRI International for a group of Hong Kong business and civic leaders, Hong Kong, 1989.

Chapter two: Banks

1 A.M. Santomero, 'Modeling the bank firm, *Journal of Money, Credit and Banking* 16 (4): 576–712, 1984.
2 J.M. Mason, *Financial Management of Commercial Banks*, Warren, Gorham & Lamont, 1979, pp. 32–62; P.F. Smith, *Money and Financial Intermediation*, Englewood Cliffs, NJ: Prentice-Hall, 1970, Chapter 12 *passim*.
3 *Banking Ordinance* (1986), Third Schedule, as modified in September 1988, Hong Kong, Government Printer, 1986; see also Hongkong Bank, *Economic Report*, July 1988.
4 Chinese Banks' Association, *Hong Kong's Banking System: Problems, Prospects and Policies*, Hong Kong, 1988, p. 89.
5 For an extensive survey see R.A. Gilbert, 'Bank market structure and competition', *Journal of Money, Credit and Banking*, 16 (4): 617–60, 1984.
6 M. Smirlock, 'Evidence on the (non) relationship between concentration and profitability in banking', *Journal of Money, Credit and Banking* 17 (1): 69–83, 1985.
7 H. Demsetz, 'Industry structure, market rivalry and public policy', *Journal of Law and Economics*, April 1973, pp. 1–9.
8 Smirlock, 'Evidence on the (non) relationship', p. 71.
9 The following are typical results of the equations using deposits as a proxy for size in explaining profitability (D denotes deposits):

$$\%RAA\ (84) = \begin{array}{c} 1.00 - 0.00043D \\ (2.60) \quad (-0.084) \end{array} \qquad R^2 = 0.0002$$

$$\%RAA\ (85) = \begin{array}{c} -3.00 + 0.009D \\ (-1.83) \quad (0.47) \end{array} \qquad R^2 = 0.007$$

$$\%RAA\ (86) = \begin{array}{c} -0.45 + 0.0024D \\ (-0.39) \quad (0.25) \end{array} \qquad R^2 = 0.002$$

$$\%RAA\ (87) = \begin{array}{c} 1.23 - 0.0008D \\ (5.52) \quad (-0.52) \end{array} \qquad R^2 = 0.009$$

The figures in parentheses are the *t* ratios. These and the rest of the results are based on A. Freris 'Size and profitability of local Hong Kong banks', in M. Ariff *et al.* (eds), *Proceedings of the Inaugural Conference on Asian–Pacific Financial Markets*, Singapore: National University of Singapore, 1989, pp. 411–24.
10 J. Kolari and A. Zardkoohi, *Bank Costs, Structure and Performance*, Lexington, MA: Lexington Books, 1987, pp. 219–21.

11 D.B. Humphrey, 'Cost dispersion and the measurement of economies in banking', *Federal Reserve Bank of Richmond Economic Review* 73 (3): 24–38.
12 For a detailed description of the Interest Rate Agreement (IRA) see S.H. Ko, *Introduction to Finance Law in Hong Kong*, Hong Kong: Vita Investment, 1983, pp. 33–6, and T.K. Ghose, *The Banking System of Hong Kong*, London: Butterworths, 1987, pp. 77–80. A comprehensive summary of the provisions of the IRA was provided in the Chinese Banks' Association, *Hong Kong's Banking System*, pp. 67–8.

> Under this arrangement licensed banks are divided into two categories. Category I consists of the Hongkong Bank Group, foreign banks as well as those local banks which are more than 25% owned by the first two groups of banks. Category II consists of the Bank of China Group and other local Chinese banks. Category II banks can offer deposits rates 0.5% point higher than those of Category I banks, though the rate or saving deposits is uniform. With effect from February 1982, deposits of HK$ 500,000 or more with maturities of three months or less have been exempt from this agreement. The agreement applies however only to licensed banks and not to DTCs; it also does not cover HK dollar deposits of over 15 months and foreign currency deposits.

13 See Chapter 6 for details.
14 The analysis and diagrams are based on J.L. Pierce, *Monetary and Financial Economics*, New York: Wiley, 1984, Chapter 7 *passim*. See also D.G. Pierce and P.J. Tysone, *Monetary Economics*, London: Butterworths, 1985 (2nd edn), pp. 93–9, and for the general issues raised A.M. Santomero, 'Modeling the banking firm, *Journal of Money, Credit and Banking* 16 (4): 576–712, 1984.
15 The simple analysis used here does not allow for the frequent cases of 'round-tripping' whereby customers (or banks themselves) borrow from banks in order to redeposit the loaned funds and exploit any differentials between the rates charged and paid.
16 Pierce, *Monetary and Financial Economics*, p. 182.
17 Hongkong Bank, *Economic Report*, April 1986.
18 T.C. Kwong and Y.K. Ho, 'The demand for liquid assets in Hong Kong', in Y.K. Ho and C.K. Law (eds), *Hong Kong Financial Markets: Empirical Evidence*, Hong Kong: University Publisher and Printer, 1983, pp. 71–107.
19 The evidence is outlined in Section 2.3.
20 'Why the HKD/USD linked rate system should not be changed', *Asian Monetary Monitor*, November–December 1984, pp. 2–17, especially p. 8.
21 Ibid., pp. 8–9. This was calculated as follows:

$$\text{Best lending rate} - \tfrac{1}{2}(\text{savings deposit rate} + 3 \text{ month time deposit rate})$$

22 For the DTC crisis see Ghose, *The Banking System*, pp. 84–6. The Carrian affair is covered in P. Bowring and R. Cottrell, *The Carrian File*, Hong Kong: Far Eastern Economic Review, 1984 (revised edn), *passim*.

23 For a discussion of the official attitude and actions towards these banks see Commissioner of Banking, Hong Kong, *Annual Reports*, 1986, 1987.

24 A.F. Freris and T.M. Ho, 'An empirical investigation of company liquidations in Hong Kong', Discussion Paper 73, Department of Economics, University of Hong Kong, April 1986.

25 For an extensive discussion of banking crises in both Hong Kong and Taiwan see Y.C. Jao, 'A comparative analysis of banking crises in Hong Kong and Taiwan,' *Journal of Economics and International Relations*, 1 (4): 299–322, 1987. For a general survey of both the banking and DTC markets which also covers the crises see Y.C. Jao, 'Monetary system and banking structure', in H.C.Y. Ho and L.C. Chan (eds), *The Economic System of Hong Kong*, Hong Kong: Asian Research Service, 1988, pp. 43–85. The Exchange Fund is described and discussed in detail in Chapter 6 of this book.

26 For one of the standard treatments of this topic see M. Parkin, M.R. Gray and K. J. Barret, 'The portfolio behaviour of commercial banks', in K. Hilton and D. Heathfield (eds), *The Econometric Study of the United Kingdom*, London: Macmillan, 1970, pp. 229–251.

27 This example is based on J.C. Francis, 'Portfolio analysis of asset and liability management small-, medium- and large-sized banks', *Journal of Monetary Economics* 4: 459–80, 1978. For a comprehensive critique and some pitfalls of this type of approach see A.S. Courakis, 'Modelling portfolio selections', *Economic Journal* no. 392: 619–42, 1988.

28 C.L. Wu, 'The economics of land sales in Hong Kong', Discussion Paper 71, Department of Economics, University of Hong Kong, April 1986.

29 Hongkong Bank, *Economic Report*, April 1986; see also the Chinese Banks' Association, *Hong Kong's Banking System*, pp. 42–52.

30 Chinese Banks' Association, *Hong Kong's Banking System*, pp. 49–50.

31 The percentage of loans made by banks in forex to total loans has risen from 33 per cent in 1982 to nearly 59 per cent in 1988.

32 See, for example, B.J. Moore and A.R. Threadgold, 'Corporate bank borrowing in the UK, 1965–1981', *Economica*, February 1985, pp. 65–78; K. Cuthbertson and N. Foster, 'Bank lending to industrial and commercial companies in three models of the UK economy', *National Institute Economic Review*, November 1982, pp. 63–77; K. Cuthbertson, 'Bank lending to UK industrial and commercial companies', *Oxford Bulletin of Economics and Statistics* 42 (2): 91–118, 1985.

33 R. Brealey and S. Myers, *Principles of Corporate Finance*, New York: McGraw Hill, 1984, Chapter 30 *passim*.

34 For a purely analytical treatment of loans and the personal consumption patterns see A. Deaton and J. Muellbauer, *Economics and Consumer Behaviour*, Cambridge: Cambridge University Press, 1983, Chapter 12 *passim*.
35 Moore and Threadgold, 'Corporate bank borrowing', pp. 67–8.
36 K. Cuthbertson, *The Supply and Demand for Money*, Oxford: Basil Blackwell, 1985, pp. 103–5.
37 See, for example, Cuthbertson and Foster, 'Bank lending', pp. 64–5.
38 This section draws from A. Freris, 'Demand for bank loans in Hong Kong 1978–1986: a preliminary investigation', *Working Paper 16*, Department of Business and Management, City Polytechnic of Hong Kong, 1987. The quarterly data on total loans used in these models have been separated into two major periods, 1978(iv)–1986(ii) and 1981(i)–1986(ii). For the period up to 1981(i) the statistics did not distinguish between loans for use in Hong Kong and outside Hong Kong. Furthermore, there were no separate statistics for loans in foreign currencies and in HK dollars. Therefore, the data spanning 1981(i)–1986(ii) cover only loans for use in Hong Kong in HK dollars. The data spanning 1978(iv)–1986(ii) include loans that might have been used outside Hong Kong or were issued in foreign currency. For both sets of data, loans to the construction and building industry and loans for the purchase of residential property have been excluded for reasons already explained. Until 1980(iv) the data included loans for the financing of import and export trade. After 1980(iv) loans for the financing of import and export trade were not included in the total of loans in Hong Kong and were shown separately. In order to ensure consistency through 1980(iv) onwards, these loans were added back to the total. The earliest consistent set of data that can be obtained is from 1978(iv). Before that date the statistics did not show loans for the purchase of residential property separately so that they could be subtracted.

To summarize, the data for total loans are in million HK dollars and include the following sectors: manufacturing, agriculture and fisheries, transport and transport equipment, electricity, gas and telephone, wholesale, retail and (re)export–import trade, mining and quarrying, and finally miscellaneous (including personal loans). The data exclude loans to building, construction, property development and personal loans to purchase property. The data for 1978(iv)–1986(ii) cover loans for use in Hong Kong and elsewhere, both in HK dollars and in foreign currencies plus loans for the financing of import and export trade minus loans relating to property, construction etc. The data for 1981(i)–1986(ii) are as above except that these are loans for use in Hong Kong only and exclude loans in foreign currencies.

The figures for the BLR are based on the daily or monthly data. These were weighted using the length of time of their duration and then averaged on a quarterly basis. For wages W, the index of industrial wages was used based on 1981(i) when used with other indexes based on the same year. The figures for exports E were at current prices in million HK dollars, seasonally adjusted. The retail sales index S was expressed in value terms, seasonally adjusted, with 1981(i) = 100. Sectoral loans were expressed in million HK dollars (current prices).

As the data spanning 1978(iv) onwards include loans in foreign currency, use of the BLR as one of the regressors may not have been appropriate. The 3 month Eurodollar lending rate (EDR) was regressed over this period against the BLR as follows:

$$BLR_t = a + b(EDR)_t \text{ or } (EDR)_{t-1}$$

with R^2 values of 0.73 and 0.83 respectively. The coefficient of EDR was significant in both equations. It now appears that the BLR could act as a proxy for the cost of loans in forex as well as in HK dollars where the equations covered periods before 1981.

39 Calculation of real interest rates is rather difficult for Hong Kong. As indicated there are three price indexes measuring consumer prices based on income levels. The calculations used here are based on the Hang Seng CPI which covers the top income groups. For loans, strictly speaking, the GDP deflator should have been used, but this is not officially available except on an annual basis. Given the frequent changes of BLR a weighted quarterly estimation using the CPI changes is the best approximation to the real interest rate available at present.

40 For an estimate of demand for deposits elasticities, see Kwong and Ho, 'Demand for liquid assets'. For the interest elasticities of UK bank loans see Moore and Threadgold, 'Corporate bank borrowing'.

41 For the medium- to long-term strategies of both these groups see the surveys in the *Far Eastern Economic Review*, 28 August 1988, pp. 50–3 for BOC and *Far Eastern Economic Review*, 22 December 1988, pp. 52–7 for the Hongkong Bank.

42 One less publicized aspect of this success has been the persistent rumours, occasionally backed by facts, that narcotics-related funds are 'laundered' through Hong Kong. One potentially substantiated case involved the fine imposed in 1985 by the US Treasury on a bank in California for failing to report a very large number of cash transactions totalling nearly US$4 billion which involved primarily Hong Kong banks. Although there was no evidence that the money was the proceeds of illegal activities, there was a strong presumption that at least part of it may well have been (*South China Morning Post*, 17 December 1988).

43 Chinese Banks' Association, *Hong Kong's Banking System*, p. 11.

44 'Developments in international capital and banking markets in 1987', *Bank of England Quarterly Bulletin* May 1988, pp. 209–19. See also related reports in *Far Eastern Economic Review*, 21 May 1987, pp. 60–1; 2 June 1988, p. 69.

45 'Developments in international capital', p. 216.

46 Y.C. Jao, 'Theories and policy implications of financial innovations', *Discussion Paper 59*, Department of Economics, University of Hong Kong, November 1985.

Chapter three: Deposit-taking companies and the capital market

1 T.K. Ghose, *The Banking System of Hong Kong*, London: Butterworths, 1987, pp. 80–90.
2 Office of the Commissioner of Banking, 'The three tier system', Consultative Paper 1, mimeo, Hong Kong, 1987.
3 Office of the Commissioner of Banking, 'RDTC – the current position', Consultative Paper 2, mimeo, Hong Kong, 1987.
4 Office of the Commissioner of Banking, 'Securities dealings', Consultative Paper 4, mimeo, Hong Kong, 1987.
5 The issue was made in 1984 at 10 per cent maturing in 1989 with the last recorded transaction in July 1986. The issue was almost exclusively held by institutional investors and banks who did not wish to part with it before maturity.
6 The first of this example was a 1–10 year bond issue by Quantas, the Australian airline, in October 1987. See *Asian Finance*, December 1988, pp. 44–6.
7 For an extensive survey of the issue see R.E. McBain, 'The Hong Kong capital market since October 19', paper presented to a Stock Exchange of Hong Kong seminar, mimeo, Hong Kong, March 1988. There is relatively little available in English on the interest rate structure of Hong Kong's money and capital markets, particularly on the time structure. On a related issue see C.K. Law *et al.*, 'A model to forecast timing of interest rate changes', in H.C.Y. Ho and L.C. Chan (eds), *The Economic System of Hong Kong*, Hong Kong: Asian Research Service, 1988, pp. 86–99.
8 D. Walker-Smith 'Hong Kong dollar debt issues', paper presented at the conference on Hong Kong's Capital Market, mimeo, International Research Institute, Hong Kong, 1989.
9 P.K. Thomas, 'Hong Kong dollar market–acorn or dwarf?', paper presented at the Conference on Hong Kong's Capital Market, mimeo, International Research Institute, Hong Kong, 1989.
10 *Far Eastern Economic Review*, 26 February 1987, 26 April 1987; *SCMP Banking and Finance Review*, 1986, 1987.
11 For a discussion see D.P.M. Chan, 'Hong Kong bond market', *Securities Bulletin, Stock Exchange of Hong Kong* No. 14, June 1987, pp. 32–3; C. Hang, 'Feasibility of developing a bond market in Hong Kong', *Securities Bulletin, Stock Exchange of Hong Kong* No. 19, November 1987, p. 25. See also *Far Eastern Economic Review*, 26 February 1987. Relevant issues are also discussed in the surveys published in *Asian Finance*, January 1988, December 1988, and the annual surveys of banking and finance published by the *South China Morning Post* for 1986, 1987 and 1988.

12 C. Hang, 'Capital market instruments in transition', *Securities Bulletin, Stock Exchange of Hong Kong* No. 24, April 1988, pp. 19–20.

13 Commissioner of Banking, 'Options', Consultative Paper 5, mimeo, Hong Kong, 1987.

14 Commissioner of Banking, *Annual Report for 1987*, Hong Kong, 1988, pp. 55–61.

15 Commissioner of Banking, 'The three tier system', mimeo, March 1989.

16 Commissioner of Banking, *Annual Report for 1988*, Hong Kong 1989, p. 2.

Chapter four: The Stock Exchange

1 For a succinct history of the equity markets in Hong Kong see T.Y. Cheng, *The Economy of Hong Kong*, Hong Kong: Far East Publications, 1982, pp. 252–73; Report of the Securities Review Committee, *The Operations and Regulation of the Hong Kong Securities Industry* (the *SRC Report*), Hong Kong, 1988, Appendix 10, pp. 371–6. For a good general introduction see A. Rowley, *Asian Stockmarkets*, Hong Kong: *Far Eastern Economic Review*, 1987, pp. 127–56.

2 *SRC Report, passim.* See also Chapter 5, Section 5.4, for an extensive treatment of these issues.

3 J.C. Francis, *Investments: Analysis and Management*, New York: McGraw-Hill, 1986, pp. 80–1.

4 These months were chosen because the trading volume in million HK dollars was high but had not reached the exceptional, and therefore unrepresentative, values of August–October 1987. Therefore, for example, the average value of turnover during these 6 months was HK$24.7 billion and this increased to HK$40.3 billion, HK$60.3 billion and HK$61.8 billion during August, September and October 1987 respectively. The turnover fell to HK$22.3 billion in November and then dropped to a low of HK$8.1 billion in September 1988. The average monthly turnover for 1988 stood at HK$16 billion. The first two months of 1989 saw a considerable increase to nearly HK$31 billion per month, but the turnover dropped again considerably after the Beijing events in May–June 1989.

5 J.H. Wood and N.L. Wood, *Financial Markets*, New York: Harcourt Brace Jovanovitch, 1985, p. 189.

6 *The Investors' Chronicle* 82 (1037): p. 18, 16–22 October 1987.

7 Wood and Wood, *Financial Markets*, pp. 188–9.

8 Board, odd, special and direct lots refer to the minimum number of shares which can be traded. According to the SEHK Regulations, a board lot is defined as the standard number of shares to be traded. Odd and special lot transactions involve less than one board lot and more than one board lot respectively. Direct lots involve transactions

where the broker acts for both the buyer and the seller. For 'non-standard' transactions different rules regarding the minimum and maximum quotations in terms of spreads may apply. See the *Rules of the Stock Exchange of Hong Kong*, 1/1–1/5, 5/3–5/7, 1/1988 edn.

9 For a good introduction see L. Cheung, 'Stock market indexes of Hong Kong', *Hong Kong Manager*, February–March 1987, pp. 25–33.

10 *A Guide to the Hang Seng Index*, Hong Kong: HSI Services Ltd, 1988.

11 There is some evidence from the USA that the price of stocks added or deleted from the Standard & Poor (S & P) 100 index did change as a result of this addition or deletion. See R.D. Arnott and S.J. Vincent, 'S & P additions and deletions: a market anomaly', *Journal of Portfolio Management*, Fall 1986, pp. 29–33. There is no evidence for any similar effects on the constituents of the HSI. If any additions or deletions effect was observed then it might have made some difference to the trading of the HSI stock index futures contract although there is, as yet, no evidence for that. The dynamics of the HSI futures market are discussed in Chapter 5, Section 5.2.

12 For the details and numerical examples see *Guide to HSI*.

13 See the discussion in F. Allen and A. Postlewaite, 'Rational expectations and the measurement of a stock's elasticity of demand', *Journal of Finance* 39 (4): 119–25, 1984; A. Shleifer, 'Do demand curves for stocks slope down?', *Journal of Finance* 41 (3): 579–90, 1986. For a related discussion of the price changes and volume causality direction in Hong Kong see K. Lam, W.K. Li and P.S. Wong, 'Price changes and trading volume relationship in the Hong Kong securities market', in M. Ariff *et al.* (eds), *Proceedings of the Inaugural Conference on Asian–Pacific Financial Markets*, Singapore: National University of Singapore, 1989, pp. 653–67.

14 'What do you know about the HKI?', *Securities Bulletin, Stock Exchange of Hong Kong* No. 25, May 1988, pp. 16–19.

15 The details can be found in 'Emerging of a New Index', *Securities Bulletin, Stock Exchange of Hong Kong* No. 30, October 1988, pp. 21–2.

16 Cheung, 'Stock market indexes', pp. 31–3.

17 It must be noted, however, that hotels showed a rise of 12.51 per cent against the overall decline of the HKI.

18 Henry M.K. Mok, 'Stationarity of returns and risk of sectoral indices in Hong Kong's stock market', Working Paper 19, Department of Business and Management, City Polytechnic of Hong Kong, August 1987.

19 H.M.K. Mok, K. Lam and I.Y.K. Cheung, 'The unique structure of stock returns in Hong Kong', *Securities Bulletin, Stock Exchange of Hong Kong* No. 35, March 1989, pp. 5–14.

20 Examples other than the Li Ka Shing group include the Y.K. Pao (Wharf and World International), Keswick (Jardine Matheson) and to a lesser extent Swire (Swire Pacific) families. These links are

further strengthened by family interlocking directorships of other major property companies such as New World Development, SHK Properties, Henderson Land and Hang Lung Development.

21 In other words the principal component analysis 'explains' 31.3 per cent of the $100 - 42 = 58$ per cent still left unexplained after the market effect is allowed for. Thus, 31.3 per cent of 58 per cent is 18.15 per cent which added to 42 per cent yields approximately 60.2 per cent.

22 Mok *et al.* 'The unique structure', p. 12.

23 See, for example, P.S. Tso, 'Sectoral groupings of stocks in the Hong Kong stock market 1978–1982', Discussion Paper 86, Department of Economics, University of Hong Kong, March 1987. Tso applied factor analysis to the daily returns of forty-seven stocks over 1978–82. The overall market effect was removed and the principal component analysis of the residuals yielded two basic sectors, a real estate sector and another which was less well defined. On average the market explained 40 per cent of variations in stock returns. Of the remaining 60 per cent the two basic groups could explain 20 per cent, leaving a 48 per cent variation accountable by company-specific factors.

24 On average only twenty-three out of the thirty-three constituent companies were included. In some cases incomplete information did not allow for consistent persentation, especially in the treatment of bank loans in the accounts of a number of firms. Also, as explained in the text, banks were excluded from the sample.

25 Y.K. Ip and M.I. Hopewell, 'Corporate financial structure in Hong Kong', *Hong Kong Journal of Business Management* 5: 21–31, 1987.

26 L.S. Tai, 'Financial policies and practices of corporations in Hong Kong', *Hong Kong Manager*, June–July 1987, pp. 6–13. The study used fifty-three responses to a questionnaire sent to quoted public firms in Hong Kong. Only sixteen of the fifty-three firms responded on the questions related to the ratio of long-term debt to capitalisation.

27 Y.K. Ip and P.Y.F. Ho, 'Dividend policy in Hong Kong', *Securities Bulletin, Stock Exchange of Hong Kong* No. 36, April 1989, pp. 32 5.

28 A.F. Freris and T.M. Ho, 'An empirical investigation of company liquidations in Hong Kong', Discussion Paper 73, Department of Economics, University of Hong Kong, April 1986.

29 'Venture capital in Hong Kong', Report of the Working Party of the Hong Kong Association of Banks, June 1987.

30 C.R. Nelson, *The Investor's Guide to Leading Indicators*', New York: Wiley, 1987, Chapter 9 *passim*.

31 S. Wadhwani and M. Mullins, 'The effect of stock market on investment: a comparative study', LSE Financial Markets Group Discussion Paper 0032, June 1988.

32 W.F. Sharpe, *Investments*, Englewood Cliffs, NJ: Prentice-Hall, 1985 (3rd edn), pp. 67–8.

33 For a brief, non-technical and fairly complete survey see C.H.F. Jing, 'Empirical evidence on Hong Kong stock market informational

efficiency', *Securities Bulletin, Stock Exchange of Hong Kong*, No.
21, January 1988, pp. 21–2. Some of the earlier studies reviewed in
this article involved random walk tests on weekly or even monthly
price changes and hence are not particularly reliable.

34 C.K. Law, 'A test of the efficient market hypothesis with respect to
the recent behaviour of the Hong Kong stock market', in Y.K. Ho
and C.K. Law (eds), *Hong Kong Financial Markets: Empirical
Evidence*, Hong Kong: University Publisher and Printer, 1983, pp.
125–57.

35 K.A. Wong and K.S. Kwong, 'The behaviour of Hong Kong stock
prices', *Applied Economics* 16: 905–17, 1984.

36 Ibid., pp. 913–14.

37 S.Y. Chan, J.P. Dickinson and G.D. Donleavy, 'Economic efficiency
and stock market unification', *Securities Bulletin, Stock Exchange of
Hong Kong*, No. 37, May 1989, pp. 30–4.

38 Ibid., p. 33.

39 Y.M. Mui and C.K. Law, 'The expectation and adjustment patterns
of stock prices to new interest rates information in Hong Kong', in
Y.K. Ho and C.K. Law (eds), *Hong Kong Financial Markets*, pp.
159–92.

40 C.K. Law and K.W. AuYeung, 'A test of takeover price efficiency in
the Hong Kong stock market', in Y.K. Ho and C.K. Law (eds),
Hong Kong Financial Markets, pp. 193–210.

41 S.M. Dawson and T. Hiraki, 'Selling unseasoned new shares in Hong
Kong and Japan', *Hong Kong Journal of Business Management* 3:
125–34, 1985.

42 S.M. Dawson, 'Secondary stock market performance of initial public
offers: Hong Kong, Singapore and Malaysia 1978–1984', *Journal of
Business Finance and Accounting* 14 (1): 65–76, Spring 1987.

43 Ibid.

44 S.M. Dawson, 'Price trends for new stock issues in Hong Kong:
1979–1985', *Hong Kong Journal of Business Management* 4: 55–66,
1986.

45 Ibid., 63.

46 S. Dawson, 'Is the Hong Kong market efficient?', *Journal of
Portfolio Management* 8 (3): 17–20, Spring 1982.

47 Ibid., p. 19.

48 S. Dawson, 'The trend towards efficiency for less developed stock
exchange: Hong Kong', *Journal of Business Finance and Accounting*,
11 (2): 151–9, Summer 1984.

49 Y.K. Ho, 'Money supply and equity prices in Hong Kong', in Y.K.
Ho and C.K. Law (eds), *Hong Kong Financial Markets*, pp. 210–33.
For a recent survey of this area see R.W. Hafer, 'The response of
stock prices to changes in weekly money and the discount rate',
Review of the Federal Reserve Bank of St. Louis 68 (3):5–14, 1986. At
this stage mention must be made of a study which examined the role
of political events on the HSI. This study can be construed as an
indirect test of the way that publicly available information may

influence such returns, the information here was newspaper headlines on the progress of Sino-British talks on the future of Hong Kong during 1980–5. Not surprisingly, it was found that favourable or unfavourable news was associated with rises or falls in the HSI. See G. Yen, 'Stock market response to political events – a case study of the Sino-British talks', in Ariff *et al.* (eds), *Asian–Pacific Financial Markets*, pp. 823–33.

50 Y.K. Ho, K.C. Leung and T. Wong, 'Further evidence on stock return seasonality in Asia Pacific markets', Working Paper MS89002, Business Research Centre, Hong Kong Baptist College, January 1988. See also Y.K. Ho and R.K.C. Leung, 'Daily trading pattern in the Asia Pacific stock market', FEC Financial Studies Series No. 1, Financial Engineering Corporation, Hong Kong, 1988. The summary of the findings in the paper by Ho *et al.* (Jan. 1988) is well worth quoting as the study covered not only Hong Kong but also other markets (Australia, Japan, Korea, Malaysia, New Zealand, the Philippines, Singapore and Thailand). The US and UK markets were also covered for the purposes of comparison:

> There exist trading day effects in most of the markets. Five out of ten Asia Pacific markets have negative Monday returns but it is only in Malaysia and Philippines that this negative effect is significant. A great majority of the markets have negative Tuesday returns but only three of them are significant (Australia, Japan, and Malaysia). The last trading day returns are usually positive, significant, and having the highest value in most of the markets. The Calendar Time Hypothesis has to be rejected except in New Zealand and Taiwan. Similarly, the Trading Time Hypothesis is not valid except in Taiwan. In general, there exists some pattern of monthly seasonal effect in that daily average returns in January are higher than that for other months but such effect does not occur during the turn-of-the-year. However, a 'reverse' turn-of-the-lunar-year effect exists before 1983 and a slight turn-of-the-lunar-year effect exists in Singapore and Malaysia after 1983.' (p. 7.)

Similar results for the 'Monday effect' in Hong Kong were obtained by K.A. Wong, T.K. Hui and C.Y. Chan, 'Day of the week effects: evidence from developing stock markets', in Ariff *et al.* (eds), *Asian–Pacific Financial Markets*, pp. 627–39.

51 For a detailed survey using microdata, i.e. intra-day returns, for the daily patterns of trading in the SEHK during 1986–9 see Y.K. Ho and Y.L. Cheung, 'Trading day and intra-daily seasonalities of stock returns on the Hong Kong stock market', in Ariff *et al.* (eds), *Asian–Pacific Financial Markets*, pp. 691–706.

Chapter five: Futures, gold, investment management and regulation

1 *Asiabanking*, October 1986, pp 16–17. The May–June 1989 events in Beijing have put these plans on hold.

2 Report of the Securities Review Committee, *The Operations and Regulation of the Hong Kong Securities Industry* (the *SRC Report*), Hong Kong, 1988.

3 Ibid., Appendix 22 *passim*.

4 'Soyabeans and sugar contracts', Hong Kong Futures Exchange, October 1988.

5 After the October 1987 crash the months of delivery were lengthened to involve the spot and three consecutive even months, whilst the price for settlement was changed to the average of the quotations for the HSI taken at 5 minute intervals during the last trading day of the contract month. See *Stock Index Futures Contract*, Hong Kong Futures Exchange, October 1988.

6 There is an extensive literature on the issue. For a good standard textbook treatment see R.W. Kolb, *Understanding Futures Markets*, Glenview, IL: Scott, Foresman, 1988 (2nd edn), Chapter 2 *passim*.

7 There are a number of equivalent ways of seeing this:
Consider the difference between buying the 100 shares in the FT-SE 100 Index and the futures contract. When you buy the shares you get the benefit of the dividend income. When you buy the futures contract, you forego any dividends. Instead you put up margin for the futures contract and earn interest on the remaining money by putting it on deposit. (*FT-SE 100 Stock Index Futures and Options*, London International Financial Futures Exchange, 1986, p. 5.)

8 Equally this could be interpreted as the cost saved by not having to purchase the underlying shares and depositing the money instead minus the dividends that would have been received on those shares.

9 R. Silk, 'The Hang Seng Index futures market', *Asian Monetary Monitor* 10 (4): 1–13, 1986.

10 M.H. Hopewell and R.H. Terpstra, 'The relationship between spot and future prices: The Hang Seng Index contract', mimeo, Chinese University of Hong Kong, 1988, pp. 1–30.

11 J. Yau, T. Schneeweis and K. Yung, 'The behaviour of stock index futures prices in Hong Kong: before and after the crash', paper presented to the First Annual Pacific-Basin Finance Conference, mimeo, Taipei, Taiwan, 1989, pp. 1–40.

12 The differences between the premiums and discounts in the studies by Hopewell and Terpstra and Yau *et al.* are indicative of the problems encountered in estimating the theoretical formula. For example, Hopewell and Terpstra use the (actual − theoretical)/theoretical ratio whereas Yau *et al.* use (actual − theoretical)/spot ratio. The former used the BLR as the interest rate whereas the latter used HIBOR. The former does not enter separate transaction costs calculations for the pre- and post-crash periods, whereas the latter does. Similarly, there are also differences in the estimation of the market impact effect. Therefore, except for the broad similarities of their conclusions, the numerical results of these two studies are not strictly comparable, even when

allowing for the differences in the samples in the post-crash period.

13 Yau *et al.*, 'The behaviour of stock index futures prices', p. 8.

14 The following draws heavily on the *SRC Report*, Appendix 23, pp. 405–20.

15 Ibid., p. 158.

16 Ibid., pp. 153–5.

17 For the evidence in the USA see, for example, R.E. Whaley, 'Program trading and expiration day effects', *Financial Analysts Journal*, March–April 1987, pp. 16–25; G.J. Santoni, 'Has program trading made stock prices more volatile?', *Review of Federal Reserve Bank of St. Louis*, May 1987, pp. 18–29; F.R. Edwards, 'Futures trading and cash market volatility: stock index and interest rate futures', *Journal of Futures Markets* 8 (4): 421–39, 1988. The absence of significant arbitrage activity in the FT-100 contract of LIFFE traded in London does not yet afford the opportunity of a meaningful test. On this see The International Stock Exchange, London, *Quality of Markets Quarterly*, Winter 1987–8, pp. 2–43. For the evidence on the effects of options see E.M. Cinar and J. Vu, 'Evidence on the effect of options expiration on stock prices', *Financial Analysts Journal*, January–February 1987, pp. 55–7.

18 D. Modest and M. Sundaresan, 'The relationship between spot and futures prices in stock index futures market: some preliminary evidence', *Journal of Futures Markets* 3: 15–42, 1983; J.J. Merrick Jr, 'Volume determination in stock index futures markets: analysis of arbitrage and volatility effects', *Journal of Futures Markets* 1987 (5): 483–96, 1987; S. Figlewski, 'Hedging performance and basis risk in stock index futures', *Journal of Finance* 39: 657–69, 1987.

19 The following draws heavily on A.F. Freris, 'The effects of the introduction of stock index futures on stock prices: the experience of Hong Kong 1984–87', in S.G. Rhee and R.P. Chang (eds), *Pacific Basin Capital Market Research*, Amsterdam: North-Holland, 1990, pp. 409–16.

20 For a more detailed discussion see A.F. Freris, 'The Hang Seng Index futures and the stability of the equity market in Hong Kong 1984–87', Discussion Paper 97, Department of Economics, University of Hong Kong, 1988.

21 The Kolmogorov–Smirnof D statistic and the zero mean t test were both significant for the whole of this time series at $D = 0.059$ with a probability of 0.01 and $t = 41.56$ with a probability of 0.0001.

22 $D = 0.047$ with a probability of 0.01 and $t = 3.67$ with a probability of 0.0002.

23 See references in note 17.

24 For a general description of the gold markets see T.Y. Cheng. *The Economy of Hong Kong*, Hong Kong: Far East Publications, 1982, pp. 238–40.

25 See Y.K. Ho, 'The variability of gold prices in Hong Kong', in Y.K. Ho and C.K. Law (eds), *Hong Kong Financial Markets: Empirical Evidence*, Hong Kong: University Publisher and Printer, 1983, pp.

249–66. Regular market reports appear in the *Securities Bulletin, Stock Exchange of Hong Kong.*

26 *South China Morning Post,* 2 July 1989.

27 For brief details see D. Lethbridge (ed.), *The Business Environment in Hong Kong,* Oxford: Oxford University Press, 1984 (2nd edn), pp. 159–60.

28 For reviews of the gold market in an Asian perspective see, for example, the *SCMP Banking and Finance Reports,* 1986, p. 39; 1987, p. 26.

29 *Asiabanking,* October 1986, pp.16–17.

30 Gold Futures Contract, Hong Kong Futures Exchange, October 1988.

31 L.S.T. Tai, 'Random walk and Hong Kong gold prices: a spectral analysis', *Hong Kong Journal of Business Management* 3: 11–17, 1985.

32 Ibid., p. 11.

33 Y.Y. Ho, 'The variability of gold prices', pp. 249–66.

34 See R.H. Scott *et al.* (eds), *Hong Kong's Financial Institutions and Markets,* Hong Kong: Oxford University Press, 1986, pp. 121–9; P. Pearson, 'Hong Kong's attraction for fund managers', paper presented to the conference on Investment Hong Kong, Stock Exchange of Hong Kong, 1987.

35 R. Thomas, 'Development of unit trusts in Hong Kong', *Securities Bulletin, Stock Exchange of Hong Kong,* No. 26, June 1988, p. 33. The following alternative set of figures is given by Pearson, 'Hong Kong's attraction for fund managers'. In 1987 there were 238 authorized funds of which ninety-one were locally established with the other 147 being overseas. They had under control US$10.6 billion of funds giving an average fund size of US$45 million.

36 Hong Kong Unit Trust Association, *Hong Kong Unit Trust Year Book 1988,* Hong Kong: Longman Hong Kong, 1988. See also the daily financial report in *South China Morning Post.* An abbreviated version of Pearson's paper referred to in note 34 appears in *Hong Kong Unit Trust Year Book 1988,* pp. 4–6.

37 P. Pearson, 'Hong Kong's attraction for fund managers'; R. Thomas, 'Development of unit trusts'.

38 'The implications of establishing a central provident fund in Hong Kong', Hong Kong Government Economic Services, mimeo, 1986.

39 'Measurement of investment performance survey for Hong Kong retirement schemes, 1988 Annual Report', Hong Kong: Wyatt Company (HK) Ltd, 1989.

40 This discussion draws heavily on the occasional reports on the insurance sector published in the monthly *Economic Report* of the Hongkong Bank. In particular see the reports for June 1986, July 1987 and September 1988.

41 Hongkong Bank, *Economic Report,* September 1988.

42 Wyatt & Company, 'Measurement of investment', pp. 17–20.

43 Ibid., *passim.*

44 G.P. Dwyer and R.W. Hafer,'Are national stock markets linked?',
   Review of the Federal Reserve Bank of St. Louis 70 (6): 3–14, 1988
   (quotation p. 9).
45 Ibid., *passim*.
46 Y.K. Ho, 'The risk and return of investing in the Far East emerging
   markets', *Securities Bulletin, Securities Exchange of Hong Kong*, No.
   33, January 1989, pp. 31–5. See also similar results obtained by Y.L.
   Cheung and Y.K. Ho, 'The intertemporal stability of the
   relationships between the Far East equity markets and the developed
   equity markets', in M. Ariff *et al.* (eds), *Proceedings of the Inaugural
   Conference on Asian–Pacific Financial Markets*, Singapore: National
   University of Singapore, 1989, pp. 213–30; R.K. Leung, D. Chan and
   S. Leung, 'Internationalization of capital markets: evidence from the
   Asian Pacific regions', in Ariff *et al.* (eds), *Asian–Pacific Financial
   Markets*, pp. 277–87.
47 D.W.W. Cheung and Y.K. Ho, 'Causal relationship between US and
   major Asian–Pacific emerging markets', in Ariff *et al.* (eds),
   Asian–Pacific Financial Markets, pp. 285–301.
48 D. Chan and R. Leung, Portfolio diversification into the Asian
   Pacific capital markets: a currency perspective', in Ariff *et al.* (eds),
   Asian–Pacific Financial Markets, pp. 243–54.
49 Y.K. Ip, Y.K. Ho, C.K. Law and N.K. Mak, 'Risk measurements
   and analysis of unit trusts in Hong Kong', FEC Financial Studies
   Series No. 2, Hong Kong: Financial Engineering Corporation, 1988,
   passim. For an earlier study covering the performance of twelve unit
   trusts active in Hong Kong during 1975–9 see K.Y. Ip, 'The
   performance of unit trusts in Hong Kong', in Y.K. Ho and C.K.
   Law (eds), *Hong Kong Financial Markets*, pp. 109–23.
50 Y.K. Ip and Y.K. Ho, 'Evaluation of performance of mutual funds in
   Asian Pacific region', in Ariff *et al.* (eds), *Asian–Pacific Financial
   Markets*, pp. 727–38.
51 J. Evans 'Does international diversification work for Hong Kong fund
   managers', *Securities Bulletin, Stock Exchange of Hong Kong* No. 15,
   July 1987, p. 17.
52 H. Choi, 'Costs and objectives of mutual funds', *Hong Kong
   Manager*, October–November 1987, pp. 6–11. A more detailed
   exposition can be found in H. Choi, 'The cost of investing in mutual
   funds', Working Paper WP-87-03, Faculty of Business
   Administration, Chinese University of Hong Kong, April 1987.
53 The following discussion draws from the *SRC Report*, Appendix 25,
   pp. 424–31.
54 K.W. Chan, 'Trade integrity', *Securities Bulletin, Stock Exchange of
   Hong Kong* No. 31, November 1988, pp. 25–6.
55 See 'Overview of the central clearing and settlement system' and
   'Preliminary systems design of the central clearing system', Hong
   Kong Securities Clearing Co. Ltd, Hong Kong, May 1989.
56 For a summary of the reforms see F. Yuen, 'Latest developments in
   the Exchange', *Securities Bulletin, Stock Exchange of Hong Kong* No.

31, November 1988, pp. 7–9.

57 There was an extensive period of consultation and discussion over this ordinance. For a summary of views expressed see various articles in the *Securities Bulletin, Stock Exchange of Hong Kong* No. 31, November 1988; No. 34, February 1989; No. 36, April 1989; No. 37, May 1989.

58 For a summary of all these developments see *Hong Kong Futures Exchange Newsletter* Nos. 144–151, September–October 1988 to April–May 1989.

59 For details see P. Phenix, 'Preparing for the age of interest disclosure', Parts I and II, *Securities Bulletin, Stock Exchange of Hong Kong* No. 35, March 1989, pp. 21–2; No. 36, April 1989, pp. 23–5. See also C. Shum, 'Insider dealing in Hong Kong', *Securities Bulletin, Stock Exchange of Hong Kong* No. 32, May 1987, pp. 8–11.

60 It is perhaps indicative of the touchiness with which the Stock Exchange Council reacts to any suggestion of closure or of disruption of trading that, on the day of the general strike which was called in protest at the Beijing massacre, the Exchange not only stayed open but limited its 'no trading' activities to a discrete ceremony before the day's trading started. The Council had stressed that it should not appear to the outside world that the Exchange was seeking for an excuse in the tragic events in China to suspend trading in order to avoid further price falls.

Chapter six: The foreign exchange rate, monetary and fiscal policy

1 For a background to these events see T.K. Ghose, *The Banking System of Hong Kong*, London: Butterworths, 1987, Chapter 1 *passim*. Some further details are contained in 'Hong Kong's financial crisis' *Asian Monetary Monitor*, November–December 1982, pp. 48–9, and also in J.G. Greenwood, 'Underlying ingredients of the recent Hong Kong dollar crisis', *Hong Kong Economic Papers* No. 15, 1984, pp. 119–24.

2 Y.H. Lui, 'A perspective on Hong Kong foreign exchange market', *Hong Kong Manager*, June–July 1987, pp. 26–39.

3 N.K. Mak, 'The behaviour of the Hong Kong foreign exchange market', M.Phil Thesis, Chinese University of Hong Kong, pp. 42–4; see also S.Y. Lee and Y.C. Jao, *Financial Structure and Monetary Policies in Southeast Asia*, London: Macmillan, 1982, pp. 19–21.

4 *Euromoney*, May 1986, pp. 191, 202. In a survey published in *Euromoney* in May 1989 the major dealers in HK dollars were listed as Hongkong Bank, Standard Chartered, Barclays, Citibank and Bank of Commerce.

5 *South China Morning Post*, 15 January 1986.

6 *South China Morning Post*, 13 November 1986; *SCMP* Banking and Finance Survey, 1987, p. 32.

7 *Asian Wall Street Journal*, 10–11 January 1986.

8 Y.K. Ho, 'The Hong Kong foreign exchange market – an analysis of the monetary approach and market efficiency', in Y.K. Ho and C.K. Law (eds), *The Hong Kong Financial Markets: Empirical Evidence*, Hong Kong: University Publisher and Printer, 1983, pp. 235–48.

9 P.M. Chan, 'Random Walk behaviour of Hong Kong dollar exchange rate', *Hong Kong Baptist College Academic Journal*, 11: 91–104, 1984.

10 Y.H. Lui, 'Empirical properties of foreign exchange rate before and after the linked exchange rate system in Hong Kong', *Hong Kong Journal of Management* 4: 5–29, 1986.

11 *Hong Kong Montly Digest of Statistics Special Review*, November 1987, pp. 99–109.

12 T.K. Ghose, *The Banking System*, pp. 22–3.

13 'Time to blow the whistle', *Asian Monetary Monitor* 5 (4): 22–3, 1981.

14 'Hong Kong's financial crisis', *Asian Monetary Monitor* 6 (6): 27–8, 1982.

15 J.G. Greenwood, 'How to rescue the Hong Kong dollar', *Asian Monetary Monitor* 7 (5): 14, 1983.

16 *Asian Monetary Monitor*, July–August 1981, p. 27.

17 Y.K. Ho, 'The new clearing system', *Securities Bulletin, Stock Exchange of Hong Kong*, No. 28, August 1988, p. 26.

18 T.K. Ghose, *The Banking System*, p. 26.

19 T.Y. Cheng, *The Economy of Hong Kong*, Hong Kong: Far East Publications, 1982, pp. 188–9; D. Lethbridge (ed.), *The Business Environment in Hong Kong*, Oxford: Oxford University Press, 1984 (2nd edn), p. 172.

20 J.G. Greenwood, 'The stabilisation of the Hong Kong dollar', *Asian Monetary Monitor* 7 (6): 28, 1983.

21 Ibid., p. 31.

22 Ibid., pp. 31–2.

23 J.G. Greenwood, 'Hong Kong's monetary system', *Asian Monetary Monitor* 12 (1): 1–13, 1988.

24 D.P.M. Chan, 'An empirical study of cash and interest rate arbitrage under the linked exchange rate system in Hong Kong', Research Paper 3, Department of Economics and Finance, City Polytechnic of Hong Kong, 1989.

25 J.C. Hsu, 'Exchange rate management without central bank: the Hong Kong experience', *Hong Kong Economic Papers* No. 6, 1985, pp. 14–26.

26 Ibid., pp. 22–3.

27 The details of the scheme with the official text is set out in J.G. Greenwood, 'Negative interest rates – a comparison of Hong Kong and Swiss scheme', *Asian Monetary Monitor* 12 (1): 25–32, 1988.

28 The official text is found in *New Accounting Arrangements between the Exchange Fund and the Hongkong and Shanghai Banking Corporation*, Hong Kong: Monetary Affairs Office, July 1988. There is also an extensive discussion in J.G. Greenwood, 'Hong Kong:

intervention replaces arbitrage – the July package of monetary measures', *Asian Monetary Monitor* 12 (4): 1–3, 1988.

29 *New Accounting Arrangements*, p. 3,

30 Y.K. Ho, 'The new clearing system', p. 26.

31 Ibid., p. 28.

32 *Far Eastern Economic Review*, 28 July 1988, p. 91. The estimate was based on an average daily NCB of HK$1 billion yielding a 5 per cent per annum return.

33 *South China Morning Post*, 8 September 1988. See also J.G. Greenwood, 'Further developments affecting the linked rate system for the Hong Kong dollar', *Asian Monetary Monitor* 13 (3): 12–21, 1989.

34 *The 1989–90 Budget*, Hong Kong: Government Printer, 1989, p. 16.

35 See, for example, the whole chapter devoted to this question in the Chinese Banks' Association, *Hong Kong's Banking System: Problems, Prospects and Policies*, Hong Kong, 1988, Chapter 5, pp. 151–82.

36 See the discussion in Y.C. Jao, 'Hong Kong intervention replaces arbitrage – the July package of monetary measures: a comment', and J.G. Greenwood, 'Hong Kong: a response to Dr Jao', *Asian Monetary Monitor* 12 (6): 1–12, 1988. See also Greenwood, 'Further developments'. For an extensive treatment which touches on a number of issues concerning the control of money stock in Hong Kong, although in a somewhat different context, see R.H. Scott, *Saving Hong Kong's Dollar*, Hong Kong: University Publisher and Printer, 1984, *passim*.

37 See, for example, K. Cuthbertson, *The Supply and Demand for Money*, Oxford: Basil Blackwell, 1986, pp. 165–7.

38 R. Coghlan, *The Theory of Money and Finance*, London: Macmillan, 1980, Chapters 8 and 9, *passim*.

39 G. Peebles, *Hong Kong's Economy*, Oxford: Oxford University Press, 1988, p. 147.

40 S.Y. Lee and Y.C. Yao, *Financial Structures and Monetary Policies in Southeast Asia*, London: Macmillan 1982, pp. 26–30, 238.

41 For an analytical approach to these issues see J. Hsu, 'Hong Kong exchange rate system and money supply', *Hong Kong Economic Papers* No. 18, 1987, pp. 43–52.

42 *Banking Ordinance*, Revised edn 1986, Fourth Schedule, Hong Kong: Government Printer, 1987, Chapter 155.

43 'The new monetary statistics', *Asian Monetary Monitor* 5 (5): 11, 1981.

44 R.H. Scott et al. (eds), *Hong Kong's Financial Institutions and Markets*, Hong Kong: Oxford University Press, 1986, p. 42.

45 This discussion draws extensively from H.C.Y. Ho, 'Public finance', in H.C.Y. Ho and L.C. Chan (eds), *The Economic System of Hong Kong*, Hong Kong: Asian Research Service, 1988, pp. 17–42.

46 Research note on the 1988 budget by B. Yates of First Pacific Securities, quoted in the *South China Morning Post*, 6 March 1988.

47 Two of the more easily accessible macroeconomic models of Hong Kong contain estimates of government expenditure multipliers but no discussion of the budget surplus (deficit) impact: see T.T. Hsueh and K.K. Chow, 'A dynamic macroeconomic model of the Hong Kong economy', *Hong Kong Economic Papers* No. 12, 1981, pp. 14–36, and T.B. Lin and W.L. Chou, 'Hong Kong model', in S. Ichimura and M. Ezaki (eds), *Econometric Models of Asian Link*, New York: Springer Verlag, 1985, pp. 9–34. The figure quoted for the marginal propensity to consume is from Peebles, *Hong Kong's Economy*, p. 253.
48 H.C.Y. Ho, 'Public finance', p. 37.
49 *The 1989–90 Budget Speech*, Hong Kong: Government Printer, 1989, p. 29.
50 H.C.Y. Ho, 'Public Finance', p. 20, Table 3.2.
51 P.K.L. Chan and J.H.Y. Wong, 'The effect of exchange rate variability on Hong Kong's exports', *Hong Kong Economic Papers* No. 16, 1985, pp. 27–39.
52 Ibid.
53 C. Chmura, 'The effect of exchange rate variation on US textile and apparel imports', *Federal Reserve Bank of Richmond Economic Review* 73 (3): 17–23, 1987.
54 J.G. Greenwood, 'Adjusting to the link', *Asian Monetary Monitor* 9 (4): 2–12, 1985.
55 *Hang Seng Economic Monthly*, February 1985, February 1986, February 1988; *Hong Kong Bank Economic Report*, October 1987.
56 T.B. Lin and W.L. Chou, 'Hong Kong model'.

Index

All Ordinaries Index 112

Arbitrage (interest rates) model
119–201

Balance of trade/payments;
current account 8
effects on pegged forex rate
223–4
Banks (licensed);
assets 45, 46, 50
CDs, holdings of 57–8
capital adequacy ratio 174
foreign 19, 21–2
interest rates (*see also* Interest
Rate Agreement) 31–2, 56, 66
liabilities 43–5, 54–8
loans 48, 58–68
local 19, 29
regulation of 173–4
reserve requirements 18, 174
Bank of China group 21
Bank Ordinances 142, 173–4
Best Lending Rate (BLR) 31, 60
Beta coefficients 115
bonds;
corporate 87, 93–4
government 87
brokerage costs 104–5
Budget surplus
size 226–8
measurement 228
effects on the economy 229–31

Capital Asset Pricing Model
(CAPM) 113, 116
cash arbitrage and the pegged
HK$ rate;
mechanism 188–9
tests of efficiency 196–204
Certificates of Deposit;
banks' role in 91–2
DTC's role in 83, 86
growth of 91–3
Clearing House 207–8
Commercial Paper (CP) 91
Commissioner of Banking 173–4
Commissioner of Securities 175–6
commodities futures 143–4
corporate finance decisions 119–25

deposits (Bank)
demand for 36–7
in forex 54–6
in HK$ 55
size of 5, 55
Deposit Taking Companies
(Licensed and Registered)
assets 84–5
CDs, holdings of 86, 94
liabilities 84–5
merchant banking 126
regulation 76–7, 95
relations with banks 50–4, 75–6
dividends 122

effective exchange rate index 185
efficiency frontier 165, 167, 168

equity market, efficiency of 127,
    139
Exchange Fund
    bills 212
    history of 186–8
    post-July '88 role 207–11
    role as central bank 212–15
    role in note issue 188–9
    role in pegged forex rate 190–1
    size 188

financial innovation 73
fiscal policies 221–8
flow of funds in Hong Kong
    119–26
foreign exchange rate (HK$) (see
    also cash arbitrage)
    forward market 119–201
    pegged 188–9
    policies towards 184–6
foreign exchange brokers 181
foreign exchange market 180–2
foreign investment 11
futures markets;
    history in Hong Kong 142–3,
        157
    regulation 143, 176–7
    role in October '87 crash 149–52

GDP, growth of in Hong Kong
    4–6
gold markets;
    Chinese market 157
    futures 159
    loco 158
    role of Hong Kong 160

Hang Seng Index 105–9
Hang Seng Index futures;
    contract 143
    development 144–5
    empirical evidence on 146–9,
        152–7
    role in October '87 crash 149–52
Hay-Davison Committee report
    (see also Securities Review
    committee) 175–7
Hongkong Bank

role in note issue 186, 188
role as quasi-central bank
    208–11
share of market 21, 29, 68–9
Hong Kong Banks Association 18
Hong Kong Dollar notes;
    issuing procedures 186–8
    pegged exchange rate 189
Hong Kong Index 110–12

Inflation 5
Initial Public Offers (IPOs) 134–5
insurance companies 163–4
insider trading 132–4
interbank lending 52, 54
interDTC lending 53
Interest Rate Agreement;
    details 31–2
    effects 32–7
    future 38
investment management;
    role of Hong Kong 161–3
    performance of managers 166–8,
        170–1

Japanese Banks 22

liquidation of companies 39
liquidity ratio 18
loans (banks)
    demand 58–68
    distribution 48
    role in assets 46–7
loans (DTCs) 84–5

money stock;
    definition 217
    determinants 218–21
    effects of pegged exchange rate
        189–96
Monetary Affairs Branch 173
Mutual Funds (see Unit Trusts)

P/E ratios 114
People's Republic of China (PRC)
    investment in Hong Kong 11, 12
    re-exports from Hong Kong 7–9
    role after 1997 13

trade with Hong Kong 10
portfolio management 165–8
property sector
    booms and slumps 48–9
    price movements 48
    role of banks 47
    role of government 49
    role in HKSE 100–1

Securities and Futures
        Commission 174–5
Securities Review Committee 177
    (*see also* Hay-Davison

        Committee Report)
Sharpe's Index 166
short selling 148
Standard Chartered Bank 188
Stock Exchange of Hong Kong
    crashes 97–8
    efficiency 139
    role in raising capital 119–26
    regulation of 175–6

Unit Trusts (Hong Kong)
    growth 160–3
    performance 170–1

For Product Safety Concerns and Information please contact our EU
representative GPSR@taylorandfrancis.com Taylor & Francis Verlag GmbH,
Kaufingerstraße 24, 80331 München, Germany

Printed and bound by CPI Group (UK) Ltd, Croydon, CR0 4YY

08/05/2025

01864369-0003